Time on the Cross

Evidence and Methods

Time on the Cross:

Evidence and Methods –
A Supplement

by Robert William Fogel
and Stanley L. Engerman

Little, Brown and Company

Boston – Toronto

First Edition

T 04/74

LIBRARY OF CONGRESS CATALOG CARD NUMBER 73-18347

Published simultaneously in Canada by Little, Brown & Company (Canada) Limited

Printed in the United States of America

Publisher's Note

This volume is a supplement to *Time on the Cross*. For the convenience of the general reader and student, *Time on the Cross* has been
divided into two volumes. This supplementary volume, subtitled
Evidence and Methods, contains all source references for the work,
together with comprehensive appendixes that discuss in detail the
technical, methodological, and theoretical bases for the writing of
Time on the Cross.

The primary volume of *Time on the Cross*, subtitled *The Economics of American Negro Slavery*, is also available. The primary
volume contains the full and complete text of *Time on the Cross,* as
well as pertinent charts, maps, and tables, an index, and all
acknowledgments.

Contents

Tables

x

Time on the Cross

Evidence and Methods

Appendix A.

Science, Humanism, and Ideology in the Interpretation of Slavery

We have tried to present the findings of the cliometricians on the economics of slavery in as dispassionate a manner as possible — although we allowed ourselves some personal latitude in the prologue and epilogue. We would be misleading our readers, however, if we left the impression that cliometricians were immune from the ideological pressures that have beset other students of American Negro slavery. The battle to disentangle private prejudices and objective knowledge is unending. That battle is not always won in the natural sciences; it is much more difficult to win in the social sciences, where the objects of investigation are not atoms but human beings.

The problem of disentangling knowledge from belief is still more acute in the discipline of history. The task which historians set for themselves cannot be achieved through social science alone. Because historians aspire to comprehend the totality of human behavior, their concerns transcend the subject matter of the social sciences and enter moral and aesthetic realms. Even with respect to those issues which fall within the scope of social science, historians frequently demand more than social science can deliver. This is certainly the case when historians attempt to combine all the elements of human behavior that concern social scientists — economic, social, political, psychological, and cultural — into a "seamless web."

Social science is incapable of producing such a seamless web. It produces, instead, particular bodies of knowledge. There is, for example, no theory which encompasses all economic behavior, but only theories which deal with such particular aspects of economic behavior as income distribution, resource allocation, and economic growth. And the theories developed to analyze these problems are far from comprehensive. Economists can deal with income distribution, resource allocation, and economic growth only under certain quite specific sets of circumstances.

The particularized character of scientific knowledge is not a special limitation of the social sciences. There is, of course, no comprehensive theory of physical behavior, but only more or less particular theories such as those of fluids, gases, light, or energy. While physical scientists strive to integrate the various particular theories into more general ones, at least along certain dimensions, they have met with only limited (but important) success. The most ambitious of these efforts, such as the attempt by Einstein and others to produce a unified field theory, have so far been inconclusive.

If we had confined our consideration of the economics of slavery purely to what can be achieved with the methods of the social sciences, this book would have been limited to appendix B, or to some more extended version of it. That appendix, which brings together many of the principal findings of cliometricians regarding slavery, demonstrates the particularized nature of quantitative research in this field.

In the main text we attempted to weave these new findings into a fairly comprehensive reinterpretation of the nature of the slave economy. To do so we were obliged to invoke assumptions which, though plausible, cannot be verified at present, and to rely on additional evidence which is too fragmentary to be subjected to systematic statistical tests. This was particularly true of our discussions of such issues as the effect of slavery on the sexual morality of blacks and the role of racial bias in the origins of the myth of black incompetence.

Where hard evidence was lacking on issues vital to the interpretation of slavery, we, like historians who preceded us, were forced into speculation. By taking advantage of the extensive quantitative work of the cliometricians, however, we have been able to reduce significantly the number of issues on which speculation was the only option. We have also attempted to separate, more explicitly than is usually done, the issues on which the evidence is strong and speculation is limited, from those on which the evidence is weak and the speculative element is predominant.

It is where the evidence is weak, where the element of speculation is most influential, that interpretation becomes most vulnerable to the influence of ideology. Comprehensive ideologies such as neoabolitionism and southern revisionism are quite tempting, because they offer an easy solution to problems of interpretation: they provide the substance needed to cover over the broad and irregular seams of an imperfect historiography and give the impression of a neat, seamless web. While we have tried to resist such temptation, we would not (and do not) claim that we have expunged all ideological influences from this book.[1]

Ideology, for example, may be involved in the way that one casts the responsibility for the burden of proof. Thus, when we suggested that there had developed among slaves a stable nuclear family which was in significant degree the consequence of black needs, rather than merely a response to the pressures of masters, we did more than just challenge the traditional view that slavery prevented the development of an independent black culture. We also, in effect, shifted the burden of proof away from those who contend that blacks constituted an independent cultural force during the antebellum era and to those who deny that slaves were capable of performing such a role. While we could have avoided meddling in such ideological contests, we did not. We meddled because a number of the principal findings of the cliometricians have contradicted central assumptions of the traditional paradigm on the slave family, and have raised the possibility that the widespread acceptance of the paradigm has diverted scholars from probing into the nature of black culture under slavery. We believe that shifting the burden of proof to the proponents of the para-

[1] As we use the words, "ideology" means a system of beliefs, "belief" means an unverified proposition which is held to be true, and "knowledge" refers to propositions which have been verified according to a set of objective criteria such as those employed in statistics or in various fields of science.

It follows from these definitions that "ideology" is a synonym for an unverified theory, or set of related theories, about historical behavior. The major ideologies are generally massive, complex, and quite loosely constructed. They are often logically incomplete.

Thus we would characterize both southern revisionism and neoabolitionism as complex, loosely constructed, and unverified theories of antebellum society. Neither ideology was subjected to rigorous empirical tests by their principal formulators. When they sought data it was rarely to test the validity of the ideology. Sometimes data were sought to enhance the plausibility of the ideology. At other times data were gathered so that they could be combined with the ideology to deduce new conclusions about behavior. In other words, these ideologists started from the assumption that their theories were true and then asked what implications could be drawn from their ideologies and certain pieces of evidence which they had uncovered.

What we frequently find in history are grand theories (ideologies) which claim to have the force of empirically valid hypotheses but which, in fact, do not. The sponsors of these rival ideologies then enter into raging debates about the interpretation of one or another set of facts, debates which cannot be settled because they presuppose what has to be proved: the empirical validity of the ideologies which are the foundation of the conflicting interpretations.

digm is not only justified by the new evidence but may be conducive to new insights.

The preceding paragraphs are an admission that the writing of history cannot be reduced merely to science. But they are also an assertion that the study of history will be advanced by combining the methods of science with the concerns of humanism. We believe that it is both desirable and possible to end the prevailing split between science and the humanities – a split that traces back at least to the Victorian era. This split, as Lionel Trilling pointed out so insightfully, was acknowledged and made official by two of the most eminent intellectuals of that age, T.H. Huxley and Matthew Arnold. It was Huxley who argued that science rather than literature "must supply the knowledge which is necessary for an age committed to rational truth and material practicality." Arnold replied that the knowledge provided by science was not useful unless it was related to man. And the service of relating "scientific knowledge to the whole life of man, is rendered by culture, which is not to be thought of as confined to literature – to *belles lettres* – but as comprising all the humane intellectual disciplines."

Over the decades the issue has been like a volcano, dormant most of the time, but always threatening to erupt. And so it did with great force in 1959, when C.P. Snow published his famous Rede Lecture, "The Two Cultures and the Scientific Revolution." Snow's simultaneous careers as scientific administrator and novelist made him acutely aware of the extent of the breach which had developed between the humanities and the sciences. In his view, humanists and scientists formed not only two vocational groups but two distinct cultures. The men who made up these cultures, though of comparable intelligence and social origins, were so far apart in intellectual, moral, and psychological climate that they ceased to communicate. They "had so little in common," said Snow, "that they might have inhabited different worlds."

Snow's treatment of the rift between science and the humanities has been widely criticized. His characterization of the "two cultures" was undoubtedly too glib. For one thing, he identified science almost exclusively with physics and chemistry. For another, he failed to emphasize the high degree of specialization within each area of thought, specialization which has led some critics of Snow to speak of an infinity of cultures. But if it is an error to exaggerate the separation between science and the humanities, it is also an error to underestimate it.

No doubt specialization in the physical sciences goes very far. And the men who work in such highly focused areas of inquiry as high energy particles, microwave spectroscopy, or ionic transport do not usually venture professionally beyond the narrow boundary of their expertise. Nevertheless, physical scientists possess a language and method which simultaneously ties them together and sets them apart from the humanists. The common tongue of the sciences is mathematics. It has been adopted because its precision removes the ambiguity that is characteristic of ordinary language. Some scientific treatises make so little use of words that a foreign physicist could understand a complex paper written by his American counterpart even though he lacked the command of English required to engage the author in a casual discussion of the weather. As for method, two of the hallmarks of physical science are the precise statement of relationships among variables (frequently in the form of equations) and the testing of these assumed relationships against data.

The humanist, by contrast, gives little thought to natural phenomena. He is concerned with the conventions, mores, institutions, language, thought, and artistic expression of man. These preoccupations are pursued in such well-established disciplines as classics, English literature, Romance languages, fine arts, and music. Departmentalization of the humanities has not been without cost. An expert in Renaissance art may have as little understanding of the technical aspects of Slavic philology as an expert in amino acids has of pulsars. Still, humanists are bound together by their common emphasis on moral and aesthetic values. Whether one studies the Peloponnesian wars or modern music, his aim is to "enrich experience" and "understanding" by reflecting "upon the nature of what is good and what is man's good." The language of humanists is delicately textured with metaphors and words of multiple connotation. These contribute much to the beauty of expression and evoke a wide range of ideas and images in readers. Such "imprecision" is not usually an accident; the ability to write with a "rich aura of connotation" is a high skill to which young authors aspire. There is no single method that is characteristic of the humanities. While all are engaged in the transmission of experience, the means of transmission varies. It may be spoken, written, visual, musical, or some combination of these basic forms. The skills required for such communication generally increase with age. Novelists, composers, painters, and philosophers tend to reach the peak of their powers in their middle or late years of life. Thus, while science is a young man's game — mathematicians and physicists are often "over the hill" by their thirties — the humanities are often dominated by older scholars.

One of the puzzling aspects of the Rede Lecture was Snow's neglect of the social sciences. Scholars laboring in this realm are trying to bridge the chasm that so alarmed Snow. They are engaged in the application of scientific methods to the study of human activity. The origins of the social sciences can be traced to the late eighteenth and nineteenth centuries. But these disciplines did not really come into their own until the twentieth century. Even now there is much unevenness in the level at which scientific methods are applied in social studies. Economics, for example, has become a relatively "hard" science. It has developed a large number of precise statements about economic behavior; the difficult problems of mathematizing such behavioral relationships have been worked out to a remarkable extent; and techniques have been devised for using data to estimate the parameters of these equations as well as to determine the domains to which the equations apply. On the other hand, fields such as sociology and political science remain relatively "soft." In these disciplines the distinction between "factual and evaluative" statements is not always sharply drawn. Behavioral models are not always made explicit, and they are rarely so sharply delineated that they can be mathematized and subjected to rigorous statistical tests.

The blending of scientific methods with humanistic concerns has not reduced Snow's two cultures to one. Instead it has produced a "third culture" — social science. And the alienation of many humanists from this third culture is nearly as great as from natural science. It is probably true that humanists speak to social scientists more often than to natural scientists. It is also true that there is within the social sciences a group of scholars who work in the humanist tradition. But they are a minority, and have not fully been able to stem the scientific onslaught. Hence, while communication exists between the humanities and the social sciences, it does not always take place on the best of terms. To many humanists, the work of the "softer" social scientists frequently appears pretentious. Very often one has to work extremely hard to decipher the jargon of a social scientist, only to discover a generalization about human behavior previously noted by Shakespeare, with fewer footnotes but with much greater wit and elegance. Still more appalling is the attempt of "harder" social scientists to describe such intricate human activities as learning, the development of language, kinship, and political conflict with equations or sets of equations. To many humanists this effort to treat man as if he were an atom is the ultimate folly. It takes no great effort on their part to ignore such prattle. And that is what many humanists do, except for an occasional snicker in the privacy of their studies when someone mistakenly sends them a reprint of a paper containing a mathematical model of the French Revolution.

But disengagement is not always possible. To live in isolation from the culture of the social sciences requires at least a modicum of cooperation from those who inhabit it. And in the case of one of the most important fields of the humanities – history – that minimum degree of restraint has been lacking. It was not only economists who invaded this field in the late 1950s; they were joined by sociologists, political scientists and others. All were armed to the teeth with statistical methods, computer programs, and mathematical models of human behavior. The main body of historians attempted to ignore this incursion, on the assumption that the invaders would flee in retreat when they realized the strength of their opposition, or else, as was true of so many previous barbarian intruders, they would become assimilated.

The invasion of the late 1950s was not the first time that historians were called on to submit to science. During the last decade of the nineteenth century, such distinguished figures as Henry Adams and Herbert Baxter Adams, deeply influenced by revolutionary discoveries in biology, especially the work of Darwin, and by the integration of biology with physics through the laws of thermodynamics, began to propound the view that "history represented a continuum with the universe of nature, and like nature, was . . . governed by law." However, their appeals for an all-out effort to discover the laws of history were largely ignored. Their own efforts and those of their students produced some interesting studies, but fell far short of their proclaimed goals. Indeed, they had to fail. The point is not merely that they were operating at a time when the social sciences were pubescent – before the era of modern statistical methods, before the age of computers, before the flowering of rigorously formulated models of human behavior. They were dead wrong in their assumption that human behavior could be described by equations as stable as those discovered in physics. They did not understand the extremely limited nature of the systematic component of human behavior, and the complex ways in which systematic and chance factors interacted with each other in political, economic, and social life. Nor did they appreciate the herculean tasks that lay ahead in the development of new mathematical systems. For the mathematical logic which served the physical scientists of the mid-nineteenth century so well was inadequate for the needs of social science.

The experience of the late nineteenth century did not repeat itself in the middle of the twentieth. With the aid of the new mathematical and statistical techniques, and by the judicious employment of behavioral models, the new generation of scientific historians made substantial contributions on several important planes of historical research. These included the study of the social mobility of various classes in Europe and America as far back as the seventeenth century, the analysis of parliamentary behavior in the nineteenth century, demographic history, the study of revolutions and other forms of collective violence, urban history, and economic history. As the cliometric record of accomplishment grew, such work received not only the considered attention of some of the leading humanists in history but also their support.

It cannot, alas, be said that the cliometricians always appreciated their indebtedness to senior historians of the humanist tradition. Self-concern and arrogance made some of us oblivious of the extent to which we stood on the shoulders of those who came before us. This was particularly true in economic history, where many senior historians encouraged their students to experiment with mathematical methods. While such aid was occasionally acknowledged, the main emphasis of many cliometricians was on the failures of our predecessors. The older economic historians, those most deeply committed to the humanist tradition, were charged with a long list of abuses. The traditional interpretation of American economic development, we said, was based on a series of unstated and unverified assumptions. Among those assumptions were implicit or explicit views of the magnitudes of crucial aspects of economic activity. However, these vicars of humanism had never engaged in the tedious work required to perform the actual measurements. Moreover, their aversion to mathematics had made them insensible to the fact that they were smuggling elaborate behavioral models into their books and articles. The traffic in covert models was especially treacherous because the underlying mathematical character of some of the most celebrated of the traditional studies was cleverly disguised by words. The unwillingness of the elders to recognize explicitly their reliance on models had led to numerous naïve, even vulgar, abuses of scientific and logical procedures.

Whatever the merit of these criticisms, the self-righteous manner in which they were made did little to aid communication between the humanists and the cliometricians. Unfortunately, many of the debates over the role of quantitative methods in history have been marred by a partisanship and dogmatism that are more appropriate to contending political ideologists than to scholars. To a certain extent, "humanism" and "social science" have taken on the characteristics of ideologies.

That ideological or quasi-ideological commitments stand as a barrier to the blending of scientific methods with humanistic concerns was emphasized by an unusual episode which occurred at the Twenty-seventh Annual Conference of the Economic History Association, held in Philadelphia in September 1967. The principal panel at that meeting, "Slavery as an Obstacle to Economic Growth," was assigned the task of evaluating the results of the cliometric effort to reinterpret the economics of slavery.

It was exactly a decade earlier that Conrad and Meyer had presented the two essays that launched simultaneously the new economic history and the review of the traditional analysis of slavery. The first paper was methodological. It set forth in a general but systematic way the case for the applicability of the mathematical and statistical models of economics to historical problems. The second paper, "The Economics of Slavery in the Ante Bellum South," utilized some of these models to determine whether the purchase of a slave constituted a profitable investment for a slaveholder.

This essay had become a cause célèbre. Its publication in April 1958 set off one of the most extensive and furious debates in the history of the discipline, and stimulated the entry into economic history of a large group of fledgling economists eager to participate in a new Reformation. Some of these would-be iconoclasts turned their attention to the problem singled out by Conrad and Meyer. The result was an extensive literature aimed at producing a "scientific" reinterpretation of the economic operation of the slave system. Since the Philadelphia meeting marked the end of a decade of work in the new mode, it was an appropriate occasion for taking stock. It was also appropriate to pivot the evaluation on the topic which the cliometricians had singled out as the primary ground for testing the validity of their approach.

The session on "Slavery as an Obstacle to Economic Growth" was called to order by its chairman, Moses Abramovitz of Stanford University. Abramovitz started by carefully outlining the procedure. There would be an opening statement of twenty minutes by Conrad and Meyer reviewing the decade of debate ushered in by their essay. This opening statement was to be followed by statements from six commentators, three of whom were favorable to the cliometric approach, three of whom were critical of it. One of the critics, Douglas Dowd of Cornell University, was to have twenty minutes. All the other commentators were allowed ten minutes each. After the opening statements were concluded, each member of the panel would be allowed to comment on, or reply to, any of the points raised in the first round. Then brief interventions would be allowed from the floor.

The care that went into the planning of the session was evident in the choice of commentators. Not only was there balance between critics and exponents of the new economic history, but there was a diversity of views among the members of each category. Two of the critics, Douglas Dowd and Eli Ginzberg of Columbia University, were economists steeped in the humanist tradition. They were both highly critical of the fascination with mathematical models that had become so characteristic of modern economics, and were scornful of the attempt to apply such models to history. But agreement on these points did not mean agreement on others. Dowd was a Marxist and a radical activist, while Ginzberg had devoted much of his career to advising such government agencies as the U.S. Army, the Defense Department, the Department of State, and the Department of Labor. The third critic, Harry Scheiber of Dartmouth College, was a traditionally trained historian with a wide range of interests. After a passing flirtation with cliometrics he had become skeptical of the usefulness of quantitative approaches and was now concentrating his effort on the investigation of the interrelationship between legal and economic change. Scheiber, at thirty-two, was the youngest of the three critics. Ginzberg was fifty-six, and Dowd forty-eight.

The age gap between the critics and defenders of cliometrics was striking. Two of the three supporters were still graduate students. Richard Sutch was a precocious young man of twenty-five who had written one of the leading contributions to the reinterpretation of the economics of slavery while he was still an undergraduate. Now, three years later, he was still working on the completion of a dissertation at M.I.T. and was about to begin his first appointment as an assistant professor of economics at the University of California at Berkeley. The other graduate student was Martin Kelso, who was working for a Ph.D. from Harvard. He was twenty-two years old and still not far enough along in his training to be ready for the job market. One of the authors of this book, Engerman, was the third cliometrician on the panel and, at thirty-one, he was the oldest of the trio.

The opening statement was delivered by Alfred Conrad for John Meyer and himself. When they had first presented the essay embodying their analysis of the profitability of slavery, he admitted, they had thought they "were disposing, once and for all" of the issue. Instead, they had provoked a new debate which was more intense than that which preceded their paper. Criticisms of their original essay fell into three categories: alleged errors in their facts, doubts about certain technical aspects of their theoretical model, and contentions that their model, even if technically correct, was irrelevant to an understanding of the fundamental questions of the slave system and could not be used to settle these questions. Conrad readily granted the existence of certain factual errors. The corrections, however, either had only minor effects on their estimate of the profitability of an investment in slaves, or else served to buttress the conclusion that such investments were profitable. The technical criticisms generally took the form of proposals for alternative, and presumably superior, ways of dealing with the issue of profitability. Conrad granted that some of these alternative models had certain advantages over the model he and Meyer had adopted. But since these alternative approaches also led to the conclusion that they reached, the new work was properly viewed as part of the process of confirming, refining, and elaborating the original finding.

Conrad's strongest objections were to the third category of criticisms — those which dismissed their work because slavery was more than "just another business," and because the behavior of planters could not be described by a model developed to explain the behavior of ordinary capitalists. Conrad objected to the contention that their models were irrelevant because they neglected the social, political, and psychological consequences of slavery which made southern agriculture inefficient; because they failed to take account of the way in which slavery corrupted the ruling class and seduced it into expending its capital on conspicuous consumption; because they failed to recognize that slavery produced an irrational aversion to modern manufacturing industry and led directly to southern stagnation. Those who argued in this way, said Conrad, missed the point:

[W]e were not attempting to prove that slaveholding was "just another business.". . . We were looking for evidence on profits, because their alleged absence has been offered as a reason why the American Civil War was unnecessary. We believe that we did find evidence of competitive profit rates in slavery and concluded, first, that they were an additional and significant reason, along with any possible Southern quixoticism and Gothic imagination, to explain the South's willingness to fight; and second that those profits could have provided the capital for further growth. . . . Now, to recognize that the economic phenomena do not explain everything is not the same as to relegate the production of material conditions to the outbuildings of history. We don't believe that slaves were simply or merely

13

capital, or that the southern gentleman was simply or merely *homo faber* [man the creator], but that does not make a capital model irrelevant . . . nor does it render the capitalization of an income stream from slaves a figment or a fiction. History passes through *homo faber*, and the production of material conditions, the production and transformation of laws, customs, beliefs, styles of civilization, even the content of consciousness — all these are mutually penetrating and fully reciprocal.

The statement by Conrad and Meyer did little to persuade Douglas Dowd. There was more than a hint of derision, we thought, in his opening remarks. "The new economic historians . . . ," he said, "put one in mind of rather light-hearted evangelists; while those who dissent from their innovations seem by comparison, stuffy, old-fashioned, fearful of the new truths, perhaps of truth itself." It was, of course, in the role of an ardent dissenter that Dowd cast himself. The profitability of slavery, he charged, was a trivial issue. By concentrating on it, Conrad and Meyer had diverted attention from the critical question of the effect of slavery on the growth and development of the southern economy. Their model served "to fragmentize an area of inquiry that requires broadening, deepening, and an enhanced sense of relevance." To Dowd, the central feature of the antebellum South was its dependence on slavery and cotton. Even before the Civil War there were signs that this dependency was inimical to the economic interests of the region. By the 1870s, the South would have been confronted with a rapidly falling price for cotton. Its difficulties would have been further complicated by the inability of the system to maintain the supply of slave labor "within economically viable magnitudes." To Dowd, the conclusion was inescapable. Economic development and sustained growth after 1860 could not have taken place under the slave system. That was the point which eluded Conrad and Meyer and the other cliometricians.

The comments of the two other critics reinforced Dowd's argument. Ginzberg and Scheiber supplemented his position by stressing five additional points. First, slavery led to the destruction of the Union. Second, slavery produced a very unequal distribution of income in the South. Third, slavery prevented or inhibited the development of human resources by making it a crime to educate slaves. As a consequence very few slaves were educated and "there was no incentive for the bulk of the Negro population in the South to improve themselves. In fact, they got into very bad habits of doing as little as possible, except under maximum coercion." Fourth, both in the long term and in the short term, the "caste system of labor and social control" reduced the productivity of southern labor. Fifth, slaves "could not be used in a factory system because factory employment and slavery did not mix."

Rather than defending the work of Conrad and Meyer, the three cliometricians reported on research aimed at extending the quantitative analysis of slavery to new questions. Sutch described a paper which attempted to estimate whether the huge outlays on slaves had diverted southern capital from investment in manufacturing plants. Kelso spoke of his efforts to extend the analysis of the employment of slaves from the production of cotton to the production of tobacco, sugar, and rice. The results of his calculations indicated that slaveholders were earning approximately the same rates of return on these crops as Conrad and Meyer found for cotton. Kelso concluded that the economy of the South was efficient in allocating capital from one activity to another. This followed not only from the fact that comparable outlays in each area of production yielded comparable returns, but also from "the fact that higher returns were earned on projects which required higher initial outlays and therefore entailed higher risks."

Engerman reported on our study of the distribution of income and wealth. We found no evidence, he said, that the income distribution was markedly less equal in the antebellum South than it was in the North. According to our estimates, the distribution of wealth was more highly concentrated in the United States in recent times than in Mississippi before the Civil War. Engerman also rejected the proposition that slavery had ground the mass of southern whites into poverty. Our computations showed that per capita income was higher in the South than in the much celebrated north central region. Nor was the slave South stagnating. Between 1840 and 1860 it was actually growing more rapidly than the nation as a whole. Another aspect of our studies was presented later on in the afternoon when Fogel, speaking from the floor, challenged Dowd's contention that the southern economy would have been plunged into crisis in the 1870s, even in the absence of a Civil War, by the unfavorable turn in the world market for cotton and by the pressure of the slave labor force on land. Our analysis, Fogel said, showed no abatement in the worldwide demand for cotton during the nineteenth century. Indeed, for sixty years after the Civil War the world demand for cotton outstripped the southern supply.

As the afternoon wore on the two of us became increasingly confident that the criticisms of the cliometric analysis had missed their target. For these criticisms were based on the supposition that quantitative methods could only be employed to deal with the issue of profitability, an issue which the critics had already dismissed as trivial. But the discussion showed that economic models could be applied, in fact were in the process of being applied, to the whole array of issues thrown up by the critics.

What we did not recognize, until it was too late, was the transformation in the tone and character of the discussion. The subtle tension that marked the opening of the meeting gradually changed into mutual irritation. Some of the critics were offended by the cold, detached attitude of the cliometricians. Slavery was a dirty business, one that of necessity had to arouse the passions of a decent man. Instead of anger, they were confronted with what almost appeared to be our fascination with a cruel system of human bondage. We, on the other hand, felt that the critics were much too emotional, too visceral. Our critics were overly concerned with "what ought to have been" rather than "what actually was." It was pure romanticism, we were convinced, that caused them to blanch before the unpleasant possibility that a backward political system, a bad social system, and a reprehensible moral system might nevertheless be a vigorous, deeply entrenched, and rapidly growing economic system.

Irritation soon passed over to exasperation. It was bad enough to argue that slavery was profitable, but now we seemed to be arguing that slavery was also efficient and produced a high rate of economic growth without having markedly distorted the distribution of income. Would we next claim that blacks were better off under slavery than freedom? Were we trying to convince them that the abolition of slavery was a mistake? Were we toying with them, using our unintelligible models to twist evidence first one way, and then the other? Did we really believe what we were arguing or were we merely trying to shock fuzzy liberals? Had we become tinged by racism? How could anyone living in 1967 be so callous about three hundred years of vicious exploitation?

Exasperation was just as deep in our camp. Why should our motives be called into question? Why should detachment in scientific research be equated with "insensitivity" and "lack of heart"? The special contribution of the cliometricians rested on the capacity to apply the statistical methods and behavioral models of the social sciences to the dissection and analysis of the relevant historical problem. Success in this operation required, no less than in the operating room of a modern hospital, the adroit use of professional skills in a cool, detached manner. In the circumstances of 1967 it was difficult enough to maintain the required objectivity without being incessantly called upon to prove one's integrity and good faith.

What mighty deeds had our accusers performed to have made them so self-righteous?

These thoughts of mutual recrimination finally burst into the open. They poured out in fiery stares, in thinly disguised insinuations of racism, in caustic charges of naïve romanticism. Faces flushed. Voices became strident. Reasoned consideration of evidence was drowned in a torrent of passionate speeches. Gesticulations became so aggressive that they were menacing. The collegiality achieved through years of work on common problems was ruptured as we turned away from each other in anger. Scholarly discussion had succumbed to the emotionalism of the times.

What caused the breakdown?

One contributing factor was the national tension over race relations. It must be remembered that 1967 marked the third successive summer in which race riots engulfed American cities with arson, violence, and death. The first major battle occurred in the Watts section of Los Angeles in August 1965, when more than ten thousand blacks took to the streets in a single night, bringing disorder to a fifty-square-mile area. Although Watts originally appeared to be an isolated incident, it was the beginning of a wave of riots that swept through Omaha, Minneapolis, Chicago, Cleveland, and Atlanta in 1966, and finally reached a crest in Newark and Detroit during the summer of 1967. The roster of cities embroiled in racial conflict during 1967 grew to well over a hundred, and the casualties – mostly black – were 83 dead and 1,897 injured.

Obviously those of us who gathered in Philadelphia to discuss "Slavery as an Obstacle to Economic Growth" on September 8 were not oblivious of the turmoil that once again threatened the integrity of the nation. A century after Appomattox, the country seemed to be tottering on the edge of full-scale civil war. This time the battle flag was unfurled not by the slaveowners but by descendants of slaves who were willing to undertake revolution to right the injustices of three hundred years. "We are going to start with guns to get our liberation," proclaimed black militant Stokley Carmichael. "Our only answer is to destroy the government or to be destroyed." There was much talk of the crisis in the corridors at the Philadelphia meeting, and concern over the crisis seeped steadily into the hall reserved for scholarly debate.

While the events of the preceding three months gave a special edge to the discussion at Philadelphia, it would be wrong to infer that the bitter emotional explosion was the result of a split between left and right, between radicals and conservatives in the usual political classifications.

Though the attack on the cliometric position was led by Dowd, a well-known radical, his principal partner was a solid member of the establishment. Moreover, the cliometricians were by no means archreactionaries. In addition to his work in economic history, Meyer specialized in urban economics and had long been concerned with the problems of black ghettos. But if his position as the president of the National Bureau of Economic Research, the nation's most prestigious research organization in economics, made his credentials unacceptable to the left, there were no such doubts about his collaborator. Conrad's claim to militant radicalism was at least as strong as Dowd's, a fact that was later emphasized by the considerable notoriety he gained as a leader of the "open enrollment" campaign at City University in New York — a campaign aimed at permitting black and Puerto Rican students to enter the university without having to satisfy the usual academic criteria. His uncompromising opposition to official policy on this question, as well as his role as the principal faculty advisor to the radical students who were leading the strikes and demonstrations, so aroused the opposition of more conservative faculty members that Conrad eventually resigned from the chairmanship of the economics department.

The issues that divided the two sides simply cannot be sorted into the usual political categories. For the radicals, reactionaries, and all of the intermediate political groupings have come to terms with the conventional interpretation of the slave system. Each group has taken from that tale what is needed to justify its political program. Radicals point to the internal economic contradictions in order to emphasize their indictment of slavery and to add the degrading conditions of labor to the reparations bill owed to black Americans. Those of another political stripe use the argument of inevitable collapse to warn against the calamities that can befall the nation as a consequence of hasty and ill-considered political interference. Still others find in the "historical record" of the inefficiency of black labor a justification for discrimination in employment.

The cliometric reinterpretation struck at the underpinnings of these varied positions with such impartiality that it antagonized representatives of every shade in the political spectrum. Members of each camp felt confronted with the need to find new justifications for cherished programs. To many in each camp, it seemed more appropriate to repudiate the unwelcome findings than to seek new rationalizations that would restore the link with history.

The bitter emotional explosion in Philadelphia, then, was caused by the interaction of a number of different elements. We quantifiers were challenging so much, and conceding so little, that any historian steeped in the conventional interpretation of the slave system *had* to be upset. Those who had devoted so many years of their lives to weaving the traditional fabric of southern history could not be expected to look upon our attacks with equanimity. We aggravated the initial wound by frequently resorting to a language that the humanists could not understand, by invoking behavioral models whose relevancy seemed dubious, and by transmuting some of the most passionate and personal of human issues into such cold, sterile terminology that they could hardly be recognized. And all of this was carried out with the arrogance that is typical of youthful upstarts.

But rudeness is as irrelevant to the intellectual issue posed by our attempt to reconstruct the economics of slavery as is the civility of the authors of the traditional interpretation. The real question is whether quantitative methods have produced a more accurate and complete portrayal of slavery than was previously available.

Appendix B.

Technical Notes

The objectives of appendix B are fourfold:

1. To present the evidence, or at least describe the nature of the evidence, numerical or otherwise, which is the foundation for statements in the primary volume of this work, *Time on the Cross: The Economics of American Negro Slavery*.

2. To qualify or amplify certain statements made in the primary volume.

3. To specify the equations or models (groups of equations) which underlie various of the statements in the primary volume.

4. To describe the procedures employed in estimating the values of the parameters and the variables of particular equations.

The following conventions are employed in appendix B:

Citations of particular studies are made directly in the text of the appendix as follows: [1, pp. 23–32]. The first number within the brackets refers to a book or paper given in the list of references which follows appendix C. The numbers following the comma refer to the relevant pages in the cited study. When several citations are made within one pair of brackets, the citations are separated by semicolons.

At the beginning of the notes to chapters 1, 2, 3, 4, and 6 we present tables of the symbols employed in the equations relevant to each of these chapters.

When the results of regressions on particular equations are presented, the numbers within parentheses immediately below the parameter values are the standard errors of the parameters. Correlation coefficients and

Durbin-Watson statistics are not presented unless their values are relevant to the point at issue. Unless otherwise stated, the correlation coefficients of the regressions are statistically significant.

The bold-faced numbers at the beginning of each note are the *note index*. The note index is used for making cross-references within appendix B. The first number or letter of the note index refers to the chapter to which the note applies ("P" refers to the prologue). The second number refers to the order of that note within the chapter. The third and subsequent numbers refer to sections or subsections of the note. Thus "See **1.3.2**" means "See section 2 to note 3 of chapter 1."

The pages, table numbers or figure numbers given in parentheses immediately following the note index indicate the parts of the primary volume to which the note applies.

Notes to the Prologue

P. 1. (p. 6). The way in which erroneous mathematical assumptions covertly entered into the traditional interpretation of slavery is well illustrated by Phillips's treatment of the question of profitability. See **3.2.1**.

P.2. (pp. 7–8). Table B.1 summarizes the main bodies of data bearing on the economics of slavery that have thus far been recovered from archives by cliometricians and are now available in machine-readable form.

P.2.1. The data described in the first seven projects listed in table B.1 came from several different schedules of the U.S. census. Information on value of farms, value and number of livestock, number of improved and unimproved acres, and the physical output of 33 crops came from the agricultural schedules. The population schedules provided data on the age and sex of free residents (including overseers) and on the value of the personal property of the head of each household. Information on the age and sex of slaves as well as on the number of slave houses per plantation came from the slave schedules. The name of the operator of each farm is common to all three schedules and, hence, could be used to link together the information in all three schedules (cf. [121; 389]).

P.2.2. The data schedules from which they were obtained, and the method of linking information were the same in the Ransom-Sutch and in the Bateman-Foust projects as those described in **P.2.1**.

P.2.3. The probate records are a voluminous source of information on

Table B.1

Major Bodies of Data Collected by Cliometricians

Nature of project and principal investigators	Sources	Geographic area and number of observations
1. The cotton economy in 1860 William Parker and Robert Gallman	Manuscript schedules U.S. censuses of agriculture, population, and slaves	5,229 farms in 11 southern states
2. The cotton economy in 1850 James Foust	Same as 1	897 farms in 11 southern states
3. The rice economy in 1860 Dale Swan	Same as 1	671 farms in Georgia and South Carolina
4. The sugar economy in 1850 and 1860 Robert Gallman and Mark Schmitz	Same as 1	1,856 farms in Louisiana
5. Southern agriculture in 1850 and 1860 Robert Gallman	Same as 1	3,745 farms in Kentuck and Tennessee
6. Northern agriculture in 1860 Fred Bateman and James Foust	Same as 1, except for slave schedules	21,118 farms in 102 randomly selected townships in the Northeast and North Central regions
7. The postbellum cotton economy Roger Ransom and Richard Sutch	Same as 6	4,693 farms in 16 southern states

Time period	*Principal information*
1860	1. Number and value of acres by farm
	2. Value of capital per farm
	3. Number and value of livestock
	4. Physical output of crops
	5. Population (free and slave) by farm, age, sex
1850	Same as 1
1860	Same as 1
1850, 1860	Same as 1
1850, 1860	Same as 1
1860	Same as 1, except for absence of slave population
1880	Same as 6

Major Bodies of Data Collected by Cliometricians

Nature of project and principal investigators	Sources	Geographic area and number of observations
8. The relative efficiency of slavery Robert Fogel and Stanley Engerman	Probate records	Approximately 80,000 slaves from 54 counties in 8 southern states
9. The inter- and intra-state slave trade Robert Fogel and Stanley Engerman	New Orleans invoices of sales	Approximately 5,000 slave sales recorded in New Orleans
10. The inter- and intra-state slave trade Robert Fogel and Stanley Engerman	Coastwise manifests of slaves shipped, U.S. bureau of customs	Approximately 20,000 slaves shipped among southern ports
11. Slave demography and plantation life Robert Fogel, Stanley Engerman, and Richard Steckel	Plantation records	30 plantations from Alabama, Georgia, Louisiana, Mississippi, North Carolina, South Carolina, and Texas
12. Slave demography Robert Fogel and Stanley Engerman	Manuscript schedules of U.S. census, mortality	Approximately 11,000 persons in 8 Southern states
13. Southern manufacturing Fred Bateman, James Foust, and Thomas Weiss	Manuscript schedules of U.S. census, manufacturing	Approximately 20,000 firms in all states

Time period	Principal information
1775–1865	1. Slave prices classified by sex, age, skill, handicap; for individuals and for families 2. Slave hires by sex 3. Prices of crops 4. Prices of livestock
1804–1862	1. Sale prices by sex, age, skill, handicap; for individuals and for families 2. Residence of purchaser and of seller 3. Credit terms
1820–1860	Slaves shipped in coastal trade, listed by age, sex, and height, by owner and consignee
1800–1865	1. Slave births by date, with names and ages of mother and (for some) father 2. Slave mortality and morbidity rates, by age, cause 3. Cotton picking by individuals, classified by age and sex 4. Slave prices by sex, age, skill, handicap 5. Daily records of work assignments of all hands 6. Records pertaining to slave maintenance costs
1850	Deaths by age, sex, place of birth, for free and slave populations
1850, 1860, 1870	1. Amounts and values of material inputs and manufacturing output 2. Value of capital stock 3. Employment and wage payments

slave prices, classified by age, sex, skills, and handicaps. It is probably the most important body of data relevant to problems of human capital that is available to economists today. The frequent listing of slaves by family units in the probate records permits the calculation of fertility rates as well as the analysis of patterns of family formation. The data on slave prices, by sex and age, in the probate records are more complete than those contained in any other currently available source, and are particularly useful because of the large number of years covered. The crop and livestock sales yield wide geographic coverage of the prices required for the preparation of county and state indexes of total output to be constructed from the data on physical output in the census tapes.

P.2.4. The New Orleans sales invoices cover the period from 1804 to 1862. These records, which are on deposit at the New Orleans Notarial Archives, provide much new material on slave capital values, the interregional pattern of slave migration, and the slave trade (cf. [309]). The bills of sale include information on the residence of buyers and sellers, the age, price, sex, skills, and physical and mental defects of the slaves sold, family relationships of slaves, credit terms, and the place of previous ownership. These data are important in estimating the effects of age, sex, and skills upon human capital values, in analyzing the effect of the slave trade on the destruction of family units, and in estimating the extent and nature of the interstate slave sales. Moreover, since the ages of mothers and their children are listed, it is possible to obtain such important demographic information as the distribution of the ages of the mothers at the time of the first surviving birth, and the spacing of surviving children.

P.2.5. Each ship carrying slaves in the coastal trade was required by law to post a manifest detailing the number of slaves carried, their sex, age, and height, as well as information concerning the ownership of the slave (see Wesley [361] for a detailed description of these manuscripts). Records in the National Archives include the incoming and outgoing manifests for Mobile, Savannah, and New Orleans. These can be used to estimate the age-sex distribution and magnitude of the movements of slaves between various southern ports over a 40-year period ending in 1860.

P.2.6. Plantation account and record books are on deposit in various historical archives throughout the South. Approximately 4,000 observations drawn from 30 plantations in various parts of the South over the entire antebellum era have been recovered from these records and put on tape. It is expected that the total number of observations from this source will eventually increase to between 7,000 and 10,000. There are entries for name of slave, mother's and father's names, date of birth, date of death, cause of death, and date of purchase, sale, and other disposition. While not all information is available for each observation, there are enough complete entries to estimate age-specific fertility rates, age-specific death rates, child spacing, and the size of completed families for a sample of slaves living on relatively large plantations. Moreover, given the diverse nature of the plantations in the sample, it is possible to examine the differences in birth and death rates by region, by size of plantation, and by primary crops produced.

P.2.7. The mortality schedules list deaths in 1850 by sex, race, slave or free, place of birth of decedent, and cause of death. This information is being used to determine differences in death patterns by age, geographic regions, sex, condition of servitude, and race. Similar data are now being collected from the mortality schedules for 1860.

P.2.8. Data drawn from the manufacturing schedules pertain to the quantity and value of firm output, investment, employment, wages, and the quantity and value of raw materials. The data in the manufacturing schedules have been linked with data in the population, agricultural, and slave schedules.

P.2.9. In addition to the bodies of data listed in table B.1, all of which exist in machine-readable form, there are a number of smaller bodies of data that are quite useful for the analysis of issues in the economics of slavery. These include data on the incidence of slave hiring collected by Claudia Goldin, on hire prices collected by Robert Evans, Jr., on slave family and marriage patterns collected by Herbert Gutman, on the inter- and intrastate slave trade collected by William Calderhead, on the operation of postbellum plantations (including wage payments to freedmen) collected by Charles Seagrave, on colonial wealth distributions collected by Alice Jones, and on antebellum wealth distributions collected by Lee Soltow.

Notes to Chapter 1

1.1. (figs. 1, 2, 3, and pp. 14–20). Until recently, estimates of the volume of the Atlantic slave trade varied widely. The most significant contribution to the improvement of these estimates was made by Philip Curtin [65]. Curtin's estimates were based on a careful consideration of the sources of earlier estimates, the consistency among estimates for various countries, the consistency between African export data and Western

Hemisphere import data, and the consistency between import figures for various Western Hemisphere colonies or countries and estimates of the African populations of these colonies at various points in time. The result of Curtin's investigation was a new set of estimates of the international slave trade far better founded than anything previously available. Nevertheless, the range of possible error in Curtin's estimates is still quite large. Curtin has placed the range of probable error for his estimates of the slave trade of individual countries at plus or minus 20 percent of the stated figure.

Table B.2

Definitions of Symbols Used in Notes to Chapter 1

P_s = the price of a slave

R = the annual net revenue derived from a slave

ψ_t = the ratio of annual net earnings of a slave during a given year to the peak-age net earnings of slaves

λ = the probability that a slave will live through a given age

B = the value of a "birthright" (the zero-age price of a slave)

ϕ = the probability of a live birth in a given year

V = the ratio of the value of the childbearing capacity of a woman of a given age to her price at that age

i = the rate of return or rate of discount

n = the expected number of years that a slave will be held; the expected number of years between age x and death

x = a subscript indicating the age of a slave

f = a subscript which indicates that the value of the variable pertains to a prime-aged hand

t = a subscript or exponent designating a year

w = a subscript which indicates that the variable pertains to females. The absence of a w means that the variable pertains to males.

Curtin's book has set off a new round of studies of the slave trade of particular countries. The corrections of Curtin's estimates thus far indicated by the new studies, most of which are still in progress, generally fall within Curtin's limits of plus or minus 20 percent, although most of the correc-

tions have served to raise rather than lower Curtin's figures [3; 201; 267].
Curtin himself has contributed to the process of revision. His new figures
for the Atlantic slave trade between 1711 and 1810 are presented in [66].

Pending completion of the studies now under way, the estimates of the
international slave trade used in this book are, with one exception, those
given in [65]. The one exception is for the United States and those colonies which subsequently formed the United States. Here we have increased
Curtin's estimate for the total volume of slave imports from 427,000 to
596,000. Since no adjustment has been made for understatement in the
trade of other colonies, the U.S. share in Atlantic slave trade is slightly
exaggerated. Our reason for correcting Curtin's estimate of the U.S. slave
trade and the procedures we employed in making the correction are given
in **1.5**.

1.2. (pp.15-16). The estimated annual rate of increase in U.S. tobacco production during the eighteenth century and the average product per hand
are based on estimates of Jacob M. Price, communicated to us in a letter
dated December 14, 1971. About the same number of hands is implied by
data in Gray [154, p. 912] and *Historical Statistics* [343, pp. 765-767].

1.2.1. The assumption that the increase of slaves required for the increase in tobacco production could only be met out of imports, biases the
import requirement upward very considerably. As pointed out in **1.5.1**, the
estimated average annual rate of natural increase in the slave population
between 1700 and 1800 was 2 percent per annum, or nearly twice as rapid
as the average rate of increase in tobacco production during the same
period. This suggests that the share of the slave labor force engaged in
tobacco production decreased during the course of the eighteenth century.
Even during the period of most rapid expansion of tobacco farming, 1725-
1775, the annual rate of increase in production (about 2.5 percent per
annum) was only slightly higher than the natural increase in the slave
population.

1.3. (p. 19). These estimates of sugar production were recently developed by McCusker [220, pp. 90-395]. McCusker's estimates pertain to
molasses and rum as well as to all grades of sugar. His unit of measurement
is equivalent pounds of muscovado sugar.

1.4. (fig. 4 and pp. 21-22). Estimates for the white and Negro population of the United States during the colonial era have been compiled by
Sutherland [343, p. 756]. The estimates of the Negro and white populations for the Caribbean are those developed by McCusker [220, pp. 548-
767].

1.4.1. Estimates of the average plantation size in the U.S. and Jamaica about 1790 are from Phillips [261, pp. 50, 84]. Phillips refers to one slave holding in Guiana of 1,598 slaves. Higman's analysis of the 1832 slave registration lists in Jamaica shows 211 holdings of between 250 and 500 slaves, and 10 holdings of between 501 and 750 slaves [179, p. 61]. However, holdings are not synonymous with plantations. It is possible that there was more than one plantation per holding. The distribution of slaves by holding in Jamaica in 1832 was as follows:

Size of holding	Percentage of slave population
1 - 50	25.9
51 - 100	13.9
101 - 250	37.5
251 - 500	20.9
501 - 750	1.8

1.4.2. Richard B. Sheridan found that the mean number of slaves in a sample of 176 Jamaican sugar plantations, during the years 1741-1775, was 181. Communicated in a letter dated January 19, 1972.

1.5. (figs. 5, 6, 7 and pp. 23-29). We have increased Curtin's estimates of slave imports into the United States for the periods 1620-1700 and 1760-1810.

Curtin assumed that all imports into the U.S. prior to 1700 came not directly from Africa but from some other slave colony in the Western Hemisphere and, hence, held that to include these slaves in the U.S. total would be to double count. Even if the assumption is true, the issue still arises as to whether the slaves in question should be attributed to the U.S. or to the other colonies. In order to guard against underestimating the U.S. share in the slave trade, we have attributed these imports to the U.S. This correction raises the U.S. total for slave imports by 20,500. We did not deduct this amount from the total for the rest of the Western Hemisphere for two reasons: It cannot be ruled out that a substantial share of these early imports did come directly from Africa; even if we are guilty of double counting, the error introduced in the total imports of the rest of the Western Hemisphere is trivial — two tenths of 1 percent.

We raised Curtin's estimate of slave imports into the U.S. between 1760 and 1810 by 148,000. For this period, Curtin took over the import estimates of Henry Carey [35]. Carey derived his estimates from figures on the total slave population in the U.S. colonies between 1760 and 1810, and the assumption that the U.S. slave population had a natural rate of increase of 2.0 percent per annum. Our quarrel is not with Carey's assumptions, but with errors he committed in performing the calculations indicated by his assumptions. Our correction arises, then, not from different assumptions but from the elimination of computational errors and better estimates [343, p. 756] than were available to Carey on the total Negro population of the U.S.

1.5.1. All attempts at quantifying U.S. slave imports rest on a shaky basis. The fundamental problem, of course, is the paucity of data, especially before 1770. Attempts to reconstruct the volume of slave imports from bills of sale and other direct evidence yield totals which virtually all scholars hold to be too low. For example, direct counts of slaves imported into Virginia and South Carolina, the two chief markets, between 1701 and 1767, amount to only 115,000 [343, pp. 769, 770]. Curtin's estimate for approximately the same period is 240,000.

The alternative approach has been to infer slave imports from estimates of the total Negro population, the best of which are those of Sutherland [343], and from an assumption regarding the rate of natural increase of the U.S. slave population. The assumption that U.S. slaves experienced a high rate of natural increase rests partly on qualitative evidence, especially the observations of travelers to the South during the colonial era. But the conclusion has also been inferred from statistical evidence from the period after 1810. Between 1810 and 1860, the U.S. slave population exhibited an average rate of increase of 2.3 percent per annum. This figure was much higher than the rate of increase during the same period in Jamaica, Brazil, and most of the other Latin American countries for which data are available. Indeed, in the case of Jamaica, the negative rate of increase in the slave population persisted for more than two decades after the close of the slave trade [58]. It was not until sometime after 1834 that the black population of Jamaica became demographically self-sustaining.

Consequently, the unresolved issue is not whether the demographic experience of U.S. slaves was better than that of slaves in Latin America, but by how much it was better and for how long. Most scholars who have taken up the issue have assumed that the demographic experience of U.S. slaves prior to 1810 was not quite as good as in the subsequent period but that it was, more or less, of a uniform level up to 1800 or 1810. To Carey, Stetson [312], and Curtin this meant a rate of natural increase in the neighborhood of 2.0 percent per annum over the years from 1620 to 1810.

We have been able to find one important piece of evidence against which to test this assumption for the period between 1780 and 1810. It comes from the birth register of the Gaillard plantation, a large South Carolina plantation, and one of the first to enter into cotton production on a large scale. Over the quarter-century from 1786 to 1810, there were 270 births on this plantation. Of this number, 65 died within the first year. The indicated infant mortality rate, 24 percent, implies a life expectation of about 35 years, only slightly less than Evans's estimate of life expectation for U.S. slaves in 1850 [105, p. 212].

1.5.2. Figure 5 was computed by taking the ratio of Africans to the total slave population at each decade. To determine the number of Africans imported at time t who survived to time $t + j$, the following schedule of survivors was used:

j	Proportion imported at time t who survive to t + j
10	0.77
20	0.63
30	0.47
40	0.30
50	0.13
60	0

This schedule is based on the assumption that those imported duplicated, as a group, the mortality experience of slaves aged 20–29 in Evans's table of survivors, except that the death rate for Africans during the first decade on U.S. soil was three times as high as for native-born slaves in 1850 [105, p. 212]. A curve based on the assumption that newly arrived Africans had exactly the same mortality experience as Creoles, would be virtually identical with the curve shown in figure 5.

1.5.3. The lower curve in figure 7 was computed on the assumption that the natural rate of decrease among slaves alive at time t was 3.0 percent per annum. In other words, slaves in the U.S. at time t would yield a population at time $t + 10$ equal to 0.737 of the initial population. The total population at time $t + 10$ is computed by adding, to the population in the U.S. carried over from time t, the estimated number of slaves imported between t and $t + 10$. For estimates of the rate of decrease in Jamaica see [58, p. 24].

1.5.4. (pp. 26–27). It is usually assumed that the fertility rates of imported slaves were below those of Creoles [58; 278] and various cultural, psychological, and physiological arguments have been advanced to explain this phenomenon. Eblen [99] has recently challenged this assumption. Pointing to a lack of direct evidence on fertility rates, he contends that what is thought to be a low fertility rate might actually be consistent with normal fertility rates but unusually high infant and female mortality rates. Eblen thus raises the possibility that the number of live births per female *who survived the childbearing ages* might actually have been as high in the Caribbean as in the United States. If Eblen's hypothesis can be substantiated, it would require a reexamination of current assumptions regarding the cultural, social, psychological, economic, and physiological circumstances of Caribbean slavery.

1.6. (figs. 8 and 9). The distribution of the slave and Negro populations in 1825 is based on an exhaustive survey of population statistics carried out by Steckel and reported in [306]. Among Steckel's principal sources were [65; 74; 220; 282; 395].

1.7. (table 1). The chronology was derived from a wide variety of sources including [9; 74; 126; 159; 306; 397]. For many countries it is impossible to present an unambiguous date for the abolition of slavery. Political turmoil and other factors frequently led to conflicting decrees or laws as well as to various interruptions and delays in the implementation of these decrees and laws.

1.8. (pp. 35-36). In order to estimate the cost of gradual emancipation schemes, it is necessary to make use of equations developed in the notes to chapter 3 (see especially 3.1.3 and 3.5). There it is shown that the equation for the price of a male slave at age x is

$$(3.6) \quad P_{sx} = (R_f) \sum_{t=1}^{n} \frac{\psi_t \lambda_t}{(1+i)^t}$$

(see table B.2 for the definitions of symbols). The equation for the price of a female slave at age x is

$$(3.29) \quad P_{swx} = (R_{wf}) \sum_{t=1}^{n} \frac{\psi_{wt} \lambda_{wt}}{(1+i)^t} + B \sum_{t=1}^{n} \frac{\phi_t \lambda_{wt}}{(1+i)^t} \, .$$

The second term of the right-hand side of equation 3.29 is the value of the childbearing capacity of a woman aged x.

1.8.1. Emancipation laws of the type instituted by New York involved no *direct* loss for owners of male slaves, since no slave alive at the time of the enactment of the emancipation law was freed. There was, however, a capital loss suffered by owners of female slaves since, as equation 3.29 shows, a share of the price of a female equal to

$$(1.1) \quad V = \frac{B \sum_{t=1}^{n} \frac{\phi_t \lambda_{wt}}{(1+i)^t}}{P_{swx}}$$

was due to her childbearing capacity.

As is shown in figure 21, the value of V rose from 10 percent at age 9 to a peak of 13 percent at age 20 and then fell gradually to 0 at age 50. On average, the ratio of the value of the childbearing capacity of women to their price was 10.1 percent.

The exact amount of the loss imposed on owners of women depended on the age of emancipation. In figure 41, it was shown that the break-even age for rearing males in the Old South about 1850 was 26 years. If that break-even age also applies to the period 1780–1804, an emancipation law which freed newly born slave children at age 26 would reduce the value of the birthright (B) of those children to zero.[1] When the effect of an emancipation law is to reduce B from a positive value to zero, the capital loss imposed on the owner of a female, expressed as a percentage of the original price of the female, is exactly V. Emancipation laws which freed children before the break-even age would make the value of B negative and would have imposed a capital loss greater than V. Emancipation laws which freed children at ages greater than the break-even age would have left B positive and, hence, imposed a capital loss less than V.

In the case of a law which freed children at the break-even age, then, the average capital loss imposed on owners of slave women would be about 10 percent. Since female slaves represented about 43 percent of the value of all slaves, the average loss on all owners of emancipated slaves would be 4.3 (10 × 0.43) percent.

1.8.1.1. The discussion in 1.8.1 was based on the assumption that slave-owners continued to provide the same treatment to slaves scheduled to be freed as had been true before the emancipation laws. This is a dubious

---

[1] For a discussion of the meaning of the variable called the value of a "birthright" designated by the symbol B, as well as of the variables on which it is dependent, see **3.5, 4.11.**

assumption. The immediacy of emancipation would have given owners an incentive to work slaves harder and to provide poorer maintenance for them, since these owners would no longer bear the consequence of any deterioration in the health of slaves that showed up after the age of emancipation. To the extent that this incentive became operative, the capital loss to slaveholders would have been reduced below 4.3 percent.

1.8.1.2. The various emancipation schemes debated and enacted in the North are described in Zilversmit [397]. The development of the age-price profiles presented in chapter 3 have made it possible to evaluate the cost to slaveholders of various schemes.

A recent paper by Goldin [147] shows that the cost of one of the emancipation schemes discussed in the North on the eve of the Civil War would have been equal to approximately 5 percent of G.N.P. in 1860. A gradual emancipation scheme similar to those actually enacted in the northern states would have cost about 1 percent of G.N.P. in 1860. Similar estimates were independently derived in a paper by West [364].

Fielding [108] has estimated the capital losses implicit in several of the emancipation schemes enacted by northern states, on the assumption that slaveholders could find no loopholes. His estimates are

State	Year of enactment of the law	Capital loss as a percentage of the original capital value of the slaves
Pennsylvania	1780	3.7
New York	1799	4.3
New Jersey	1804	6.2

These figures should be considered upper limits for two reasons. First, Fielding assumed that during the period 1780–1804, as in 1850, the birthright was positive prior to the passage of the emancipation laws and equal to 5 percent of the peak-age price of a female (see **4.11.4** and **4.11.5**). However, the relatively sluggish movement in demand during 1790–1800, the unlimited supply of slave imports, and the relatively low ratio of female-to-male prices all suggest that the market for slaves was probably at, or near, a long-run equilibrium. If this were true, the birthright (B) would have been zero and emancipation at age 26 would have not involved any capital losses whatsoever.

Second, Zilversmit notes the failure of officials to close loopholes which permitted owners of slaves in states with emancipation laws to sell their slaves in the South. In this connection, it is worth noting that there was a sharp decline in the rate of increase of the Negro populations in these states after the closing of the international slave trade in 1807. Table B.3 gives the rates of growth of the black population in three emancipation states between 1810 and 1820, and compares these with the rate of growth of the black population in the same states between 1790 and 1810, as well as with the growth rates of the southern slave population and the total U.S. black population.

Table B.3

The Relative Rates of Growth of the Negro Population in Emancipation States between 1810 and 1820 Compared with That of Other Populations (percent)

	Decade rates of change Negro population (slave & free)		Decade rates of change in the slave population	
	1790–1810	*1810–1820*	*1790–1810*	*1810–1820*
New York	+24.6	– 2.4	–16.1	–32.8
New Jersey	+14.8	+ 7.1	– 2.5	–30.4
Pennsylvania	+50.6	+30.6	–53.9	–73.5
The North	+25.2	+12.0	–17.5	–30.5
The South	+33.5	+30.0	+31.0	+30.5
The U.S.	+32.8	+28.6	+28.7	+29.1

Note: The South includes Louisiana between 1810 and 1820, but not between 1790 and 1810. The North includes all states in the Northeast and the North Central regions except Missouri, which is included in the South.

The entries in table B.3 strongly suggest that slaveholders in New York and New Jersey were selling their slaves to the South, especially between 1810 and 1820. These sales were probably motivated by the sharp rise in slave prices, which again made the birthright positive and permitted slaveowners to obtain capital gains in excess of the transactions costs involved in slave sales. Thus it is probable that, to a substantial degree, the decline of slavery in the North was brought about not by the freeing of slaves but because northern slaveholders were cashing in on capital gains by selling their chattel in southern markets.

Notes to Chapter 2

2.1. (pp. 38–41 and fig. 10). The occupational distribution of all males over age 15 in 1870 was tabulated from [342]. Ideally, we would have preferred to compare the occupational distribution of slaves in 1850 with whites in the same year. However, 1870 is the first year for which an occupational distribution of the labor force is sufficiently detailed to permit the breakdown into the 4 skill categories used in figure 10.

Unfortunately, the data needed to separate the occupations of whites from blacks are not available for 1870. This limitation is not as serious as it might seem, since it is unlikely that the occupational distribution of white labor would have been much different from that of all labor in 1870. Indeed, for reasons indicated below, it is likely that the comparison in figure 10 understates the skill composition of the slave labor force relative to that of the white labor force in 1870.

2.1.1. The share of skilled and semiskilled laborers in nonfield occupations on plantations was determined from a sample of 33 estates, ranging in size from 3 to 98 slaves, retrieved from the probate records. This sample revealed that 15.4 percent of slaves over age 15 were engaged in such occupations. The percentage of skilled slaves was fairly constant over plantation size, as is indicated by the regression

$$(2.1) \quad S_k = -0.194 + 0.165 L_a$$
$$(0.537) \ (0.024)$$

which can also be written as

$$(2.2) \quad \frac{S_k}{L_a} = 0.165 - \frac{0.194}{L_a}$$

It can be seen that over the range $L_a = 10$ to $L_a = 100$, S_k/L_a varies between 0.146 and 0.163. Moreover, the intercept of equation 2.1 is not statistically significant. Hence we used $S_k/L_a = 15.4$ percent for all plantations.

Table B.4

Definitions of Symbols Used in Notes to Chapter 2

S_k = the number of skilled and semiskilled slaves

L_a = the number of male slaves in the labor force over age 15

L_h = the number of slaves (male and female) in the labor force over age 10

Y_i = the annual yield per slave hand (L_h) in the ith crop or other occupational activity

L_{hi} = the man-years of slave labor devoted to the ith crop or activity

L_{ho} = the man-years devoted to all occupational activities except the raising of cotton, corn, and livestock

Q_c = the output of cotton in bales

Q_m = the output of corn in bushels

Q_a = the value of livestock, in dollars, which is assumed to be proportional to the output of livestock

U = number of childless females in selling states before sale

U' = number of childless females from selling states sold in New Orleans

M = number of females with child in selling states before sale

M' = number of females with child from selling states sold in New Orleans

W = the proportion of females in the selling states who were childless

α_1 = the proportion of U bought by New Orleans

α_2 = the proportion of M bought by New Orleans

M_a = number of women with both husbands and children in selling states before sale

M_d = number of widowed females with children in the selling states before sale

M'_d = number of widowed females with children from selling states in the New Orleans sample

β_1 = the proportion of M_d bought by New Orleans

β_2 = the proportion of M_a bought by New Orleans

$\bar{\delta}$ = the male share of the total interstate migration

δ_s = the male share of interstate sales

δ_m = the male share of the interstate movement of whole plantations

γ = the share of sales in the total interstate migration

2.1.2. The probate records thus far processed do not provide an adequate basis for determining the proportion of slaves on each plantation who were drivers. Our estimate of the share of males over 10 who were drivers is based on the conventional ratio of one driver to every 30 slaves [112, p. 143; cf. 154, p. 546; 289, p. 8]. This ratio was applied to all plantations with 30 or more slaves. On plantations with 11 to 30 slaves, fractional drivers were computed. However, fractional (part-time) drivers were assumed to have a lower skill composition (to be, in effect, assistant drivers) than full drivers and hence were classified as semiskilled workers rather than as managerial personnel.

Since virtually all drivers were male, on plantations with 30 or more slaves, one out of 15, or 6.7 percent of all males, were drivers. Only 68 percent of all males were age 10 or over, and 55 percent were age 15 or over. If we define the labor force as including all persons over age 10, then drivers were 9.7 percent of the male labor force on plantations of 51 or more slaves. If we define the adult labor force as those who are 15 years of age or over, drivers formed 12.2 percent of adult males on these large estates. With another 1.6 percent of adult men working as overseers (see chapter 6 and **6.5**), roughly 14 percent of the adult males on large plantations fell into the slave managerial class. An additional 11.9 percent were craftsmen, while 3.5 percent were semiskilled workers. Thus, between a quarter and a third of all adult male slaves on large plantations fell into the upper occupational stratum.

Black overseers were assumed to have existed only on plantations of 50 or more slaves. No doubt many drivers on smaller plantations performed the role of overseers, but for the purposes of the occupational categories given in figure 10, it is not necessary to distinguish between drivers and overseers on the smaller plantations.

The distribution of slave occupations in the entire farm sector is presented in table B.5.

2.1.3. Our estimate of the distribution of occupations in urban areas is based on the Charleston census of 1848 [83]. It shows that 22 percent of all male slaves over 10 were in crafts or semiskilled occupations. The indicated share of skilled workers among adult males would then be 27 percent.

There is some possibility that the share of skilled persons in the slave labor force was lower in Charleston than in the rest of southern cities. Wesley [360, p. 142] and Stavisky [305, p. 258] argue that blacks were 80 percent of all southern artisans during the antebellum era. In Charleston, however, blacks were only 44 percent of all craftsmen. It may be that in Charleston white artisans were particularly successful in limiting occupational opportunities for slaves. The white artisans of Charleston were well-

Table B.5

The Derivation of the Occupational Structure of Adult Male Slaves on Farms

Slaves per plantation	(1) Percent of the total male slave population age 15 or over on each size plantation	Percent on each size plantation who are					
		(2) "ordinary" field hands	(3) slave drivers	(4) slave overseers	(5) nonfield craftsmen	(6) nonfield semiskilled	(7) assistant drivers
1. 1–10	14.88	84.6	0	0	11.9	3.5	0
2. 11–30	31.61	72.4	0	0	11.9	3.5	12.2
3. 31–50	20.79	72.4	12.2	0	11.9	3.5	0
4. 51 or more	32.71	70.8	12.2	1.6	11.9	3.5	0
5. Percentage of all male farm slaves 15 or over who hold occupations given in cols. 2–7		73.7	6.5	0.5	11.9	3.5	3.9

Method of computation: The percentages in column 1 were multiplied by the percentages in cols. 2–7 to obtain the weighted average share of the slaves in each occupational category over all slave plantations. These weighted average shares are given in line 5.

The percentages in column 1 were computed from the Parker-Gallman sample.

organized and extremely active politically. There was hardly a year during which they did not petition the Charleston city council for some new restriction against slave artisans [305, chap. 6].

The Charleston census reveals no slaves who are managers or professionals. Yet it is known that in at least some industries, at least some slaves were engineers and foremen or department heads.

Moreover, it seems likely that the economic factors which led large planters to put 14 percent of the labor force in supervisory posts would have carried over to urban industries. Indeed, Starobin [304, p. 168] argues that the ratio of one manager to 30 slaves prevailed in industry as on plantations. He also argues that white managers "were scarce." Accordingly, we assume that among firms using slaves, 72 percent of managers and foremen were slaves (the proportion used for overseers on plantations over 51 slaves; cf. chap. 6, pp. 200, 211-212 in the primary volume) and that there was one manager or foreman to every 30 unskilled hands other than domestics.

Applying these proportions to the Charleston data leads to the conclusion that 1.0 percent of male slaves in the urban labor force were managers. It should be noted that this figure has little effect on the estimate of the overall proportion of slaves in the managerial and professional class. If we assumed that there were no slave managers whatsoever in urban areas, the overall proportion of slaves in the labor force who were managers would still be 7.0 percent, when the proportion is given to two significant digits.

2.1.4. The agricultural and urban occupational distributions were combined by using 0.94 as the weight for agricultural workers and 0.06 for urban workers. We include as urban, cities and towns with 1,000 or more persons.

2.1.5. We have indicated several reasons for believing that the distribution shown in figure 10 understates the relative skill composition of the slave labor force. Two additional reasons should be stressed.

First, the labor force participation rate was higher among slaves than among whites among the ages 15-19. Since these are ages at which the skill composition is relatively low, this asymmetry tends to make the slave population relatively less skilled than it would have been if we defined the adult labor force as consisting of those aged 20 or over.

Second, most of the whites included in the category "professional and managerial" were farmers, many of whom operated very small farms. It is doubtful that such petty farmers (say those who operated farms of less than 40 acres) had greater skills as farmers than the slave agriculturalists we have classified as "laborers."

In this connection the caveat made in the text should be repeated: ordinary field hands engaged in virtually all the many-faceted activities of raising crops and livestock, and had most of the skills normally identified with farming.

2.2. (pp. 41–42). It is possible to use equation 2.3 to determine the distribution of slave labor among various plantation activities:

$$(2.3) \quad L_h = \sum_{i=1}^{n} \frac{1}{Y_i} (L_{hi} Y_i)$$

which may be written as

$$(2.4) \quad L_h = L_{ho} + \frac{1}{Y_c} Q_c + \frac{1}{Y_m} Q_m + \frac{1}{Y_a} Q_a.$$

The parameters of equation 2.4 were estimated from data in the Parker-Gallman sample for plantations with 10 or more hands (i.e., plantations with approximately 15 or more slaves). The resulting regression

$$(2.5) \quad L_h = 8.378 + 0.09658 Q_c + 0.00218 Q_m + 0.00142 Q_a$$
$$(0.00535) \qquad (0.00030) \qquad (0.00025)$$

together with the mean values of the variables

$$L_h = 24.8$$
$$Q_c = 87.0$$
$$Q_m = 1973.4$$
$$Q_a = \$2592.0$$

implied the following distribution (in percent) of labor time (measured in man years) among the principal plantation activities:

cotton	34
corn	17
livestock	15
other activities	34.

Of the 34 percent of the labor allocated to other activities by equation 2.5, about one half was accounted for by the nonfield occupations of males (see **2.1.2**, especially table B.5) or by such nonfield occupations of women as cooks, seamstresses, servants, and nurses. On the sample of plantations described in **2.1.1** some 20 percent of the women over age 10 were in nonfield occupations (see [137, p. 339] for nearly identical results from a regression based on other data). The balance of the labor time compounded in "other activities" was devoted to the improvement of land, the erection of fences and other structures, and the raising of minor crops.

2.3. (p. 43). The data on the skill composition of runaways during 1736–1801 were collected by Mullin [239]. Analysis of advertisements on runaways for the late antebellum period is now under way. Since the occupational structure of the overall slave population during that period is now known, it will be possible to determine the degree to which skilled slaves were overrepresented among runaways.

2.4. (figs. 12, 13 and pp. 44–47). The interregional movement of slaves by decades between 1790 and 1860 was estimated by Claudia Goldin. As she points out, the estimates for the later decades are more reliable than the estimates for the earlier decades. In **2.4.1** and **2.4.2** we present Professor Goldin's description of her estimation procedures. For other applications and discussions of the "survivor" method of estimating interstate migration, see [205; 209; 317].

2.4.1. The Survivor Technique. The interregional movement of slaves, 1790 to 1860, was computed using a statistical method commonly employed in demographic work known as the "survivor technique." This method is especially useful where data on actual migration are severely limited, but where reliable population censuses have been taken over a period of time. This method takes the population in an area, here slaves in the total U.S., as one which is closed. That is, imports of slaves into, or exports from, the U.S. are assumed each to be zero or to balance exactly, as was approximately the case between 1810 and 1860. The analysis is more accurate if the census population figures are broken down by sex and age.

Because of deaths, only part of the total U.S. slave population in any age category will survive to the next census year. For example, 78 percent of the female slaves between the ages 20 to 29 in 1850 lived to be 30 to 39 years old in 1860. These survivor rates by age category and sex are computed using information in two successive federal population censuses. For 1850 to 1860 this calculation was made for each ten-year age group, although the previous censuses were treated differently (see below) because the age classifications in the printed federal censuses were very broad. These survivor rates by age group and by sex are then applied to population data for individual states. Each age group by sex in every state is assumed to survive as the total U.S. age and sex category did. The survivor percentages are applied to the population in the earlier year and a prediction is made concerning how many slaves should have survived to the next decade. This number is then compared to the actual population figure found in the printed federal census. If the actual number is greater than the predicted number, the state is assumed to have had a net in-migration. Similarly, if the actual number is less than that computed, the state is assumed to have lost slaves during the decade. This computation is performed for all states for each ten-year period. The total number of "exported" slaves is exactly equal to those which were "imported," by definition.

The net migration figure shown for each decade is the number of slaves who migrated during that period. This computation results in a net figure because it only considers the location of a slave in each of the end years. For example, if a slave was in South Carolina in 1850 and moved to Tennessee in 1855, and then to North Carolina in 1860, only one move is counted. Furthermore, if the slave returned to South Carolina, no change is recorded. In addition, if a number of slaves of age 20 moved from South Carolina to North Carolina and an equal number of slaves age 20 migrated the other way, no net change is recorded. This implies that the migration figures given are probably underestimates of the actual movement, as well as of the number of persons engaged in these movements. The extent of the underestimation of persons is probably small because it is improbable that much crosshauling occurred. But to the extent that slaves migrated more than once in a ten-year period, gross movement is underestimated.

No adjustment was made for the migration of children who were born within the ten-year periods. This also introduces a small downward bias in the estimates.

In all survivor-technique work the states or regions are assumed to have the same survivor rates. To the extent that these are in fact different, states with higher life expectations will be taken to be importing slaves and those with low ones will appear to be exporting them. This can bias the estimates upward, for more movement is measured than actually occurred. For example, assume we have two states, with one healthier than the other. Slaves did not migrate, but their number grew more slowly in one state than in the other. The survivor technique as employed here would allocate the difference in growth to slave movement and not to differences in health conditions. The assumption of a closed population will be discussed in detail in the following decade-by-decade description of the survivor method as applied to the U.S. slave population.

2.4.2. The Survivor Technique Applied to Slave Population Data. Because of variations in the nature of the age breakdowns given in the various censuses of population between 1790 and 1860, it was necessary to modify the application of the survivor technique in the various decades. The most detailed information is contained in the censuses of 1850 and 1860. Hence the most reliable estimates of slave migration are for the decade 1850–1860.

2.4.2.1. 1850 to 1860. The 1850 and 1860 published federal census accounts list slaves by sex for 14 age categories. The survivor technique was applied by computing the percentage of slaves in most of these age groups who survived to the next decade. The first group is of slaves aged 0–4 in 1850 who survived to ages 10–14 in 1860; the second group is of slaves aged 5–9 in 1850 who lived to 15–19 in 1860. The remaining slaves were enumerated in ten-year age intervals which I followed, except for the tail end where the number of slaves 60 and above in 1850 was compared to those 70 and above in 1860. These survivor rates calculated from these cohorts were applied to all slave states listed in the population censuses.[2]

2.4.2.2. 1840 to 1850. The 1840 published population census lists slaves by broad age categories — 0 to 9, 10 to 23, 24 to 35, 36 to 54, 55 to 99, and 100 and above. It was, therefore, impossible to perform calculations by as small age groups as was done for 1850 and 1860. Instead, a very wide age classification was used. Those slaves living in 1840, male and female separately, were compared to those over ten years of age who survived to 1850. The ratio was calculated, using the published federal censuses, to have been 0.876 for males and 0.870 for females. These survivor rates were then applied to the various state figures.

The use of these very broad classifications brings in biases additional to those discussed above. If the states differ substantially in their age compositions, then applying the national survivor rate will yield incorrect results. For example, if one area has a very young population, say due to a large

---

[2] Richard Sutch [317] has also computed net slave migration using the same data and technique. My figures differ only trivially from his. The differences are fully accounted for by three factors. One is an adjustment for certain minor printing errors in the census. Sutch also had an "age unknown" category for which he calculated a survival rate. I instead allocated those of unknown age among the known ages on a proportionate basis. The third source of differences is due to rounding errors.

percentage of children, its survivor rate will actually be higher than the national average. By applying the average survivor rate a bias toward a net in-migration results. This would not be the case if cohort survivor rates were used, for then each state would have some weighted average of the national cohort survivor rates. This problem is quite similar to that of differential mortality among the states discussed above.

Texas entered the Union in 1850, although slaves existed in that area for many years before. If Texas slave figures are counted for the first time in 1850, the migration estimates for 1840–1850 will be biased upward. Therefore, I assumed that 18,529 (9,025 males and 9,504 females) slaves were brought to Texas prior to 1840, with the rest having moved into the state between 1840 and 1850.

2.4.2.3. 1830 to 1840. The same technique was used here as in **2.4.2.2**. The rates employed for slaves in 1830 who survived to 10 and above in 1840 were 0.82 for males and 0.83 for females. Texas was assumed to have gained all of its 18,529 slaves (which I allotted it for 1840) within the period 1831 to 1840. Therefore, all those over 10 were included in the total migration figures.

2.4.2.4. 1820 to 1830. The technique of **2.4.2.2** was again used here, with the total survivor rates calculated at 0.85 for males and 0.87 for females. Florida was included in the federal population census for the first time in 1830, and I allocated its slave population back another decade. That is, I assumed that Florida began acquiring slaves in 1820. Florida is given 9,346 slaves (4,899 males and 4,447 females) as of 1820, which implies that its slave population grew at an equal rate during both decades, 1820 to 1830, and 1830 to 1840. The direction of this assumption is again justified, although its magnitude is a guess. However, an error in the guess will affect, not the estimate of total migrations, but merely the distribution of the migrants between the two decades.

2.4.2.5. 1810 to 1820. Although a method similar to that of **2.4.2.2** was used for this decade, additional calculations were performed because the 1820 census lists only slaves aged 0–14, rather than those aged 0–9. Therefore, the 1820 figures were adjusted to yield the number of slaves 10 and above. This adjustment was made by assuming that 10 percent of the slaves in the entire slave population were 10–14 years old. This figure was chosen on the basis of the slave age breakdowns in the 1860 census and an allowance for a slightly older group of slaves due to recent imports. The resulting figures compare favorably with others computed by using trends in age distributions for later years. The total survivor rates used were 0.85 for both males and females together, because the 1810 census did not list male and female slaves separately. It was assumed that Florida began acquiring slaves in 1810, and that by 1820 it had 6,316 slaves above 10 years of age. Alabama and Arkansas, which entered in 1820, were pushed back to 1810 in exactly the same way as was Florida.

There are two additional problems with the computations for 1810–1820 which should be noted. First, all slaves in the North in 1820 were assumed to have been manumitted. This is, of course, not true. Many were transferred South during the remainder of this period (see **1.8.1.2.**). My assumption, therefore, introduces an upward bias in the total migration figures by the amount of slaves shipped South. Although the bias is small in comparison with the total figures, it may amount to over 15,000 slaves. The second problem is far more complicated and involves the assumption of a closed population. If the system was not closed, then the biases which enter the work depend upon how the illegal imports were scattered across the states. If a few states gained the bulk of these arrivals (as was probably the case), then they are computed as having a net in-migration, and other states are assumed to have lost slaves. If, instead, the slaves are scattered evenly across the states, each state will survive at the national average and no migration will be recorded. It is possible that 1820 to 1830 was a period of smuggling, for the high survivor figure for females is suspect.

2.4.2.6. 1800 to 1810. I used the 1820 figure minus two percentage points for the percentage of total slaves who were 0 through 9 years of age. The survivor rate chosen was 0.80, slightly lower than that for the period 1830 to 1840. This yielded a positive residual of over 100,000 slaves who are assumed to have been imported during this period. Louisiana and Missouri entered in 1810 and were not extrapolated back to 1800. Therefore, if some slaves were in these areas in 1800, imports should be decreased for 1800–1810 and increased for the period 1790 to 1800. Given the survivor rate figure of 0.80, interstate migration is not affected by this assumption.

2.4.2.7. 1790 to 1800. I used the 1820 figure minus three percentage points for the percentage of slaves 0 through 9. A survivor rate of 0.80 was used, which yielded about 60,000 slaves imported during this period.

During both the decades 1790–1800 and 1800–1810, any decreases in the northern slave population beyond the hypothetical survivor figures were attributed to the migration of slaves to the South, although some were manumitted. Certainly, if one anticipated northern legislation, 1790 to 1800 would have been the optimal period for selling slaves South, although the extent of this movement is not known.

The migration estimates are probably least reliable for the earliest periods, 1790 to 1800 and 1800 to 1810. Two gross assumptions had to be made for these decades. First, the percentage of slaves less than ten years old was extrapolated from other census figures. Secondly, the rate at which persons in the earlier year survived to the later date was assumed to have been 0.80. This survivor rate figure yielded net import figures which may be low, but are not unreasonable (cf. fig. 6 and 1.5 which give estimate for the period from 1790 to 1810 that are about 15 percent higher than mine).

2.4.3. The lower curve in figure 13 was computed on the assumption that during each decade, beginning in 1810, the slave population of the importing states increased at the same rate as was observed for the entire slave population during that decade.

2.5. (pp. 48–50 and fig. 14). The New Orleans sales invoices contain data which bear on such important issues as the effect of the interregional slave trade on the destruction of slave families, the effect of color on slave prices, and the volume of the slave trade. The analysis of these data are still at a preliminary stage. Not all of the information in them has yet been mined. Furthermore, the findings presented in this note should be considered provisional, although we believe that it is unlikely that refinements of the computations now under way will significantly alter the conclusions.

2.5.1. The New Orleans slave invoices contain no direct statements regarding the marital status of slaves, except when slaves were sold in complete families. In particular, they contain no statements regarding whether or not slaves sold without husbands (or wives) were separated from their spouses as a consequence of being traded. Even if the New Orleans invoices did contain statements regarding previous marital status, such information could hardly be considered reliable. Not only would economic (and possibly moral) considerations have led to false reporting, but we would not be willing to assume that the only valid slave marriages were those recognized by slaveowners or white officials who accepted the behavioral norms of slaveholders.

We consider as slave marriages all unions that the slaves involved intended, or expected, to be "stable" (for our purposes, this term need not be defined), regardless of what view others may have had of these unions. For the purpose of estimating the breakup rate, we take as evidence of such intent, the existence of a child. In other words, we consider every case of a slave woman who is sold with a child but without a husband to be a broken marriage. Since some women with children did not intend to have stable unions with the fathers, this assumption tends to exaggerate the degree to which the slave trade destroyed marriages. However, because we are attempting to show that the breakup rate was low, it is appropriate that we choose a criterion of marriage that biases the result against the case we are trying to make.

Our conclusions on the proportion of slave marriages broken up by the interregional slave trade are based on inferences drawn from the demographic data contained in the New Orleans sales records, data which are a by-product of commercial transactions. A reason for care in the recording of these data is that they formed the legal basis for claims of ownership, and for suits in the event a trader needed to recover damages.

The crucial aspect of our estimating procedure is the following comparison: From the New Orleans sales records we can compute the percentage of women at each age who have one or more children. We compare these age-specific rates with the corresponding rates in the slave population as a whole. For example, in the slave population as a whole, about half of the women aged 20–24 had one or more children. However, among the slaves traded in New Orleans, less than 20 percent of women aged 20–24 had one or more children. Since women with infants or young children were virtually always traded together with their offspring, the "shortage" of women with children in the New Orleans sales indicates that traders were not indifferent to whether women were married, but strongly preferred unmarried women.

The actual mathematical procedure employed to convert the observed differences in the relative frequencies into an estimate of the proportion of female slaves who were forcibly separated from their husbands is as follows:

2.5.2. Method of Estimating the Proportions of Single and Married Women from Selling States Who Were Traded in New Orleans.

$$(2.6) \quad U' + M' = \alpha_1 U + \alpha_2 M$$

$$(2.7) \quad \frac{U'}{U' + M'} = \frac{\alpha_1 U}{\alpha_1 U + \alpha_2 M} = \frac{\alpha_1}{\alpha_1 + \alpha_2 \dfrac{M}{U}} = \frac{1}{1 + \dfrac{\alpha_2}{\alpha_1} \cdot \dfrac{M}{U}}.$$

If $\dfrac{U}{U + M} = W$, $\dfrac{U'}{U' + M'} = X$, and $\dfrac{M}{U} = Z$, then

$$(2.8) \quad \alpha_1 = \frac{XZ}{1-X} \alpha_2 \text{ or } \frac{\alpha_1}{\alpha_2} = \frac{XZ}{1-X} .$$

Substituting (2.8) into (2.6) yields

$$(2.9) \quad \alpha_1 = \frac{U' + M'}{U + \dfrac{1-X}{XZ} M} = \frac{(U' + M') / (U + M)}{W + \dfrac{(1-X)(1-W)}{XZ}}$$

$$(2.10) \quad \alpha_2 = \frac{U' + M'}{\dfrac{XZ}{1-X} U + M} = \frac{(U' + M') / (U + M)}{\dfrac{WXZ}{(1-X)} + (1-W)} .$$

Now U', M', and X can be estimated from the New Orleans data. But M, U, W, and Z cannot be estimated directly. They can, however, be estimated indirectly by combining information contained in probate records with information contained in the census. In this connection, it is important to note that the observed variables for the selling states are not W and Z but $\hat{W}$ and $\hat{Z}$, where

$$(2.11) \quad \hat{Z} = \frac{M - \alpha_2 M}{U - \alpha_1 U} = \frac{M}{U} \times \frac{1 - \alpha_2}{1 - \alpha_1}$$

$$(2.12) \quad \hat{W} = \frac{\hat{U}}{\hat{U} + \hat{M}}$$

$$(2.13) \quad \hat{U} = (1 - \alpha_1)U; \quad \hat{M} = (1 - \alpha_2)M.$$

Moreover, if we let

$$(2.14) \quad \hat{\alpha}_1 = \frac{U' + M'}{\hat{U} + \dfrac{1-X}{X\hat{Z}} \hat{M}}$$

$$(2.15) \quad \hat{\alpha}_2 = \frac{U' + M'}{\dfrac{X\hat{Z}}{1 - X} \hat{U} + \hat{M}} \, ,$$

it follows that

$$(2.16) \quad \alpha_1 = \frac{\hat{\alpha}_1}{1 + \hat{\alpha}_1}$$

and

$$(2.17) \quad \alpha_2 = \frac{\hat{\alpha}_2}{1 + \hat{\alpha}_2} \, .$$

Thus when $\hat{\alpha}_1$ and $\hat{\alpha}_2$ are small, $\alpha_1 \approx \hat{\alpha}_1$ and $\alpha_2 \approx \hat{\alpha}_2$.

2.5.2.1. The values of the critical variables shown in equations 2.6–2.10 for women aged 20–24 have been estimated from data in the New Orleans sample and in the probate records, except for $M + U$ which was estimated from census data. The results are:

$W \quad = 0.47$

$1 - W = 0.53$

$X \quad = 0.843$

$1 - X = 0.157$

$Z \quad = 1.13$

$\alpha_1 \quad = 8.54 \times 10^{-4}$

$\alpha_2 \quad = 1.41 \times 10^{-4}.$

From these figures it can be seen that slaveholders were *six times* (α_1/α_2 = 6.1) more likely to buy an unmarried woman than a married one. In other words, although the number of married women in the East potentially available for sale (in the age category 20–24) was slightly larger than the number of single women, New Orleans traders bought six single women for every married woman that they purchased. Clearly such a strong preference for unmarried women indicates the influence of powerful economic and social forces which militated against the disruption of families (see chapter 4, in the primary volume).

2.5.3. Method of Estimating the Proportion of Women with Children in the New Orleans Sample Who Were Widowed. The discussion thus far has assumed that all women with children were married. However, some women with children were widowed. Moreover, it seems likely that the same economic and social forces that led slaveholders to prefer single to married women would have led them to prefer widowed to married women. On this assumption it is possible to estimate the share of the women with children who were widowed.

Assume

$$(2.18) \quad \frac{\beta_1}{\beta_2} = \frac{\alpha_1}{\alpha_2}.$$

Then

$$(2.19) \quad \frac{M'_d}{M'} = \frac{1}{1 + \frac{\beta_2}{\beta_1} \cdot \frac{M_a}{M_d}} = \frac{1}{1 + \frac{\alpha_2}{\alpha_1} \cdot \frac{M_a}{M_d}}.$$

2.5.3.1. From Evans's survivor table [105, p. 212] it was estimated that $M_a/M_d = 18.3$ for women aged 20–29. From the previously cited records it was estimated that $\alpha_2/\alpha_1 = 0.165$. It follows from equation 2.19 that among women 20–29, approximately 25 percent of those with children, but without husbands, were widows. The share of women with children who were widows, of course, was higher for women aged 30 or more.

2.5.4. Some women without children were married but had not been married long enough to bear children. The previous computations need to be adjusted for this group. Probate records indicate that among married women 20–24, approximately 10.2 percent were married during the previous year. If we assume that 75 percent of such women were without children, and still assuming that $\alpha_2/\alpha_1 = 0.165$, the proportion of married women in the New Orleans sample may have been not 11.8 percent (15.7 × 0.75 = 11.8) but 13.1 percent (15.7 × 0.75 + 1.5 × 0.843 = 13.1). (For an estimate of the share of marriages broken from all sales and from bequests see **4.8.3**.)

2.5.5. The New Orleans data do not contain information which permits a division of males into married and unmarried groups. It seems likely, however, that the strong preference for unmarried slaves carried over into the trade in men. The economic and other forces which caused slaveowners to hesitate to tear women away from their husbands should have been equally compelling in thwarting the temptation to tear men away from their wives. Indeed, since runaways were predominantly men, slaveowners might have been more reluctant to purchase men who were forcibly separated from their wives than wives who were forcibly separated from their husbands.

2.6. (pp. 48, 53, 54). The total slave trade (sales) can be disaggregated into two components: interstate and intrastate.

2.6.1. The interstate component can be estimated from equation 2.20

$$(2.20) \quad \bar{\delta} = \gamma\delta_s + (1 - \gamma)\delta_m.$$

Goldin (see **2.4**) found that over the period 1820-1860, $\bar{\delta}$ was equal to 0.511. It may be assumed that $\delta_m = 0.5$. Three estimates for δ_s exist. These are:

$$\delta_s' \quad = 0.57 \text{ (from New Orleans invoices)}$$

$$\delta_s'' \quad = 0.61 \text{ (from coastwise manifests to New Orleans)}$$

$$\delta_s''' \quad = 0.64 \text{ (from coastwise manifests to Mobile).}$$

Substituting these variables into equation 2.20 yields values of γ ranging from 15.7 percent to 7.8 percent.

2.6.1.1. Calderhead [34] has used bills of sale and probate records to estimate the number of slaves from Maryland who were sold out of state between 1830 and 1860. If these are combined with Goldin's estimates of the net migration out of Maryland during the same period, the value of γ for Maryland is 16.2 percent.

2.6.2. Calderhead indicates that the ratio of local to interstate sales was 5.2. The New Orleans data show a ratio of 1.8.

2.7. (fig. 14 and pp. 49-51). The age distribution of migrants was computed from Sutch [317].

Some historians have argued the New Orleans data give a biased view of child sales, since Louisiana had a law which made it illegal to sell slave children under 11 without their mothers unless they were orphans. This presumes that it was legal rather than economic constraints which explain the underrepresentation of children under 11 in the New Orleans sales.

Two factors lead us to doubt this interpretation. First, there is little evidence that the law was invoked. The absence of evidence of enforcement suggests either that economic rather than legal factors were the main constraint on child sales or that the law was not taken very seriously.

Second, data recorded in the coastwise manifests indicate that the share of children among slaves shipped into Mobile by traders was even smaller than the share of children shipped into New Orleans. This finding strongly suggests that the principal constraints on child sales were economic or social rather than legal.

2.8. (p. 56). Estimates of the incidence of hiring were constructed by Claudia Goldin. Communicated in a letter dated February 8, 1973.

2.9. (p. 57). The migration rates of the slave and free populations are compared in [205].

Notes to Chapter 3

3.1. (pp. 67-71). In this note we present the basic models required to interpret the debate on the profitability and viability of slavery. In **3.2** we summarize and comment on the arguments of some of the leading disputants. In **3.3** we evaluate the debate and provide some new evidence bearing on the points at issue.

3.1.1. It is assumed that the slave-using sector may be described by a Cobb-Douglas production function.[3]

$$(3.1) \quad Q = AL^{\alpha_1} K^{\alpha_2} T^{\alpha_3} ; \alpha_1 + \alpha_2 + \alpha_3 = 1.$$

The marginal product of labor is then

$$(3.2) \quad \frac{\partial Q}{\partial L} = \alpha_1 \frac{Q}{L} = \alpha_1 AK^{\alpha_2} T^{\alpha_3} L^{-(\alpha_2 + \alpha_3)}.$$

3.1.2. The Rental Market. Since the slave-using sector had the characteristics of a competitive industry, the annual gross rental price (which included not only the payment to the owner, but also the cost of maintain-

---

[3]There is no contradiction between our assumption of constant returns to scale here and our argument in chapter 6 for increasing returns to scale. Increasing returns existed only on the level of the firm, not on the level of industry. For a fuller discussion of this issue see **6.1-6.3**.

Table B.6

Definitions of Symbols Used in Notes to Chapter 3

Q = output

L = input of labor

K = input of capital

T = input of land

A = efficiency index of the production function

α_j = output elasticities of the inputs; $\Sigma\alpha_j = 1$

P = price

H = annual net hire rate of a slave

P_{sn} = price of a slave n years after his acquisition

i = rate of return or rate of discount

n = the expected number of years that a slave will be held

M = average annual maintenance cost of a slave

X = $1 - 1/(1 + i)^n$

θ_1 = ratio of gross revenue derived from slaves to the net revenue in the base period; $\theta_1 = H_g/H$

θ_2 = ratio of maintenance cost of slaves to the net revenue in the base period; $\theta_2 = 1 - \theta_1$

λ_t = the probability that a slave will live through year t

ψ = the ratio of the net earnings of a slave of a given age to the average peak-age net earnings of a slave

R = the annual net revenue derived from a slave

C = price of a slave plus the land and equipment that he used

E = annual rental value of the land and equipment used by a slave

ρ = the ratio of the price of a slave of a given age to average peak-age price of a slave

B = value of the "birthright" (the zero-age price of a slave)

ϕ = the probability of a live birth in a given year

V = the share of the price of a female which is due to her childbearing capacity

I = number of infants (children under one year of age)

F = number of females aged 15–45

D = intercept of a demand function (all the variables that cause the demand function to shift); an index of demand

S = the intercept of the supply function (all the variables that cause the supply function to shift)

ϵ = elasticity of demand

γ = elasticity of supply

$\bar{w}$ = wage rate

r = rental rate on land

m = rental rate on capital

$\bar{P}$ = the long-run equilibrium price

$*$ = an asterisk over a variable indicates the rate of change of that variable

c = a subscript denoting cotton

s = a subscript denoting slaves

g = a subscript denoting the gross rather than the net value of a variable

e = a subscript denoting the expected value of that variable

f = a subscript denoting that the variable pertains to prime-age hands; e.g., L_f = input of labor measured in equivalent prime-age male hands

w = a subscript which indicates that the variable pertains to a female

y = a subscript indicating a particular calendar year

$\bar{y}$ = a subscript indicating average value of a variable over a particular set of years

b = a subscript indicating that the net earnings are due to childbearing

x = a subscript indicating the age of a slave

t = a subscript or exponent designating a year

---

ing the slave) was equal to the value of the marginal physical product of a slave. When the slave-sector production function is described by equation 3.1, the demand curve for slave hires, *including the reservation demand of owners,* is

$$(3.3) \quad H_g = \alpha_1 P_c Q L^{-1}.$$

It is frequently more convenient to work with the rate of growth transformation of equation 3.3, which is

$$(3.4) \quad \overset{*}{H}_g = \overset{*}{P}_c + \overset{*}{Q} - \overset{*}{L}.$$

3.1.2.1. When equation 3.3 is interpreted to include the reservation demand, the supply curve for the rental slaves is perfectly inelastic and L is equal to the entire slave population of working age. This is a crucial point since it is the crux of Evans's argument (see **3.2.4**) and Butlin's vacillation on this point [31, chap. 4] is responsible for his misinterpretation of Evans's argument.[4]

3.1.2.2. That the interpretation we have given to equation 3.3 is warranted can be demonstrated with the aid of figure B.1.

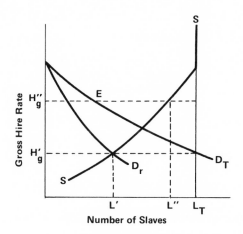

Figure B.1

The total number of slaves available for hire at any time was limited to the number of slaves of working age in existence at that time. Of course, most slaves were actually employed by their owners rather than by renters. Whether or not a slaveowner would hire his slave out depended on the relationship between the hire rate and the value of the slave to him. In order to induce an owner to hire out a particular slave, one would have to offer that owner a rental fee equal to at least the value of the marginal product of the slave to the owner. It follows that the supply curve of rental slaves relates the value of the marginal product of slaves (as envisioned by owners) to the quantity of slaves. Such a curve (identified as *S*) is shown in figure B.1. The supply is positively sloped until the quantity of slaves supplied becomes equal to the total stock of slaves. Then the supply curve becomes vertical. The positively sloped section of the curve reflects the

---

[4] However, many of Butlin's criticisms of Evans were warranted. See **3.2.4.2.**

fact that as owners are asked to rent out more and more slaves, the value to them of the remaining slaves will increase. The vertical section of the supply curve means that once the number of slaves rented becomes equal to the total stock of slaves, no further increase in the hire rate can increase the number of slaves offered for hire.

The supply and demand curve together determine the rental price of slaves. In figure B.1, the demand schedule of renters is shown by curve D_r. The intersection of this demand curve with the supply curve yields a hire rate of H_g'. At this price owners will rent out L' slaves and retain $L_T - L'$ for their own use.

That owners retain some slaves is evidence of the existence of a *reservation* demand. The reservation demand is described by a schedule or curve which relates the number of slaves that owners want to hold to the hire rate. This schedule is implicit in figure B.1. It is derived by subtracting the supply curve of hire slaves from the total stock of slaves. Thus, at a gross hire rate of H_g'', owners will want to supply L'' number of slaves and retain $L_T - L''$ slaves. The $L_T - L''$ represents the reservation demand of owners at a price of H_g'', just as $L_T - L'$ represents the reservation demand of owners at a price of H_g'.

If one adds the reservation demand of owners to the demand of renters, he obtains a total demand curve for slave labor service. The construction of this curve can also be demonstrated in figure B.1. At a price of H_g'' the reservation demand is $L_T - L''$. If we add this amount to the demand of renters, we obtain point E, which is one point on the total demand curve for slave hires. The rest of the curve can be generated in the same way. In figure B.1, the total demand for slaves is shown by D_T. This total demand curve intersects the one representing the total stock of slave workers at a price of H_g', the same price obtained by the intersection of demand curve D_r and supply curve S.

It follows that the analysis of the determinants of slave hire prices can be carried on with either curves D_r and S or with the total demand (D_T) curve and the curve representing the stock of slaves. Thus, the interpretation given to equation 3.3 in **3.1.2.1** is warranted. At the margin, the annual hire rate is identical with the value of the marginal product of slaves to slaveholders who retain slaves — hire slaves out to themselves. Equation 3.3 may, therefore, be interpreted as the total demand curve for annual slave hires. It may be employed to explain either the hire rate paid by renters or to estimate the value of the marginal product of non-rental slaves.

3.1.3. The Purchase Market. In purchasing a prime field hand, a slaveholder was acquiring an asset with a long expected life. Consequently, the price he would be willing to pay for that asset is equal to the discounted present value of the net income to be derived from it. Thus

$$(3.5) \quad P_s = \sum_{t=1}^{n} \frac{\lambda_t R_t}{(1+i)^t} + \frac{\lambda_n P_{sn}}{(1+i)^n} \ .$$

It is sometimes convenient to express R_t as $\psi_t R_f$. Then equation 3.5 can be written as

$$(3.6) \quad P_s = (R_f) \sum_{t=1}^{n} \frac{\psi_t \lambda_t}{(1+i)^t} + \frac{\lambda_n P_{sn}}{(1+i)^n} .$$

In the case of investors who held on to slaves until their death, equation 3.5 reduces to

$$(3.7) \quad P_s = \sum_{t=1}^{n} \frac{\lambda_t R_t}{(1+i)^t} = (R_f) \sum_{t=1}^{n} \frac{\psi_t \lambda_t}{(1+i)^t} .$$

If slaveholders based their purchase decisions on the assumption that the expected net revenue in future years would be equal to the average earned over some past period, equation 3.7 could be written as

$$(3.8) \quad P_s = \frac{R_e}{i} \left[1 - \frac{1}{(1+i)^n} \right] .$$

Since the net revenue from a slave is equal to the difference between gross revenue and maintenance costs, an alternative form of equation 3.8 is

$$(3.9) \quad P_s = (-M_e i^{-1} X) + (\alpha_1 P_{ce} Q_e i^{-1} X) L^{-1}$$

which, of course, is the demand curve for slaves in the purchase market.

3.1.3.1. In the short run the number of slaves, or the number in such sub-categories as prime hands, who entered the labor force was unresponsive to changes in their price. The factors which make the supply of free labor elastic did not apply to slaves. The slave labor force could not be increased through a decrease in the number of youths in school since it was the practice to set slaves to work as soon as they were mature enough to work. Nor could the slave labor supply be affected by the work decisions of females. Unlike free females who may move in and out of the labor force in response to family desires and market incentives, female slaves had no such option. A final source of elasticity in the free labor force is immigration. However, from 1807 on, the importation of slaves was prohibited. Since virtually every slave that could be in the labor force was in it, the short-run supply of slave workers is represented by the vertical line identified as S_s in figure B.2.

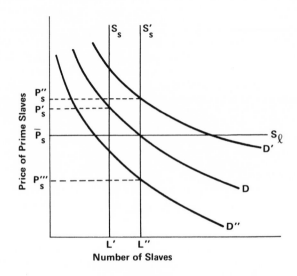

Figure B.2

The curve labeled S_ϱ in that diagram is the long-run supply. Given enough time, the number of slaves could increase at a rate determined by the natural growth of the slave population. Because slaves were deprived of the choice between leisure and work, the shape of the long-run supply of slaves was determined in the same way as that of livestock or of any commodity produced for sale on the market — that is, by the nature of the slave-rearing production function and the prices of the inputs used to raise slaves. Since slaves were raised on a large number of farms, no one of which held more than a very small percentage of the slave population, it seems clear that the slave-raising "industry" was characterized by constant returns to scale. The real price of the main input in slave rearing (food) remained constant between 1820 and 1860, although the population of the nation tripled. This suggests that the long-run supply of food to the slave-rearing "industry" was infinitely elastic. According to Robert Zevin, the long-run supply of the other main input, clothing, was infinitely elastic [396]. Hence it follows that the long-run supply curve of slaves must also have been infinitely elastic at a price $(\bar{P}_s)$ equal to the cost of producing a mature slave.

Figure B.2 may be interpreted as a description of the market for prime hands of age eighteen. The price of such slaves in any given year was determined by the intersection of the demand curve with the short-run supply curve. If the initial demand for slaves is given by D and the supply by S_s, the market price of eighteen-year-olds will be P_s'. Since P_s' exceeds the cost of producing eighteen-year-olds, suppliers of slaves will be earning a "pure profit" or a "capitalized rent" (a profit in excess of the normal one). The pure profit will be equal to the discounted present value of the annual difference between the net earnings of a slave and the amount that could be earned by investing a sum equal to the cost of producing slaves at the normal rate of return.[5] If the demand for slaves does not change, the growth in the short-run supply of eighteen-year-olds will eventually eliminate the capitalized rent. Thus, in figure B.2, a growth in the supply of labor from S_s to S_s' (L' to L'') drops the price of a slave from P_s' to $\bar{P}_s$, to the cost of production. However, if the demand for slaves increases more rapidly than the supply, the capitalized rent will increase over time. This case is illustrated by the shift in the demand curve from D to D'. The increased demand intersects the increased supply at a price of P_s'', which is in excess of P_s'.

Of course the demand for slaves could also fall over time. If the demand curve shifted from D to D'' at the same time that the supply increased from

---

[5] If H_j is the net earnings of mature slaves in year j, c_j the net cost of rearing an immature slave in year j, λ_j the probability that a slave will survive the jth year, $\bar{P}_s$ the cost of producing slaves, P_s' the market price of slaves, r the prevailing market rate of return, n the year of the sale, and k the life expectancy of slaves aged n, profit is

$$P_s' - \bar{P}_s = \sum_{j=n+1}^{n+k} \frac{\lambda_j H_j}{(1+r)^j} - \sum_{j=0}^{n} \lambda_j c_j (1+r)^{n-j} .$$

S_s to S'_s, the equilibrium price of eighteen-year-old slaves would drop to P'''_s. Since this price is below the cost of producing slaves ($\bar{P}_s$), owners would not want to continue the raising of slaves if they expected P'''_s to persist. The production of slaves could have been ended through manumission, birth control, or some similar measure.

From the foregoing discussion it is apparent that the short-run equilibrium price of slaves in the purchase market is determined by the intersection of the demand curve for slaves, represented by equation 3.9, with a perfectly inelastic supply curve. The value of L in equation 3.9 is, therefore, merely the number of slaves in the labor force.

The rate of growth transformation of equation 3.9 is

$$(3.10) \quad \overset{*}{P}_s = \theta_1 (\overset{*}{P}_{ce} + \overset{*}{Q}_e - \overset{*}{L}_e) - \theta_2 \overset{*}{M}_e - \overset{*}{i} + \overset{*}{X}$$

which reduces to

$$(3.11) \quad \overset{*}{P}_s = \theta_1 \overset{*}{H}_{ge} - \theta_2 \overset{*}{M}_e - \overset{*}{i} + \overset{*}{X}$$

and

$$(3.12) \quad \overset{*}{P}_s = \overset{*}{H}_e - \overset{*}{i} + \overset{*}{X}.$$

3.1.4. Conspicuous Consumption. If slaves were held not merely for productive purposes but as status symbols, as objects of conspicuous consumption, the preceding analysis would have to be modified. The modification is necessary not because some slaves were servants. Servants can be treated with the models previously set forth merely by considering the servant market as one distinct from the productive input market. A special problem arises, however, if slaves who are used as productive inputs, say prime field hands, are simultaneously desired as objects of conspicuous consumption by the people who employ these same slaves in the fields; that is, there is a conspicuous consumption demand for field workers by plantation owners.

Figure B.3 shows the modification required in this case. The modification turns on the existence of two separate sources of demand for the same hands, a producers' demand and a consumers' demand. These demands are represented by curves D_p and D_c respectively. Since the same people want the slaves for both purposes, the aggregate demand curve (designated as ABC) is obtained by adding D_p and D_c vertically. The intersection of the aggregate demand curve with the supply curve gives the equilibrium price

(P_s). It will be noted that if slaves were desired only for use as productive inputs, the price would be P_s'. Hence, if conspicuous consumption exists,

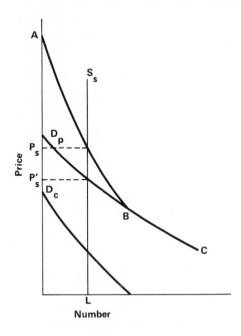

Figure B.3

the observed market price of slaves exceeds the value of the marginal product of slaves as productive inputs.[6]

It follows that equation 3.6, or one of its variants, can be used to test the proposition that conspicuous consumption inflated the market price of slaves and made an investment in slaves, for ordinary business purpose

---

[6]We have drawn the consumption demand curve with a negative slope. This does not rule out the proposition that slaves were a "snob" good. The *aggregate* consumption curve will be upward sloping only if snobbery is limited to individuals in the highest income bracket. If all income groups harbor this attitude, the aggregate curve will have the usual negative slope. A fall in the price of Cadillacs, for example, might lead some current buyers to switch to Continentals. However, the price decline will also lead (presumably more) people who previously bought Buicks, and other comparable cars, to switch to Cadillacs.

alone, unprofitable. All that is necessary is to solve that equation for i, substituting the observed market price of slaves for P_s and the value of the marginal product of slaves in business activity alone for R_t.

It might be argued that those who purchased slaves for conspicuous consumption were a different group of people from those who purchased slaves for productive purposes and, hence, that the demand curves should be added horizontally rather than vertically. This viewpoint, while novel, has nothing to do with the point at issue. For if conspicuous consumers were different from productive users of slaves, there is no basis for expecting conspicuous consumption to have pushed the rate of return of planters below the market rate of return. When the demand curves are added horizontally, P_s and R_t both rise, leaving i unchanged.

In any event, the thesis that there were separate markets for conspicuous consumption and for productive activity is historically unwarranted. There is not, nor has there ever been, any evidence or alleged evidence, that any significant number of slaves were held as "objets d'art," freed from all productive responsibilities. Arduous measurements are not needed to reject that hypothesis. The usual form of the hypothesis of conspicuous consumption is interesting precisely because it cannot be rejected by mere inspection. The fact that all, or nearly all, slaves were used in productive pursuits does not dispose of the contention that a substantial part of the income of their owners took a nonpecuniary form.

3.2. Phillips initiated the modern debate on the profitability of ordinary investments in slaves [257; cf. 374]. The issue was not really joined until the appearance of the paper by Conrad and Meyer [53]. The principal critics of Conrad and Meyer on the issue of profitability have been Saraydar [287], Genovese [139], Sutch [316], Foust and Swan [122], Butlin [31], and Yasuba [392]. An extremely important, but much neglected paper, was published by Evans [105]. Working independently of Conrad and Meyer on the issue of profitability, Evans's approach avoided many of the computational problems which beset Conrad and Meyer.

3.2.1. To support his contention that slaves were an unprofitable investment, Phillips assembled time series on the prices of slaves and raw cotton. These series showed that from 1815 on, slave prices rose more rapidly than cotton prices. According to Phillips, that fact was sufficient to establish the proposition that the profitability of slavery must have declined over the period. Indeed, since the ratio of slave to cotton prices was much higher in 1860 than it had been in 1815, he drew the conclusion that by the eve of the Civil War, slavery had become unprofitable.

Equation 3.13 is the algebraic representation of the Phillips argument:

$$(3.13) \quad \overset{*}{i} = \bar{b}(\overset{*}{P_c} - \overset{*}{P_s})$$

where $\bar{b}$ is a constant. Thus Phillips's central argument for the unprofit-ability of slavery rested on the implicit assumption that the rate of change in profit was related to the rate of change in the ratio of cotton to slave prices by the simplest of all possible equations — a linear equation with a zero intercept.

We do not mean to give the impression that Phillips was naïve. Quite the contrary, the issues in the economics of slavery which have occupied so much of the attention of econometric historians during the past decade are those which he defined. It is surprising that Phillips knew as much about capital theory as he did. Not only is equation 3.13 related to equation 3.8, but in one of the footnotes of *American Negro Slavery*, Phillips explicitly referred to that equation.[7] Phillips was fully aware of the similarity be-tween an investment in a slave and in a long-term security such as a bond, and built much of his argument on that similarity.

It can be shown that the expression for the change in the rate of profit implied by equation 3.8 is not equation 3.13 but

$$(3.14) \quad \overset{*}{i} = \bar{b}[\theta_1(\overset{*}{P_c} - \overset{*}{P_s}) + \theta_1(\overset{*}{Q} - \overset{*}{L}) + (1 - \theta_1)\overset{*}{M}].$$

Here $\bar{b}$ is a constant close to 1; its exact magnitude depends on the base-period values of i and n.

A comparison between equations 3.13 and 3.14 reveals that equation 3.13 is merely a special case of equation 3.14. Equation 3.14 will reduce to equation 3.13 when $\theta_1 = 1$ and $\overset{*}{Q} - \overset{*}{L} = 0$. Consequently the evaluation of the Phillips thesis comes down to the question of whether Phillips was justified in implicitly assuming that $\theta_1 = 1$ and $\overset{*}{Q} - \overset{*}{L} = 0$. For only then is information on the change in the ratio of cotton to slave prices *alone* suf-ficient to determine that profits were declining.

3.2.2. Most participants in the debate on the profitability of slavery have assumed that Conrad and Meyer represent a sharp break with Phillips and with the traditional interpretation of slavery. This is incorrect. While Conrad and Meyer differed with Phillips on a number of important empiri-cal issues, the basic conceptual approaches of the three scholars to the problem of profitability were quite similar. Moreover, to the extent that

[7]The equation is presented in Gibson [142]. Phillips cites Gibson and then states that his own discussion is "mostly in accord with Gibson's analysis" [261, p. 359].

Conrad and Meyer differed with Phillips on empirical matters, their positions made them more direct continuers of the traditional interpretation than was Phillips.

3.2.2.1. "From the standpoint of the entrepreneur making an investment in slaves," wrote Conrad and Meyer, "the basic problems involved in determining profitability are analytically the same as those met in determining the returns from any other kind of capital investment." This, of course, is the way in which Phillips posed the problem. Conrad and Meyer sought to go beyond Phillips by actually estimating the value of i on the basis of data available in the secondary literature. Thus they put into operation the capital equation to which Phillips alluded but never actually used.

Conrad and Meyer based their computations not on equation 3.8 but on a slightly modified form of that equation, namely

$$(3.15) \quad C = \frac{R_e + E}{i} \left[1 - \frac{1}{(1+i)^n} \right].$$

It easily can be shown that equation 3.15 reduces to equation 3.8. Since

$$(3.16) \quad C - P_s = \frac{E}{i} \left[1 - \frac{1}{(1+i)^n} \right],$$

it follows that

$$(3.17) \quad P_s = C - \frac{E}{i} \left[1 - \frac{1}{(1+i)^n} \right] = \frac{R_e}{i} \left[1 - \frac{1}{(1+i)^n} \right].$$

The choice of equation 3.15 instead of 3.8 was unfortunate, since it involved Conrad and Meyer in the difficult but unnecessary task of attempting to estimate $C - P_s$. It also confused some scholars who failed to recognize the identity between equations 3.15 and 3.8.

3.2.2.2. Their search of the secondary literature led Conrad and Meyer to the conclusion that there were significant differences in the $(C - P_s)$ among plantations and that corresponding to the differences in $(C - P_s)$ were differences in the value of $\alpha_1 Q/L$. Thus they divided slave plantations into four classes, according to the corresponding values of $(C - P_s)$ and $\alpha_1 Q/L$. Moreover, to simplify the computation they assumed that, within each class, the average physical product per slave equaled the marginal physical product per slave.

This last point has confused some scholars. Butlin, for example, argues that Conrad and Meyer believed that slave plantations were characterized by fixed proportions [31, pp. 82–85]. However, this interpretation of Conrad and Meyer is inconsistent with their emphasis on substitution possibilities between factors and their acceptance, as acknowledged by Butlin, of the Evans model, which is explicitly based on a neoclassical production function [53, pp. 50–53; 31, pp. 82–85].

Table B.7

Estimates of Conrad and Meyer

Investment class	$C - P_s$ ($)	P_s ($)	P_c (cents)	$\alpha_1 Q/L$ (bales)	M ($)	i (%)
1	450	925	8	3.75	20.5	5.2
2	675	925	8	4.5	20.5	7.0
3	350	925	8	3.0	20.5	3.9
4	775	925	8	7.0	20.5	12.0

Source: [53, pp. 61, 64]

The estimates of the basic variables employed by Conrad and Meyer, and the values of i (when $n = 30$) implied by these estimates are shown in table B.7. It will be noted that two of the investment classes, 1 and 3, exhibit rates of return below 6 percent — the figure which Conrad and Meyer argued was the best approximation to the market rate of return. Conrad and Meyer identified their investment classes as follows:

Class 1: average for the South

Class 2: somewhat better land than the Southwide average

Class 3: worn lands of Upper South

Class 4: best land in the cotton belt, such as the Mississippi alluvium.

Conrad and Meyer also estimated the rate of return on female slaves on average land and found it to be somewhere between 7.1 and 8.1 percent, depending on the average number of children per female. With this high rate of return on females, the average rate of return of planters in investment classes 1 and 3 was (using the average of the 7.1 and 8.1 figures for females) 6.4 and 5.8. Thus, Conrad and Meyer concluded that even plantations with relatively low values of $\alpha_1 Q/L$, such as those in investment class 3, were able to achieve normal rates of profit by engaging in slave-breeding.

3.2.2.3. The congeniality of the findings of Conrad and Meyer with the traditional interpretation is obvious. Olmsted, Cairnes, and Phillips were all prepared to admit high rates of return for large slave plantations in the New or Lower South (Conrad and Meyer investment classes 2 and 4). Cairnes and Olmsted also believed, with Conrad and Meyer, that slave-breeding permitted Upper South plantations to raise their profits to normal levels [see chapter 5, in the primary volume]. Conrad and Meyer differed with Phillips mainly on the issue of slave-breeding – the same point on which Phillips differed with Olmsted and Cairnes. Since Phillips rejected the existence of slave-breeding and its significance as a source of income for planters in the Upper South, he held that the overall rate of return of investors in classes 1 and 3 was below normal levels.

3.2.2.4. Conrad and Meyer presented their results as the average rates of return actually earned on investments in slaves during 1830–1860. This widely accepted interpretation of their result is wrong. For slaves purchased after 1835, in the case of males, and after 1827, in the case of females, would have been freed before the expiration of the earnings period ($n = 30$ or 38) stipulated by Conrad and Meyer in their analysis. Nor can their computation be taken to be representative of slaves purchased before these dates. For the average price of slaves purchased before 1835 was considerably below the level assumed in their analysis.

What Conrad and Meyer did was to provide the answer to a question somewhat different than one usually presumed. That question is: "If investors during 1846–1850 believed that a prime slave would continue to be as productive as such slaves had been on average during the previous decade, and if they thought that the price of cotton as well as slave maintenance costs would also continue at the average level of the late forties, was the 1846–1850 price of a slave justified by business considerations alone?"[8] The computation of Conrad and Meyer answered this question in the affirmative for both male and female slaves. It showed that a person who purchased a prime slave during 1846–1850 at the prevailing market price could, if he based himself on recent experience, expect to earn about the same rate of return on his investment in slaves as was being earned on alternative long-term investment opportunities.

Although the Conrad and Meyer study did not reveal what planters actually earned from their investment in slaves, it did provide an answer to the question originally posed by Phillips. Phillips had argued that the prices of slaves after 1815 were generally unjustified by the income planters could obtain from employing slaves in the production of crops. Conrad and Meyer replied that the evidence in the secondary literature showed that the price of slaves was fully justified by the value of the crops they produced and income from slave-breeding. Consequently, they rejected as unwarranted Phillips's contention that the price of slaves was inflated by wild speculative flights and conspicuous consumption.

3.2.3. As with most pioneering studies, the findings of Conrad and Meyer were open to criticism. There were many rough approximations in their estimates of the variables which enter into equation 3.15. Critics have not only disputed the values which they assigned to C, R_e, E, and n but have also objected to their use of equation 3.15 as an approximation to equation 3.7. Most of the fire has been directed towards those aspects of the Conrad and Meyer computations which are believed to have biased upward the estimate of the rate of return. For convenience of discussion we have grouped the various issues into three categories.

The first concerns the standard used to judge the relative profitability of an investment in slaves. Conrad and Meyer argued that the appropriate standard was the return on capital that would have prevailed in the absence of slavery.[9] They also held that this rate was approximated by the prevailing (and relatively low) short-term interest rate. As Yasuba and Evans both

---

[8] Yasuba and Evans pointed out that the price of slaves and of the value of other variables which Conrad and Meyer estimated in computing i from equation 3.15 pertain to about the period 1846–1850.

[9] The same position was recently taken by Harry Scheiber [54].

pointed out [392; 105], this position is erroneous. What is at issue is not the social profitability of slavery, but the profitability to the individual investor. Consequently, the appropriate standard of comparison is the rate of return which prevailed on alternative investments actually open to private investors. On this basis, an investment in slaves would be judged profitable only if the return equaled or exceeded the return that could have been earned on another investment which had the same degree of risk as the ownership of slaves. Since high-grade, short-term securities are relatively riskless, this rate may be too low to be the appropriate standard of comparison. To guard against biasing the findings in favor of their argument, one could instead choose the earning rate on capital in railroads or in manufacturing industry. These rates exceeded those observed for high-grade, short-term securities by 30 to 60 percent.[10]

The second category of issues is demographic. Critics have challenged the assumptions of Conrad and Meyer regarding the longevity of slaves, the net reproduction rate, and the percentage of live births that reached age 18. Evans pointed out that the assumption that all eighteen-year-old slaves lived the average length of life exaggerated the rate of return. For "the income lost due to early deaths must be made up by income gained from those who live beyond the life expectancy age. . . . Even if it were physically possible, the capitalized value of extra income would be less than the capitalized value of the lost income" [105, p. 209].

The most thorough consideration of the demographic issues is contained in Noel Butlin's series of essays, *Ante-bellum Slavery* [31]. Like Evans, Butlin criticized the substitution of an average age for the distribution of survivors. Even more devastating, however, is Butlin's attack on the Conrad-Meyer assumptions regarding the reproduction rate of slaves. He points out that even if females between age eighteen and the end of their period of fertility had a successful pregnancy every other year, the high rate of infant and child mortality precluded the possibility that an average of ten of these children would survive beyond their eighteenth year. Considering actual fertility experience and the observed rate of growth of the slave population, it is likely, on average, that the female slave produced less than five children during her lifetime who survived to age eighteen. Consequently Conrad and Meyer biased their estimate on the rate of return on females upward in three major respects. They overestimated the income from the sale of off-

---

[10]These rates may be too high to serve as a standard, since some have argued that manufacturing and railroad enterprises in the South were more risky than cotton production.

Table B.8

Differences[1] with Conrad and Meyer Estimates for Male Slaves

	(1) Investment class	(2) Difference in $C - P_s$ ($)	(3) Difference in P_s ($)	(4) Difference in P_c (cents)	(5) Difference in $\alpha_1 Q/L$ (bales)	(6) Difference in M ($)	(7) Difference in i (percentage points)
Saraydar[2]	1	+315	0	0	-0.55	+11.5	-3.7
Saraydar[2]	4	+ 93	0	0	-3.4	+11.5	-9.7
Saraydar[2]	3	+111	0	0	-1.0	+11.5	-3.7
Genovese	not specified	not specified	not specified	not specified	not specified	+43.75	not specified
Foust and Swan[2,3]	1	+260	-295	+1.0	+0.65	- 5.0	+1.0
Foust and Swan[2,3]	4	-135	-295	+1.0	-3.4	- 5.0	-6.5

Sources: [287; 139; 122]

[1]The entries in cols. 2–7 were computed by subtracting, from the estimates of either Saraydar or Foust and Swan, the estimates for the corresponding variables of Conrad and Meyer.

[2]These estimates are per *average* hand rather than per *prime* hand as in Conrad and Meyer.

[3]We have deducted from the rates of return presented in [122, table 5], the 2.2 percent which Foust and Swan attributed to breeding in order to make their estimates comparable to those of Conrad and Meyer.

spring. They underestimated the cost of producing salable progeny by failing to include the cost of those children who died between birth and age eighteen.[11] They failed to take account of the fact that not all eighteen-year-old females lived through the end of their childbearing period. Butlin's correction of these errors dropped the rate of return on females from between 7 and 8 percent to only 4.5 percent.

The third category of issues concerns the estimation of the net earnings of prime hands [of $R_f = H_f = \alpha_1 P_c(Q/L_f) - M_f$] and of the average amount of capital per prime hand $(C - P_s)$. Disputes on the appropriateness of the values of these variables have occupied more of the attention of the critics of Conrad and Meyer than either of the other two categories of issues. Table B.8 indicates the range of differences with Conrad and Meyer on the estimation of R_e and its determinants. Table B.8 shows how much of an effect differences in the estimates of the indicated values have on the estimated value of i, even within the framework of equation 3.15 and with $n = 30$.

3.2.4. Working independently of Conrad and Meyer, Evans set out to use equation 3.6 instead of equation 3.15 to estimate i. This substitution of equations improved upon the Conrad and Meyer approach in three respects: it circumvented the problem of estimating $C - P_s$; it took account of the effect of mortality on profits by including the variable λ_t; and it permitted Evans to finesse the problem of estimating the value of ψ_t during advanced ages by taking advantage of the relationship

$$(3.18) \quad P_{sn} = (R_f) \sum_{t=n}^{\infty} \frac{\psi_t \lambda_t}{(1 + i)^t}.$$

Evans also sought to finesse the many thorny problems involved in building up an estimate of R_f from its determinants $(P_c, \alpha_1 Q/L_f, \text{ and } M_f)$. His tactic was to make use of annual rental contracts for slaves which he discovered were generally listed in documents at net hire rates (H_f). Then he could make use of the identity

$$(3.19) \quad H_f = H_{gf} - M_f$$

and equation (3.3) to show that

[11] The same point was also made by Yasuba [392].

$$(3.20) \quad H_f = \alpha_1 P_c(Q/L_f) - M_f = R_{ft}.$$

Moreover, by confining himself to the interval $t = 0$ to $t = 30$ (where $0 =$ age 20), Evans thought that it would be safe to assume $\psi_t = 1$.

In order to carry through his estimation procedure, Evans gathered a sample of 6,600 slave hire prices for both the upper and lower South over the years from 1830 through 1860. He also collected a sample of slave prices which, he argued, showed that Phillips had underestimated the rate of increase in slave prices. Evans's estimates of slave hire rates and prices are shown in table B.9, and the rates of return which he derived from these figures are shown in table B.10.

Table B.9

Five-Year Averages of Hires and Weighted Prices of Slaves, 1830–60

Period	Upper South		Lower South	
	Hire	*Price*	*Hire*	*Price*
1830–35	$ 62	$ 521	$127	$ 948
1836–40	106	957		
1841–45	83	529	143	722
1846–50	99	709	168	926
1851–55	141.5	935	167	1,240
1856–60	142	1,294	196.5	1,658

Source: [105, p. 216]

Like Conrad and Meyer, Evans interpreted his estimates of i as the rates of return actually earned by investors in slaves. However, this cannot be the proper interpretation of the figures in table B.10. For in his computation Evans assumed that the average hire rate prevailing in the year that a slave was purchased would remain constant throughout the period that the slave was held, although the actual hire rates fluctuated quite widely, as table B.9 shows. Moreover, slaves purchased after 1835 could not have been held for the full term of 30 years, since all slaves were freed in 1865.

Table B.10

Average Rate of Return on Slaves Estimated by Evans, 1830–60 (percent)

Period	Upper South	Lower South
1830–35	10.5	12.0
1836–40	9.5	
1841–45	14.3	18.5
1846–50	12.6	17.0
1851–55	13.8	12.0
1856–60	9.5	10.3

Source: [105, p. 217]

Like Conrad and Meyer, Evans produced not a series of estimates of the rate of return actually earned by purchasers of slaves, but a reply to Phillips. Phillips had argued that the prevailing prices of slaves could not be justified by the prevailing hire rates; that is, Phillips believed that at prevailing hire rates, the prevailing prices of slaves were so high that a purchaser of slaves would be unable to earn a normal rate of return on his investment. Evans produced estimates which showed that the Phillips conjecture was false for every quinquennium from 1830 through 1860.

3.2.4.1. Govan criticized the rates of return shown in table B.10 on the grounds that they moved countercyclically. "But the results from this equation [equation 3.6]," said Govan, "seem to me truly astonishing. From 1830 to 1835, a most prosperous period except for the winter of 1833–34, the rate of return on capital invested in slaves is said to be 12%, but in the period from 1841 to 1845, when operators of plantations, businesses, and factories in the United States were barely getting by, the rate of return is said to be 18.5%" [151, p. 246].

The paradox arose because Govan accepted Evans's unwarranted claim that the computation revealed the actual rates of return earned by slaveowners. But Evans's computation merely shows whether or not the current price of slaves was justified by their current earnings. For periods during which the price of slaves was below that justified by current earnings because investors were pessimistic about the future — as occurred during

1841–1845 — Evans's computation will yield an inappropriately high rate of return. This is merely a way of stating that with the 1841–1845 earnings, the prices of slaves were too low. Investors who took advantage of the prevailing pessimism by buying slaves at the depressed prices could hardly have avoided making a "killing." What Evans's computation revealed is the rate of return such purchasers could expect to earn if they bought slaves at the depressed price and if earnings continued at the 1841–1845 level during the years that followed.

3.2.4.2. Butlin has raised a series of objections to Evans's calculation. One objection pertains to the representativeness of the sample of hire rates. Butlin argues that prior to 1852 the sample is too small to be representative and that after 1845 too large a part of the sample comes from a small number of urban firms. The small size of the sample *per se* does not necessarily bias the estimates, although their uneven distribution over years may distort the temporal movement of hire rates. Distortions might also be introduced by the shifting weights of various geographic regions in the sample. Given state and city differences in hire rates, shifts in weights would cause the index of slave hires to change, even when hire rates within states or cities were unchanged.

Another possible source of error is that the hire rates were not really net rates. If the hire rates are to be a measure of the value of the marginal product of slave labor to the lessor, netness must be evaluated from his point of view. However, the hire rates listed in contracts were net only with respect to food, clothing, and shelter. Butlin points out that they are not adjusted for any greater risk when hired out than when retained by the plantations of owners. The greater risk arises not so much from abuse as from the overrepresentation of urban hires in Evans's sample. For urban death rates were significantly greater than rural death rates. Butlin also notes that Evans failed to take account of the time lost while lessors were waiting to find lessees. Two other costs of leasing not netted out by Evans were the fees to brokers which ran about 7.5 percent of the annual hire rate and the cost of medical insurance, which usually had to be provided by the lessor.

3.3. The basic economic problem posed by the historical literature is not what slaveowners actually earned on their investments, but whether prevailing slave prices were generally justified by the pecuniary income derived from slaves by their owners. Obviously owners who acquired or held slave capital of the average "vintage" during the last two decades of the antebellum era all suffered capital losses. For, as shown in figure 32, the slaveowning class did not foresee, nor could it have been expected to have foreseen, the utter collapse of the peculiar institution that came with the close of the Civil War.

The really important historical question was not the capacity of the slaveholding class to read crystal balls, but whether business or nonbusiness – pecuniary or nonpecuniary – considerations dominated their transactions with respect to slave capital. This is the problem explicitly posed by Phillips and which, as we have shown in chapter 5, was also posed, although more obliquely, by Olmsted and Cairnes.

The problems standing in the way of a resolution of this issue have been both theoretical and empirical. While Phillips understood the basic theoretical issues, as his allusion to Gibson's book makes clear, his treatment of the question was so obscure that it misled his followers, many of whom failed to appreciate that Phillips's solution was correct only under certain very definite assumptions regarding the values of θ_1 and $\overset{*}{Q} - \overset{*}{L}$.

Most of the basic theoretical issues were made explicit by Conrad and Meyer who conceived of equation 3.15 as a reasonable approximation to equations 3.5 or 3.6. With the appearance of Evans's paper, the statement of the basic theoretical issues involved in answering the problem posed by Phillips was, more or less, complete. Since that time the central issues have been empirical.

While the empirical problems standing in the way of an adequate solution to Phillips's problem are not irresolvable, they are certainly very difficult. The most intractable problems have been the estimation of the values of $\alpha_1 Q/L_f$ and M_f. Little progress could be made as long as scholars relied on evidence in the secondary literature for estimates of these variables. The point is not merely that estimates in the secondary literature varied widely, but that they confused Q/L with Q/L_f and M with M_f. Still another problem arose from the fact that not all slave labor was employed in the production of agricultural output, even on plantations. Or to put the issue differently, not all pecuniary income originating in agriculture was measured in the output usually described as agricultural production. It was therefore necessary either to allocate an appropriate part of L_f to such nonagricultural activities as domestic services and manufacturing, or to increase Q by an appropriate amount, or to do both. These were all quantitatively important adjustments and difficult ones to make. As Butlin pointed out, no real progress could be made on these issues without "hard fact-gathering" [31, p. 96].

3.3.1. Evans was the first of the cliometricians to gather a substantial new body of evidence and to bring it to bear on the questions at issue. His sample of over 6,000 hire rates was the largest addition to the available body of data bearing on the economics of slavery in four decades — since Phillips's work on the collection of slave prices prior to and during World War I. Although Evans's clever stratagem for finessing the host of problems impeding reliable estimates of $\alpha_1 Q/L_f$ and M_f was not without its own difficulties, it clearly pointed out a new path of research. Moreover, Evans's analysis of the sensitivity of errors in the hire rates to estimates of i revealed that the errors would have to be in excess of 50 percent to push the value of i to a level consistent with the Phillips hypothesis. Since errors in the Evans data of such a magnitude were unlikely, his paper represented a significant contribution to the resolution of the issue of profitability.

Evans's paper was also important because it launched the work on the distribution of λ_t. Indeed, while not without its shortcomings, Evans's life table [105, p. 212] is still the best one currently available for the slave population. Butlin's application of the Jamaican life table from 1879 to 1882 to the U.S. slave population in 1850 is of dubious merit. His contention that the Jamaican table more accurately describes the U.S. slave mortality experience than Evans's table [31, pp. 26-28] assumes what has to be proved. In any case the Jamaican life table is so close to Evans's table that the substitution of one for the other has little effect on substantive issues. We do not mean to slight the need for further work on slave life tables but to suggest that progress on this issue lies not through resort to model life tables, whether Jamaican or otherwise, but in the exploitation of available demographic data in plantation and probate records, along the lines now being pursued by Steckel [307].

3.3.2. The basis for a direct approach to improved estimates of $\alpha_1 Q/L_f$ and M_f was laid when Parker and Gallman launched their project to obtain and put into machine-readable form data from a sample of 5,000 southern farms drawn from the manuscript schedules of the 1860 census (see table **B.1** and **P.2.1**). By 1967 the processing of these data had reached a point that made their exploitation feasible. Two early papers based on this sample were those by Battalio and Kagel [14] and by Foust and Swan [122].

Battalio and Kagel made a notable step forward in estimating $\alpha_1 Q/L_f$. On the basis of the data in the secondary literature they worked out a rough distribution of the values of ψ_t. With data obtained from the Parker-Gallman sample they were able to determine that rather than being deficit producers of food, slave plantations actually produced a small surplus of food, equivalent to approximately 1.3 bales of cotton per equivalent full hand. The main limitation of the Battalio and Kagel study was that it was based on a relatively small subsample of the Parker-Gallman data, a sub-sample limited just to South Carolina. The validity of their findings for the rest of the South thus remained in question.

Foust and Swan added to the Battalio and Kagel finding by producing estimates of bales per average hand for the entire South. Drawing on the entire Parker-Gallman sample, they estimated average Southwide product per equivalent full hand (in 400-pound bales) in 1860 as 5.75 bales [122, pp. 45, 54–55] or 53 percent higher than the estimate of Conrad and Meyer. For the year 1850 their upward adjustment was based on a smaller sample drawn from the manuscript schedules of 1850. Their 1850 figure was 17 percent higher than the Conrad and Meyer estimate.

The full significance of the Foust-Swan findings was diminished by two unfortunate decisions. The first was to use 0.5 as the estimate of the ratio of average hands to slaves instead of using the Battalio and Kagel figure of 0.39 to convert to equivalent prime hands. The second was the decision to base their calculation of i on equation 3.15 instead of equation 3.8. Thus, they needlessly became involved in the thorny problem of attempting to estimate the average value of land and capital per equivalent full hand. On this matter they overshot the mark by an even larger amount than Conrad and Meyer. Nevertheless, Foust and Swan found a Southwide average rate of return on slaves (net of income from slave-rearing) of 1.0 percentage points in excess of what Conrad and Meyer conceived of as the typical case.

3.3.3. On the basis of new data we have been able to use equation 3.7 to estimate the value of i. To use equation 3.7 it is necessary to know the distribution of ψ_t. Our method of deriving the distribution of ψ_t involves an iterative procedure, described in **3.4.2.1,** which simultaneously yields the value of i and the distribution of ψ_t.

Our computation resulted in an estimated value of i equal to approximately 10 percent. This figure is lower than those indicated by Evans but higher than the estimates of Foust and Swan.

3.3.3.1. Evans was too high for the reasons outlined by Butlin (see **3.2.4.2**).

3.3.3.2. We have also reestimated the values of the variables which entered into the Foust-Swan computation for 1860. The two sets of estimates are compared in table B.11. Our estimate of output per equivalent prime hand is 85 percent greater than that employed by Conrad and Meyer, and 19 percent greater than the estimate of Foust and Swan. It should be stressed that Q/L_f included not only cotton *per se* but the output of other farm products expressed in equivalents of 400-pound bales (with cotton valued at 10 cents per pound).

Table B.11

A Comparison of the Values of Some of the Variables Relevant to the Computation of the Rate of Return on Slave Capital

Variable and unit of measurement	(1) Estimates of Fogel and Engerman	(2) Estimates of Foust and Swan
1. α_1	0.58	not estimated
2. Q/L_f (bales)	6.9	5.8
3. M_f (dollars)	61	35
4. $C_f - P_{sf}$ (dollars)	1140	1438

Sources:

Column 1: Line 1, **6.2**, **6.3.1**. Line 3, **4.10.1**, **6.7.1.2**. Lines 2 and 4 were computed from data in the Parker-Gallman sample (see table B.1).
Column 2: Taken from data for 1860 in [122].

Perhaps the most surprising feature of table B.11 is the high value of M_f. It exceeds the Foust-Swan figure by 74 percent and is even higher than the amount suggested by Genovese (cf. table B.8), although Genovese presented his estimate as a lower bound.

3.4. (pp. 73–78 and figs. 15–19). The age-price and age-earnings profiles were developed from data in the probate records. Separate profiles were computed for males and females for both the Old South and the New South. The basic shape of the age-price profiles were quite robust to differences in the trend of slave prices. An age-price profile computed from data for the period 1838–1843 (when slave prices were falling quite rapidly) was quite similar to one computed from data for the period 1850–1860 (when slave prices were rising quite rapidly).

What effect should differences in expectations have on the shape of the age-price profile? The answer to that question is more complex than might appear on the surface. Work on the theoretical issues posed by the question is still under way. Our initial findings suggest that the effects, if any, will be slight, and not of magnitudes that would affect the significance of the age-specific price estimates which have thus far been derived from the age-price profiles nor the interpretation of any of the issues based on these estimates.

3.4.1. In this section we describe the basic procedure employed in computing the age-price profiles for males. The procedure for females was similar except that P_{sfw} was defined over the age interval 16 to 25.

3.4.1.1. For each calendar year the value of P_{sf} was computed by averaging the prices of males in the ages 20 to 29 during that calendar year.

3.4.1.2. A price relative (ρ_t') was then formed by dividing the price of a slave of a given age by the average peak-age price; i.e., $p_t' = P_{st}/P_{sf}$.

3.4.1.3. All of the values for ρ_t' were then averaged for each age to produce $\bar{\rho}_t'$, where

$$(3.21) \quad \bar{\rho}_t' = \frac{\sum_{j=1}^{q} \rho_{tj}'}{q} \, .$$

In other words, each of the entries in figure 16 was obtained by averaging the values of all the entries in the corresponding column in figure 15.

3.4.1.4. A sixth order polynomial on age (equation 3.22) was then fitted to the values of $\bar{\rho}_t'$. This fitted curve (equation 3.22) yielded the smoothed values (ρ_t) of the age-price profile

$$(3.22) \quad \rho_t = \eta_o + \sum_{v=1}^{6} \eta_v t^v.$$

3.4.2. The age-earnings profile was derived from the age-price profile by making use of the relationship

$$(3.23) \quad P_{st} = \frac{(\lambda_{t-0.5}/\lambda_{t-1})R_t}{(1+i)^{0.5}} + \frac{(\lambda_t/\lambda_{t-1})P_{s(t+1)}}{(1+i)}$$

which when solved for R_t yields

$$(3.24) \quad R_t = \frac{(1+i)^{0.5}}{\lambda_{t-0.5}/\lambda_{t-1}} P_{st} - \frac{\lambda_t/\lambda_{t-0.5}}{(1+i)^{0.5}} P_{s(t+1)}$$

and

$$(3.25) \quad \psi_t = \frac{R_t}{R_f} = \frac{\dfrac{(1+i)^{0.5}}{\lambda_{t-0.5}/\lambda_{t-1}} P_{st} - \dfrac{\lambda_t/\lambda_{t-0.5}}{(1+i)^{0.5}} P_{s(t+1)}}{R_f}.$$

It can be seen from equation 3.25 that if i is known, ψ_t follows directly.

3.4.2.1. Since i was not known, it was necessary to resort to an iterative procedure which simultaneously yielded the distribution of ψ_t and i. The iterative procedure involves equations 3.7 and 3.25.

First, equation 3.7 was used to compute i', accepting Evans's assumption that $\psi_t = 1$ for $t = 0$ to $t = 30$. However, before the computation, adjustments suggested by Butlin (see **3.2.4.2** and **3.4.2.2**) were made in R_f and λ_t.

Second, the value i' was then inserted into equation 3.25 to produce a vector of estimates of ψ_t'.

Third, the distribution of ψ_t' was then inserted into equation 3.7 to yield a new estimate of i; namely i''.

The iterative procedure was continued until $i^u = i^{u-1}$ and $\psi_t^u = \psi_t^{u-1}$.

3.4.2.2. The following adjustments were made in Evans's data.

1. The urban distribution of λ_t, taken from [190], was substituted for Evans's distribution of λ_t.

2. Evans's value of R_f was reduced by 7.5 percent (see [11, p. 151]) to take account of the agency hiring fee that was charged to the lessor. An allowance of $3.00 was made for medical insurance, which also was charged to the lessor. It was assumed that an amount of time equal to 5 percent of the work year (about 13 days) was lost in the search for a suitable placement for hands let out to hire.

3. Since we wanted to estimate i for periods of "average" expectations, we further adjusted the value of P_{sf}/R_f in such a manner as to be consistent with average expectations. The adjustment factor was based on the ratio of P_{sf}/R_f from 1846 to 1855 to a simple average of the values P_{sf}/R_f for the entire period from 1830 to 1860. The average value of P_{sf}/R_f between 1830 and 1860 may be taken to approximate expectations during the early 1850s.

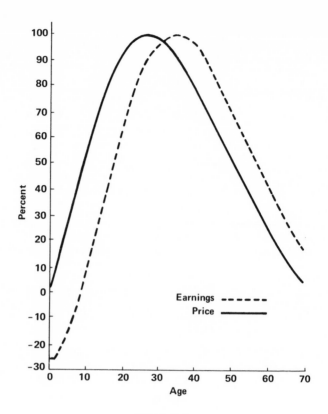

Figure B.4
A Comparison of the Price and Earnings Profiles for Males, Old South

Note that, as with the distribution of ρ_t, the shape of the distribution of ψ_t is quite robust, and hence may be applied to virtually any time period.

The dollar value of R_t was obtained from

$$(3.26) \quad R_{ty} = \psi_t \left(\frac{R_{f\bar{y}}}{P_{sf\bar{y}}} \right) P_{sfy}$$

with P_{sfy} set at \$1,000, the value observed during the early 1850s, and $R_{f\bar{y}}/P_{sf\bar{y}}$ taken as the value that prevailed in the early 1850s. The dollar value of R_t can be converted from time y to time $y + j$ merely by multiplying R_{ty} by the ratio $P_{sf(y+j)}/P_{sfy}$.

3.4.3. The relationship between the age-price and age-earnings profiles is shown in figure B.4. While net earnings were negative during ages 0–8, prices were positive. The positive price at birth reflected the expectation of positive earnings in future years. Prices rose as the burden of maintaining children declined and as the children drew closer to the age at which net losses would be transformed into net gains. Prices reached a peak at age 27, or 8 years sooner than earnings. After age 27, prices began to decline, even though earnings were still rising, because the price of a slave depended not only on the amount of net earnings but on the length of the period over which he would produce these earnings. Thus prices rose between age 9 and age 27 because the increase in annual income outweighed the shortening of the period of future earnings. However, prices declined from age 27 to age 35 because the shortening of the earnings stream outweighed the increase in the annual income during these years. The decline in prices accelerated after age 35 because both annual income and the length of the earnings stream were decreasing.

3.5. (pp. 78–86 and figs. 20–22). The fact that slaves had a positive price at birth is of considerable importance. It is not clear whether all of this price is net of pregnancy costs. Resolution of this issue is extremely complex and involves problems quite similar to those encountered in discussions on the burden of the debt (cf. [107]). From 1810 on, however, the zero-age price was clearly greater than pregnancy costs, so that at least part of the zero-age price, which we call the value of a "birthright," was a rent. This rent was equal to the present value of the difference between expected gross earnings and expected maintenance costs over the life of the slave, as shown by equation 3.27:

$$(3.27) \quad B = \sum_{t=0}^{n} \frac{(H_{get} - M_{et})\lambda_t}{(1+i)^t}$$

Since, for the late antebellum period, pregnancy costs were a small fraction of the zero-age price, we treat B as being equal to the zero-age price of slaves, without prejudicing the issues as to whether the zero-age price is net of all such costs.

3.5.1. Given the value of B, it is possible to divide the price of a woman at any age into two parts: that part of her price which is due to the value of her work in the fields and that part of her price which is due to her childbearing capacity. Since the net earnings due to a female's childbearing capacity in a given year is equal to

(3.28) $\quad R_{wbt} = \phi_t B,$

the price of a woman at age x will be

$$(3.29) \quad P_{swx} = (R_{wf}) \sum_{t=1}^{n} \frac{\psi_{wt}\lambda_{wt}}{(1+i)^t} + B \sum_{t=1}^{n} \frac{\phi_t\lambda_{wt}}{(1+i)^t} .$$

The first right-hand term of equation 3.29 is represented by the vertical distances between the age axis and the dashed curves in figures 20 and 21. The second right-hand term of equation 3.29 is represented by the vertical distances between the dashed and solid curves in the same figures.

3.5.2. The distribution of ϕ_t was taken from a population model [45, p. 30]. Work is currently under way to estimate ϕ_t from information in probate and plantation records.

3.5.3. Both the share of the value price of females represented by the childbearing capacity (V) and the dollar value of VP_{swx} were greater in the New South than in the Old South. This finding not only refutes the contention that pregnancy was considered undesirable by slaveholders in the New South but shows that slaveowners in the New South had greater reason to encourage child rearing than those in the Old South. In other words, while the opportunity cost of pregnancy was relatively high in the New South, the net benefit of children was enough to compensate slaveowners for this cost and still leave them with a higher rent on a new child than could be achieved by slaveholders in the Old South.

Note that B is a function of M from time zero on. Hence all time lost by mothers in nursing children has already been charged to children and should not again be deducted from the net earnings of mothers. One could of course shift the charge for nursing from children to mothers. While this would reduce the first right-hand term of equation 3.29, it would increase the second right-hand term by a like amount, leaving P_{swx} unchanged.

3.5.3.1. Figure 18 shows that prior to age 10 the prices of males and females were equal and in the pre-teens they were nearly equal. Not until the late teens do the prices of females fall substantially below those of males.

This pattern of prices found a reflection in the trading data at New Orleans. Although children under 10 were underrepresented in the trade, more very young females than males were imported into New Orleans. In the twenties, however, substantially more males than females were imported. The peak of female imports was reached during the middle and late teens, about four years earlier than the peak of male imports.

3.5.3.2. The New Orleans data also serve to explain why the *measured* fertility rates of the New South are lower than those for the Old South. Since the fertility rate is measured by the ratio

$$\frac{I}{F}$$

the fact that a disproportionately large percentage of women without children were shipped from east to west reduced F more than I in the Old South and raised F more than I in the New South. Hence even if *actual* fertility was the same in both regions, the use of the ratio I/F to measure fertility would lead to the conclusion that fertility was higher in the old region than the new one.

3.6. (pp. 86–89 and figs. 23, 24). The index of demand used in figure 24 was derived by solving the demand equation for slaves

$$(3.30) \quad Q_s = D_s P_s^{-\epsilon}s$$

for D_s,

$$(3.31) \quad D_s = Q_s P_s^{\epsilon}s \; .$$

Since Q_s and P_s are known, D_s could be computed, if ϵ_s were known.

For the period 1820–1860, Claudia Goldin has estimated $\epsilon_s = 0.1$. This value seems too low for the period prior to 1810 when cotton was only a minor crop, and the special features of slaves and plantations which made the demand for slaves extremely inelastic were weaker (see **6.6**). Consequently we computed D_s on the assumption that $\epsilon_s = 0.75$. The argument based on figure 24 would be somewhat stronger if we used a lower value of ϵ_s. However, the basic pattern of the curve shown in figure 24 remains over values of ϵ_s ranging from 0.1 to 1.0.

The current prices of slaves were computed from the probate records. These were deflated by the Warren-Pearson price index [343, pp. 115–116] to put P_s in real terms.

3.7. (pp. 90–92 and figs. 25–28). If we represent the demand and short-run supply for cotton by

$$(3.32) \quad Q_c = D_c P_c^{-\epsilon}c$$

and

$$(3.33) \quad Q_c = S_c P_c^{\gamma c} \ ,$$

the index of the demand for cotton will be given by

$$(3.34) \quad D_c = S_c P_c^{\epsilon c + \gamma c} \ .$$

Since the supply of cotton in the short run was perfectly inelastic, equation 3.34 reduces to

$$(3.35) \quad D_c = Q_c P_c^{\epsilon c} \ .$$

Figure 26 shows that the long-term trend of prices was downward. Given equation 3.1, the long-run supply curve for cotton is

$$(3.36) \quad \bar{P}_c = A^{-1} \bar{w}^{\alpha_1} r^{\alpha_2} m^{\alpha_3} \ .$$

3.7.1. Since the real values of $\bar{w}$ and r were generally rising over the period in question and m remained fairly constant, at least after 1830 (see [67, p. 178; 185, pp. 304–305; 150, pp. 518–519], it seems probable that the main reason for the decline in P_c was the rise in A.

Cooper, Barton, and Brodell [57, p. 3] estimate that $\overset{*}{Q} - \overset{*}{L} = 0.79$ percent per annum over the period 1800–1840. The rate of decline in the trend price of cotton was 0.71 percent per annum.

3.7.2. We interpret the deviations of observed price from the trend value of price as a proxy for $P_c - \bar{P}_c$. Our justification for this interpretation is that movements in the short-run supply of cotton lagged behind movements in demand. This lagged relationship was demonstrated econometrically by Wright [387, pp. 157–202; cf. 390]. It can also be seen in figure 28. In about three quarters of the cases in which supply is above demand, supply decreases in the next period. And when demand is above supply, supply generally increases in the next period. Given this lagged relation between demand and short-run supply, the long-term downward movement in P_c must be due to downward shifts in the long-run supply curve.

3.7.3. When the long-run supply is shifting downward, and $\bar{P}_c$ is declining, a rise in the ratio of short-run to long-run price means that demand is increasing. Hence our index for demand in figure 28 is

$$(3.27) \quad D_c = Q_c (P_c / \bar{P}_c)^{\epsilon c}$$

with $\bar{P}_c$ assumed to be equal to the trend value of P_c. The index of short-run supply, again because $\gamma = 0$, was merely Q_c.

3.7.4. Wright [387, pp. 157-202] has produced estimates of ϵ_c ranging from 0.5 to 1.0. We used the mid-value of this range for ϵ_c. However, our index of demand was robust to variations of ϵ_c in this range. All values of ϵ_c within this range lead to the same interpretation of the historical issues.

The current values of P_c, which were taken from [354], were deflated by Taylor's Charleston index [343, pp. 120-121] for use in figures 26-28.

3.8. (pp. 94-99 and fig. 29). The index shown in figure 29 was computed from equation 3.10. $\overset{*}{P}_{ce}$ and $\overset{*}{Q}_{ce}$ were estimated from [354, pp. 10-13], $\overset{*}{L}_e$ from [343, p. 9], $\overset{*}{i}$ from [343, p. 656].

3.9. (pp. 99-102). Figures 30 and 31 are computed from data in Goldin [146; cf. 148]. See **6.6** for a summary of her findings.

3.10. (pp. 103-106 and fig. 32). Figure 32 was computed from price-hire ratios in table B.9.

Notes to Chapter 4

4.1. (p. 107). The word "exploitation," while widely employed in describing the condition of slaves, is not a well-defined term. The term is probably most common in the vaguer of the two senses cited in the text — that is, when it is used to denote the unjust, unfair, or improper use of another person for one's own advantage. For reasons indicated in **4.1.2**, the possibilities for the measurement of this aspect of exploitation are quite limited.

There are, by contrast, two well-known measures which correspond to the second sense of "exploitation" that is cited in the text — the utilization of labor power of another person without giving an equivalent return. Karl Marx defined that part of the value of the product of labor which was not paid to workers as surplus value (s) and that part which was paid to them as "variable capital" (v). He proposed to measure the "rate of exploitation" by the ratio s/v [98, part IV; 280, pp. 21-22]. A comparable concept of exploitation was put forward by Joan Robinson [279, pp. 281-283]. She measured the amount of exploitation of labor by the difference between the marginal product of labor valued at market prices ($\alpha_1 P_c Q L^{-1}$ in the Cobb-Douglas case) and the wage rate.

4.1.1. It is easier to deal precisely with the notion that part of the value

Table B.12

Definition of Symbols Used in Notes to Chapter 4

---

s = surplus value

v = variable capital

F = the output of fluid milk

$\bar{B}$ = the output of butter

C = the output of cheese

γ_1 = pounds of fluid milk required to produce a pound of butter

γ_2 = pounds of fluid milk required to produce a pound of cheese

g = ratio of total fluid milk production to fluid milk consumed in the production of butter and cheese

δ = the ratio of the production of fluid milk to the output of butter

ϵ = the proportion of slave children fathered by white men (the white "participation" rate)

β = the percentage of white "blood"

$\bar{\rho}$ = the share of slaves with $\beta \geq 1/8$

ρ = the share of mulattoes in the total slave population as reported in the 1850 census

Δ = the number of mulatto parents who can give birth to a mulatto child even when their mates are pure blacks

$\bar{\Delta}$ = the number of mulatto parents who can give birth to a mulatto child only if their mate is a mulatto or a white

a = $\Delta / (\Delta + \bar{\Delta})$

w = the proportion of mothers in $\bar{\Delta}$ who mate with fathers in $\bar{\Delta}$

x = the proportion of mothers in Δ who mate with fathers in Δ

y = the proportion of mothers in Δ who mate with whites

v = $x + y$

T = total slave births = total number of fathers = total number of mothers

δ = number of mulatto births with $\beta \geq 1/8$

$\hat{\delta}$ = number of mulatto births as determined by the criterion employed in the U.S. census

e = $\rho/\bar{\rho} = \hat{\delta}/\delta$

$\bar{M}$ = the share of "Caucasian" genes presently found in U.S. Negro populations

m = the average rate of transmission of "Caucasian" genes to Negroes

k = the number of generations of gene intermixture

D = the probability that a marriage would be broken by trade before it was terminated by the death of one of the partners

z = the probability that a marriage will survive a given year without being broken by trade

B = the value of a "birthright"

λ_t = the probability that a slave will live through year t

P = price

Q = output

L = input of labor

M = average annual maintenance cost of a slave

i = rate of return or discount rate

n = the expected number of years that a slave will be held

R_g = annual gross revenue derived from a slave

E_x = the rate of exploitation

s = a subscript denoting the South

c = a subscript denoting cotton

t = a subscript or exponent designating a year

---

of the product which slaves produced was expropriated from them than with the vaguer notion of unfair general treatment. However, as pointed out in section **4.11**, neither the Marxian nor the Robinsonian measures of exploitation are appropriate to the slave case, since both are based on the assumption that exploitation always takes place during a very short time period in which the rate of exploitation is always positive. In the case of slavery, measurement of exploitation involves consideration of the slave's productive activities, and payments to him over his entire life. This creates a special complication, since the rate of exploitation not only varied over a slave's life but was actually negative at certain times.

In **4.11** we present an alternative measure of exploitation which takes account of the special features of slavery. This measure is more closely related to Robinson's measure than to Marx's, although it could be interpreted to be the analogue of either one.

4.1.2. It is not possible to obtain a measure which encompasses all aspects of the more vague conception of exploitation. The problem is not merely that "unfair" general treatment is rarely, if ever, specified to a degree that would make it measurable. When used in this vague sense, exploitation has moral and psychological aspects which, even if they were precisely specified, would be beyond the capacity of the tools of cliometricians.

"Exploitation" is, thus, frequently used as a synonym for "oppression." But oppression clearly has not only a material dimension but a psychological one; it involves the "feeling of being heavily weighed down, either mentally or physically" [237, p. 922]. Exactly the same material conditions may, therefore, involve "oppression" in one set of circumstances but not in another.

There is also the question as to whose sense of burden is relevant. Is the slave's sense of oppression or the antislavery critic's sense the relevant standard? For as Frederick Douglass pointed out [81, p. 160; cf. 81, pp. 96–99; cf. also 131], the two did not always coincide. Is oppression or exploitation absent if the slave fails to sense it or explicitly denies its existence? The resolution of these questions involves moral values. If antislavery critics viewed slavery as oppressive and exploitative even when material conditions of slaves were relatively high and even when slaves expressed a preference for bondage over freedom, it was because slavery violated *their* (the critics) moral precepts — because these critics defined oppression and exploitation according to *their* moral values.

While quantitative methods will not resolve these psychological and moral dimensions of exploitation, they are useful in clarifying the issues which remain to be debated. They are especially helpful in separating out the material aspects of treatment from the psychological and moral aspects (cf. **6.1** in appendix C).

In chapter 4 we therefore focus on the material aspects of slave treatment and on the impact of this treatment with respect to certain narrowly defined, but important, consequences. In limiting ourselves to measurable conditions and effects, we do not in any way mean to minimize the significance of conditions or possible consequences which we cannot measure. Rather, we aim to separate out those issues which can be resolved by quantitative methods from those which cannot and which must be dealt with along other lines.

4.1.3. The limitations imposed on the choices of bondsmen were among the most important features of exploitation under slavery. Some aspects of these restrictions are quantifiable. See chapter 6, pp. 244–246 in the primary volume, and **6.8**.

4.2. (pp. 109–115 and figs. 33 and 34). The fallacy in the position of those who argue that slaves were poorly fed stems from the failure to recognize the implications of the fact that the South in general, and big plantations in particular, produced large quantities of food in addition to pork and corn. If these other foods were not being consumed by slaves, where were they going? It is clear that they were not being exported from the South in any substantial degree, except for Texas beef. It is now well established that the South was, on balance, a food-importing region. While the exact level of southern food imports has not yet been precisely determined [102; 109; 110; 114; 115; 135; 212; 243], it is clear that such imports formed only a quite small proportion of the total southern food consumption. The agricultural sector of the South was not only self-sufficient in food but produced nearly enough of a surplus to feed the non-farm population of the South.

It is also clear that, at least on large plantations, whites could not have been the consumers of the large quantities of sweet potatoes, peas and beans, and grains (other than corn) that were being produced. For whites formed less than 10 percent of the population of plantations with over 50 slaves (see fig. 44). Moreover, only relatively small quantities of potatoes, grains, peas and beans, etc., were being shipped from such plantations to the cities, especially when these plantations were remote from cities.

It follows that planters were feeding large quantities of vegetable foods (other than corn) either to their livestock or their slaves. To conclude that slaves were not consuming large amounts of potatoes, peas, wheat, and fruits, one must be willing to believe that either out of ignorance or meanness planters were giving to livestock a more varied diet than to slaves.

Stampp has suggested that ignorance was responsible for the narrow diet of slaves. He argues that while there was sufficient bulk to the slave diet, the "few supplementary items" to corn and pork led to an "improper balance" in their diet. "The slaves who consequently suffered from dietary deficiencies were sometimes the victims of penurious masters, but probably they were more often the victims of ill-informed masters — of the primitive state of the science of dietetics" [303, p. 282].

The notion that stinginess would have led masters to have fed various grains, vegetables, and fruits to livestock rather than slaves is too farfetched to be plausible. Since most livestock were bound, eventually, for the stomachs of the slaves, masters would hardly have saved money by depriving slaves of sweet potatoes, peas, or fruits while feeding these foods to swine. Moreover, planters who pursued such a policy must have been ignorant not only of "the science of dietetics" but also of rudimentary economics and animal husbandry. To have substituted peas, potatoes, and fruits for corn and other grains in the diet of livestock, southern planters would have had to have gone against widely accepted (and generally correct) beliefs of farmers regarding the relative efficiency of various animal feeds, and to have preferred expensive to inexpensive feeds, even when the expensive feeds were less efficient than the inexpensive ones. In other words, the policy implied by Stampp's position required not only an ignorance of human dietetics but also that planters were extremely poor farmers.

4.2.1. The technique which we have employed for estimating the food consumption of slaves was developed by the U.S. Department of Agriculture during World War II in order to appraise food requirements and to determine resource allocations. U.S.D.A. estimates of the national consumption of foods for each year between 1909 and 1948 were first published in 1949 [345]. These estimates were subsequently revised, on the basis of improved procedures, and extended to 1952 [346]. In addition, the U.S.D.A. publishes food consumption estimates annually which keep the series current. Comparable estimates of national food consumption for the census years between 1879 and 1899 have been constructed by the Food Research Institute at Stanford University [18].

The technique employed by the U.S.D.A. to estimate per capita food consumption is called the "disappearance" method. Under this method, human consumption of food is obtained as a residual from data on production and utilization. The following is the U.S.D.A.'s brief description of its procedures [346, pp. 1–2]:

Official estimates of the United States Department of Agriculture of per capita consumption of food in this country are derived as residuals from data on production and utilization. From the annual supply of each food (production plus beginning stocks plus imports) are deducted feed and seed use, industrial use, other nonfood use, exports and shipments, Government purchases for export, and ending stocks. The residual is considered to be civilian consumption. . . .

Strictly speaking, estimates of this sort should be designated as supplies moving through trade channels for domestic consumption. Because of the perishability of most foods, however, changes in disappearance may be presumed to be closely associated with changes in actual consumption, provided the estimates of disappearance are reliable. The disappearance data for food have proved accurate enough to permit measurement of the average level of food consumption in the country as a whole, to show year-to-year changes in consumption of the principal foods, to permit calculation of the approximate nutrient content of the food supply, to establish long-time trends, and to permit statistical analyses of effects of prices and incomes on consumption of the principal foods.

Despite the fact that the existing estimates of disappearance permit the measurement of a number of significant aspects of food consumption in this country, several limitations on these estimates need to be fully recognized.

The basic disappearance data for the several foods are obtained at various levels of distribution; for example, meat in terms of dressed weight where slaughtered and fruits and vegetables in terms of farm weight. . . . To approximate more closely the actual consumption level, it is necessary, in most instances, to convert the estimates of disappearance at the primary distribution level to approximate weight at the retail level by the application of average waste factors. . . .

Ideally, estimates of consumption at the retail level should undergo a further adjustment for food wastes in the home, but data for this purpose are sketchy and unreliable. Therefore, both the index of per capita food consumption and the nutritive value of the per capita food supply are calculated in terms of food as purchased at retail.

In addition to the gap between the disappearance data in terms of primary distribution weights and actual consumption in the home and elsewhere, certain limitations of the disappearance data themselves should be noted. . . . The degree of accuracy in the production estimates varies considerably. Moreover, although production of major items, such as citrus fruits, is estimated with care, no estimates are made of production of minor foods, as some of the berries. Federally inspected livestock slaughter is reported regularly, but information on year-by-year farm slaughter is estimated from sample reports. Beyond the production level, important information is lacking on the nonfood utilization of certain items; and the nonavailability of crucial data regarding stocks presents insurmountable problems in estimating the disappearance of some food commodities. Finally, the per capita estimates are subject to statistical errors made in the course of estimating production, changes in stocks, foreign trade, and military takings.

Furthermore, estimates of per capita disappearance are subject to limitations not connected with the statistical accuracy of the basic data. These estimates are national averages which do not reflect changes in the make-up of the population; for example, the proportion of babies in the population and the withdrawal of younger men into the armed services during World War II. . . .

As national averages, the per capita consumption estimates also obscure the differences between seasons of the year, regions, urban and rural habits, family size and income, age composition, occupational differences, and wartime anomalies such as black markets in rationed commodities. Furthermore, differences between household consumption and consumption in restaurants, hotels, and private institutions, are not indicated.

4.2.2. Previous applications of the disappearance method to the estimation of southern food consumption have been made by Gallman [135], Hutchinson and Williamson [187], and Swan [318]. Our procedures were the same as those followed by Gallman, with the exceptions listed in **4.2.2.1–4.2.2.5.**

Our modifications arise from the fact that Gallman, as well as Hutchinson and Williamson, were largely concerned with demonstrating that the South was basically self-sufficient in the production of food. Hence they deliberately used procedures which biased their estimates against their hypothesis. The biases included substantial overestimation of grains fed to livestock and underestimation of meat production.

A second reason for the modification in previous procedures is the need to distinguish between the consumption of slaves and free persons. This was not an issue for Gallman, Hutchinson and Williamson, or Swan, since they were interested only in the overall consumption and not with the disaggregation of consumption by the legal status of persons. Moreover, they were not interested in the variety of the diet but only in its total energy value. Hence, they could tolerate procedures which distorted the composition of the diet as long as it did not affect the overall level.

4.2.2.1. In order to be able to separate free from slave consumption, we derived our estimates from a sample of large slave plantations (over 50 slaves). In order to separate consumption on these plantations from the sales of surpluses to cities, we further restricted the sample to plantations that were in counties at least 50 wagon miles away from the nearest cities. In other words, the slave consumption estimates shown in figure 33 apply to blacks on plantations with 51 or more slaves that were at least 50 wagon miles from a city.

These restrictions limit the sample to plantations that were clearly beyond the milk shed of these cities and were probably beyond the shed for truck gardens and, perhaps, meats to a significant degree. Not only during the antebellum era, but down to 1900, nearly all milk was delivered to southern cities by wagon. Even in a city as large as New Orleans, 86 percent of milk was shipped in by wagon [352, pp. 10–11, 54–55]. Consequently, plantations beyond a 50-mile radius of cities were, for practical purposes, excluded from urban milk markets.

It is possible that meats, which could more easily be preserved than milk, and which were high in value relative to bulk, were sold in cities by plantations beyond the 50-mile radius. To allow for this possibility, we assumed that 30 percent of all beef production and 15 percent of all pork production on the plantations in our subsample were sold off of the plantation. Since just under 10 percent of the southern population was in cities, and southern cities imported a substantial part of their food supply from the Northeast and Northwest [109; 110; 114; 115; 212], we have undoubtedly overestimated sales of meat by plantations to urban areas and, hence, underestimated the consumption of meat by slaves.

To separate white from slave consumption, we overfed the whites living on the plantations. It was assumed that whites consumed twice as much beef as the national average and 1.5 times as much milk as the national average. This overfeeding resulted in an average intake per white of about 5,300 calories — a figure which is clearly in excess of any feasible level of consumption for the relatively inactive, upper-class whites living on large plantations. While the overfeeding of whites leads to an additional underestimation of slave consumption, the error is relatively small (less than 5 percent of the per capita consumption of slaves), since whites formed a small percentage of the population of large plantations.

4.2.2.2. Feed and seed allowances for grains were taken from Towne and Rasmussen [329] for all grains and crops except corn. Their allowances probably lead to an overstatement of animal feeds and hence an understatement of human consumption. However, since only a relatively small share of these crops were consumed as feed, the error has only a minor effect.

In the case of corn we lowered Gallman's estimate of the amount of corn fed to hogs by 30 percent. Gallman's estimates of corn consumption were appropriate for hogs with live weights of about 220 pounds. However, as indicated in **4.2.2.3**, 1860 hog weights averaged well under 200 pounds.

4.2.2.3. Following Gallman we estimated the live weight of hogs at 160 pounds. Parker (cited in [139, pp. 122–123]) has indicated this figure may be too low, since the weights contained in plantation records probably are slaughter, rather than live, weights.

We differed from Gallman also by increasing the slaughter-to-inventory ratio to 0.83 and by reducing the ratio of dressed- to live-weight to 0.53. These ratios are based on data in [113, p. 43; 183; 315, p. 119; 347, pp. 283–284]. Gallman's slaughter ratio was derived from the assumption of an average life of 20 months, a figure about two thirds higher than that used by the U.S.D.A. [315, p. 119]. Gallman's procedure is inconsistent with the fact that the marginal weight gain per pound of corn fed to hogs declines with both the weight and age of the hog [298, pp. 143–144]. Given the growth curve of hogs and the feed rates (even when reduced by 30 percent, as indicated in **4.2.2.2**), hogs should have reached Gallman's slaughter weights well within a twelve-month period. Under these circumstances, a twenty-month lapse between birth and slaughter would imply gross waste on the part of southern farmers and is difficult to justify.

4.2.2.4. Gallman assumed that the average live weight of southern cattle at the time of slaughter was just 550 pounds or about half the weight of northern cattle implied by data in Towne and Rasmussen [329, p. 283]. We increased the live weight of southern cattle to 750 pounds, a figure consistent with the average weight reported by Gray [154, p. 846] for the late 1850s. Even at this weight the average live weight of northern cattle at slaughter exceeded that of southern cattle by more than one third.

4.2.2.5. We followed Bateman's procedure [13] for estimating milk production from butter production, with the following modifications:

Bateman used equation 4.1,

$$(4.1) \quad F = g(\gamma_1 \bar{B} + \gamma_2 C)$$

to estimate total fluid milk production from census data on butter and cheese production. The values of γ_1 and γ_2 were those for the nation as a whole. However, virtually no cheese was produced on the plantations in our subsample. Consequently, we used equation 4.2 to estimate F_s,

$$(4.2) \quad F_s = \delta \bar{B}_s.$$

The value of δ was derived from Bateman's ratio of $F/\bar{B}$ for the North.

To get fluid milk production per cow, we applied equation 4.2 only to free farms in the Parker-Gallman sample. Since butter was a relatively expensive way to feed milk to slaves, it is to be expected that $\bar{B}/F$ would be lower for slave than free farms [180, p. 61]. Consequently application of equation 4.2 to all farms in the Parker-Gallman sample would lead to an understatement of milk production in the South and on slave plantations in particular.

An average yield per cow was obtained by dividing the total milk production on free farms by the total number of milk cows on these farms. Milk production on slave farms was obtained by multiplying the yield per cow by the number of cows on slave farms.

Bateman believes that his estimates of southern milk production per cow are much too low, and it is doubtful that our procedures have adequately compensated for the underestimation. Our computations result in a southern milk yield per cow which is less than half as high as the estimated national average yield (and a bare 35 percent of the northern yield). But in 1900 the ratio of southern to national yield was 80 percent [341, p.

Table B.13

Per Capita Food Consumption of Slaves in 1860 Compared with the Per Capita Food Consumption of the Entire Population in 1879

Food	Slaves, 1860		Total Population, 1879	
	lbs. per year	calories per day	lbs. per year	calories per day
Beef	43	108	62	152
Pork	88	543	86	521
Mutton	2	5	7	21
Milk*	171	144	367	267
Butter	3	30	15	135
Sweet potatoes	318	424	27	36
White potatoes	22	19	157	137
Peas	101	427	13	55
Corn	507	2,265	146	652
Wheat flour	34	156	225	1,019
Miscellaneous grains	14	64	29	132
All other foods	—	—	481	614
Totals	1,303	4,185	1,615	3,741

Sources: See **4.2.3**.

*Calories per pound of fluid milk were higher in 1860 than in 1879 because of differences in the quality of milk.

clxxv]. Thus slave milk consumption may be understated by as much as 60 percent.[12]

4.2.3. The estimates of average consumption per slave of each of 12 foods (in pounds per annum) are shown in table B.13. Calories per pound for each food was estimated from data in [355] except for miscellaneous grains which was taken from [18, p. 116].

Food consumption (in pounds and calories) for the entire population is from [18].

Both the slave diet and the 1879 diet give the energy value of raw foods without allowances for losses in food preparation.

4.2.4. The recommended dietary allowances for 1964 are from [120]. Since these allowances are for an adult male age 18–35, the food consumption levels shown in table B.13 had to be converted from an "average per slave" basis to the average for adult males 18–35. The conversion factor, which was calculated from the age-specific consumption weights given in [366, p. 52–53], was 1.28. This is the lowest of the conversion factors suggested by various studies of food consumption. If we had used the Atwater weights [366, pp. 52–53], the conversion factor would have been about 1.4. Thus our procedure tends to understate the nutritional value of the raw food consumed by prime-aged male slaves.

On the other hand, the recommended daily allowances for 1964 were based not on raw foods but on actual consumption. Since there was some waste of food, and some destruction of nutrient values in the cooking process, slaves did not receive all of the nutrient value of the raw food. The losses in nutrient value through food preparation were probably not very large during the antebellum era. Virtually all parts of all foods were consumed on farms [398, pp. 81–82] as was the liquid in which the food was cooked [197, p. 129; 180, p. 51]. For most of the nutrients listed in figure 34, the losses in cooking would have had to have been improbably high to have driven the actual nutrient consumption of slaves below recommended

[12] Since this paragraph was written we received a letter from Bateman (dated March 27, 1973) informing us that he had independently recomputed his published figures and had arrived at a revised Southwide estimate of average milk yield per cow which differs from ours by less than one half of one percent. Bateman's revision is based on a county by county analysis of reporting errors in the census. His revised estimate was obtained by excluding from the computation those counties which suffered from "poor census data or lack of sufficient evidence on fluid milk consumption in the region." Bateman points out that the new adjustments were not made in his original paper [13], since they had little effect on the central problem of that paper, "which was to examine dairying nationally." Bateman's original estimates "were low only for states of the Deep South, all relatively unimportant in the national dairy economy."

levels. Calcium, the nutrient with the lowest relative shown in figure 34, does not appear to undergo significant loss in cooking, and the cooking loss of riboflavin, the second lowest nutrient level indicated in figure 34, is on the order of 15 to 30 percent [323, p. 266].

It should also be noted that a number of foods consumed by slaves were not taken into account in computing the nutrient relatives shown in figure 34. These omitted foods constituted about 15 percent of the energy content of the national diet in 1879.

4.2.5. It has frequently been presumed that "clay eating" among slaves was a measure of either an insufficient diet or of a mineral (most generally iron) or vitamin deficiency, or else that it was a response to the presence of hookworm. A recent article by Twyman [333], however, draws upon some recent medical research to argue that "no hard evidence has ever been produced that hookworm causes clay eating; and contrary to the assumptions of some historians, the practice does not necessarily arise from an insufficient diet or a vitamin or mineral deficiency." He notes that it is "a craving and a habit," "as in smoking or drinking," one which "has been practiced continuously over the years apparently by hundreds of thousands of southerners among both races and both sexes, and is still prevalent in the South today from Maryland to Texas." "[C]ontrary to earlier assumptions," he points out, "many clay eaters suffer no apparent ill effects from their habit."

4.3. (pp. 114-116 and fig. 35). The distribution of persons per slave house on large plantations was computed from data in [224; 225]. Description of the dimensions and construction of slave houses are contained in [64; 68; 112; 266; 293; 320; 324; 325]. The median number of square feet of sleeping space in New York City in 1893 was computed from [344].

In assessing the quality of housing, it is important to distinguish between the appearance of houses and their capacity to provide adequate shelter. Despite the flimsy appearance of their cabins, slaves probably were provided with better shelter than free urban workers. This anomaly is explained by the relatively low density of slave housing. For in an era of primitive methods of sanitation, both the incidence of disease and the death rate were closely correlated with the number of square (or cubic) feet of space per person. Overcrowded housing and inadequate sanitation facilities made cities deathtraps. As indicated by figure 36, in the primary volume, the life expectation of free workers in the three largest cities of the North in 1830 was about a third less than that of slaves.

The poor quality of housing for free urban workers persisted throughout the nineteenth century. While the data on housing are more systematic for the end of the nineteenth century than for the antebellum era, that evidence which is available indicates that the tenement problem was at its worst during the late 1850s [217, pp. 170-180; 276, pp. 9-20] . As Martin [217, pp. 170, 173] points out:

> The rapid growth in the urban population of industrial workers [during the 1850s] brought with it, as one result, a terrific pressure upon the housing available to that class. The resulting overcrowding, with great masses living in miserable tenements, cellars, and attics, was like nothing before or since in American history. . . . While tenement conditions in Brooklyn do not seem to have become serious by 1860, housing in Boston, Providence, and other industrial cities was little better than that of New York.

4.4. (pp. 116-117 and table 2). The clothing standard for New York workers is from [40, pp. 165-167] . The "typical" slave issue on large plantations is based on information culled from plantation records and from descriptions in [64; 68; 112; 266; 293; 320; 324; 325; 326] .

4.5. (pp. 117-126 and fig. 36). The caveat in the text regarding the preliminary nature of explorations into available morbidity and mortality data for slaves should be re-emphasized. The mortality figures in the census are clearly understatements. The 1850 census appears to be more seriously deficient than the 1860 census, especially with respect to the under-reporting of white deaths. It has not yet been determined whether the 1850 census merely understates levels or whether there are also biases in the relative frequencies of certain causes of death. Our tentative estimates are based on the assumption that relative frequencies are unbiased, except in the case of infant mortality.

Evans [105] and Jacobson [189] have corrected the slave and white mortality schedules of 1850 for level at each age. We have employed their corrected death rates in our tentative estimates. Both may be understated but not necessarily in the same degree. However, preliminary investigation suggests that the understatement is not consistent in all age categories. The understatement is probably greatest for infants. On the other hand, deaths may be overstated in later ages.

4.5.1. The slave morbidity rate was computed from the sample in [266, pp. 148-150] . This sample covers experience on 15 plantations ranging in size from 8 to 140 hands. The observations are heavily concentrated in the 1850s. The average morbidity rates on individual plantations ranged from a low of 4.3 days lost per year to a high of 21.3 days. For individual years, however, the morbidity rates ran as high as 40 days lost. Efforts are now under way to expand the sample both with respect to temporal and geographic coverage.

The slave morbidity rate of 12.0 days compares favorably with more recent morbidity rates. The National Health Survey for 1968 [348] reported that disability due to illness for workers aged 17 and over averaged 12.7 days per year. Unfortunately no breakdown was given by race. However, the national survey for 1935–36 [182] did give such a breakdown. This survey found that the average number of disabled days for persons over age 15 was 15.8 for blacks, 10.0 for whites. Finally, data collected in a survey organized by the Department of Labor in the late 1890s [349] indicate that the average annual number of days of sickness for blacks due to disease was 13.6; when illness due to childbirth and accidents is included, the average rises to 14.8 days per year. This study does not explicitly specify what was meant by "sickness." However, days of illness of adult males who did not lose any time from work were counted as zero. This suggests that only disabling illnesses were included in the definition.

4.5.2. The 1850 census mortality schedules indicate that 9.7 percent of all deaths among slave women aged 20–29 were due to childbearing. Among southern white women in the same age group, 18.2 percent of all deaths were due to childbearing.

Evans [105, p. 212] placed the overall death rate of slave women aged 20–29 at 11.93 per thousand. Hence 0.097 × 11.93 or 1.16 per thousand died due to childbearing. Since about 20 percent of women in the same age group gave birth each year, it follows that out of every 1,000 slave women who gave birth in 1850, only 6 died.

4.5.3. Analysis of data in the 1860 census indicated that the infant death rate of whites in slave states was 21 percent higher than the infant death rate of whites in the North. This factor, applied to 1850, yields an infant death rate among southern whites of 177 per thousand — just 6 per thousand less than the infant death rate of slaves.

4.5.4. Virtually all of the difference between the free and slave suffocation rates might be explained by what has recently been identified as the "sudden infant death" syndrome. One estimate placed the death rate from this disease today at 12.5 per thousand for Negro infants, and at 2.8 per thousand for all infants [19, p. 778].

4.5.5. The life expectations given in figure 36 are from [105; 169; 334].

4.6. (pp. 132–133). Table B.14 shows that, on the basis of the census classification, mulattoes increased from 7.70 percent of the slave population in 1850 to 10.41 percent of the slave population in 1860. Table B.14 also shows that 15.20 percent of all slave births in the U.S. during 1850–1860 were mulattoes, as defined by the census criterion.

It is not possible on the basis of census data alone to establish either a least upper bound or a greatest lower bound on the proportion of slave children fathered by whites (ϵ). However, by making certain plausible assumptions it is possible to identify the nature of the information needed to interpret the census data and to establish plausible realms within which upper and lower bounds of ϵ might be located.

The discussion which follows is based on memorandums prepared by Jorge Marquez-Ruarte.

4.6.1. In order to establish the value of ϵ (or even upper and lower bounds on ϵ) from census data, it is necessary to know not only the distribution of fathers and mothers among the three color categories (blacks, whites, mulattoes) but also the color preferences of potential mating partners, the proportion of mulattoes who can produce mulatto children even when they mate with pure blacks, and the census criterion for distinguishing between mulattoes and blacks. Since this information is unavailable, it is not possible to establish precise upper and lower bounds on ϵ from census data alone but only to indicate plausible domains within which these bounds might fall. Reasonable limits to the domains can be established under the following assumptions:

1. No bias is introduced into the calculation if we treat all births occurring between 1850 and 1860 as if they occurred in one year, provided each parent is counted as many times as he or she is responsible for a birth.
2. The share of mulattoes among mothers and fathers was equal to the share of mulattoes in the population in 1850.
3. Mulattoes are persons with $1/8 \leqslant \beta < 1$; blacks are persons with $\beta < 1/8$; whites are persons with $\beta = 1$.
4. The only whites who mate with Negroes are men.
5. The share of mulattoes among male slaves displaced by white fathers is the same as the share of mulattoes in the slave population in 1850.
6. The value of e was stable over time, which entails that $\hat{\delta}/\delta$ was stable.

Under these assumptions, the number of mulatto births is given by equation 4.3.

Table B.14

Data on the Slave Population in 1850 and 1860

	Mulattoes	Total
Population in 1850	246,656	3,204,313
Population in 1860	411,613	3,953,760
1850 population which survived to 1860[1]	194,254	2,523,554
Births during the decade 1850–1860[2]	217,359	1,430,206

Source: [338, p. xii]

[1] The average annual mortality rate implied by the Evans survivor table [105, p. 212] is 2.36 percent. Hence the proportion of the 1850 population that survived to 1860 is equal to $(1 - 0.0236)^{10} = 0.78755$.

[2] Births are the difference between the 1860 population and the survivors from the 1850 population.

$$(4.3) \quad \delta = \epsilon T + a(1 - \epsilon)\frac{\rho}{e} T + w(1 - a)\frac{\rho}{e} T - (x + y)a\frac{\rho}{e} T + a\frac{\rho}{e} T.$$

Equation 4.3 was derived from the following cross classification by summing the entries shown in column 3, column 4, row 3, the cell designated by the intersection of (row 2, col. 2) and then subtracting the cells designated by the intersections: (row 3, col. 3), (row 3, col. 4)

Mothers \ Fathers	(1) Blacks	(2) $\bar{\Delta}$	(3) Δ	(4) Whites	Σ
1 Blacks					$(1 - \frac{\rho}{e})T$
2 $\bar{\Delta}$		$w(1 - a)\frac{\rho}{e} T$			$(1 - a)\frac{\rho}{e} T$
3 Δ			$xa\frac{\rho}{e} T$	$ya\frac{\rho}{e} T$	$a\frac{\rho}{e} T$
Σ	$(1 - \epsilon)(1 - \frac{\rho}{e})T$	$(1 - a)(1 - \epsilon)\frac{\rho}{e} T$	$a(1 - \epsilon)\frac{\rho}{e} T$	ϵT	T

Substituting $\hat{\delta}/\epsilon$ for δ and solving equation 4.3 for ϵ yields

$$(4.4) \quad \epsilon = \frac{(\hat{\delta}/T) + \rho[a(v-2) - (1-a)w]}{e - a\rho}.$$

4.6.1.1. Since $(\partial\epsilon/\partial v) > 0$ and $(\partial\epsilon/\partial w) \leqslant 0$, and since $0 \leqslant v \leqslant 1$, $0 \leqslant w \leqslant 1$, we obtain a lower bound for ϵ when $v = 0$, $w = 1$. Thus

$$(4.4.1) \quad \epsilon_L = \frac{(\hat{\delta}/T) - \rho(1+a)}{e - a\rho}.$$

It will be seen that only the values of $(\hat{\delta}/T)$ and ρ can be determined from the census. The values of a and e are unknown. If we assume that the census criterion for mulatto was equivalent to $\beta \geqslant 1/8$ and use the value of a indicated for the eighth generation in table B.15 ($a = 0.2$), then $\epsilon_L = 6.05$ percent. If the census criterion was equivalent to $\beta \geqslant 1/16$, and again using the relevant values of a and e from table B.15 ($a \approx 0.5$, $e \approx 2.0$), then $\epsilon_L = 1.86$ percent.

4.6.1.2. The upper bound on ϵ is obtained by letting $v = 1$, $w = 0$. Thus

$$(4.4.2) \quad \epsilon_U = \frac{(\hat{\delta}/T) - a\rho}{e - a\rho}.$$

Again, only the values of $\hat{\delta}/T$ and ρ can be determined from the census. Now if we assume that the census criterion was equivalent to $\beta \geqslant 1/8$ and that $a = 0.2$, $\epsilon_U = 13.9$ percent. If the census criterion was equivalent to $\beta \geqslant 1/16$ and if $a = 0.5$, $e = 2.0$, then $\epsilon_U = 5.79$ percent.

4.6.1.3. Other plausible values of ϵ_L and ϵ_U, for various values of e and a are as in the chart on the facing page (the top rows give the values of ϵ_L and the bottom rows the values of ϵ_U). The ranges of reasonable values of ϵ_U and ϵ_L depend on the assumptions under which the limits were generated. What can be said about the way in which the assumptions listed under **4.6.1.** affected the domains of ϵ_U and ϵ_L?

The effect of assumptions 1 and 2 turns on the possibility that as the age distribution of the population changes, differences in birthrates among age groups might lead to a change in the ratio of mulatto parents to all parents. To test this possibility we simulated the change in the ratio of mulatto to all parents over a ten-year interval for a wide range of age distributions and survivor rates. The simulation showed that this ratio was

a \ e	0.5	1.0	1.5	2.0
0.2	12.30	6.05	4.01	3.00
	28.19	13.87	9.20	6.88
0.3	10.88	5.31	3.51	2.63
	27.03	13.19	8.73	6.52
0.4	9.42	4.56	3.01	2.24
	25.83	12.51	8.25	6.15
0.5	7.91	3.80	2.50	1.86
	24.59	11.80	7.77	5.79
0.6	6.35	3.02	1.98	1.47
	23.31	11.09	7.28	5.42
0.7	4.73	2.23	1.46	1.08
	21.99	10.37	6.78	5.04
0.8	3.06	1.43	0.93	0.69
	20.62	9.63	6.28	4.66
0.9	1.32	0.61	0.40	0.30
	19.20	8.89	5.78	4.28

quite insensitive to variations in assumptions, and that if it moved at all, it would rise, hence lowering the estimate of ϵ.

The upper bound estimate of ϵ is also insensitive to the effect of manumissions and runaways, even if disproportionately large portions of such slaves were mulattoes. Data in the 1860 census indicates that roughly 20,000 slaves were manumitted and half as many escaped during the period 1850 to 1860. To maximize the effect of this disappearance on the value of ϵ, we assume that all 30,000 were manumitted or escaped just before the count of the 1860 census. We also assume that mulattoes were twice as likely as all blacks to be manumitted or to escape. Under these assumptions mulatto births between 1850 and 1860 would rise from 217,359 to 222,998, total births would rise from 1,430,206 to 1,460,206, and the share of mulatto births in total births would increase from 15.20 percent to 15.28 percent. As a consequence, in the case where $e = 1$, $a = 0.4$, the upper bound estimate of ϵ would increase from 12.5 to 12.6 percent.

The assumption that the only whites who mated with Negroes were men, biased ϵ upward. If we knew what percentage of mulattoes were the progeny of unions between white women and Negro men, we could reduce the value of ϵ in both the upper and lower bound cases. In other words, what we have called a lower bound may not actually be a lower bound.

4.6.1.4. By far the most critical issue in establishing the domains of ϵ_U and ϵ_L is the value of e. The assumption that e was stable over time is justified if the census criterion for designating mulattoes was the same in 1850 and 1860, if counting errors were no greater with respect to mulattoes than other slaves, and if $\hat{\delta}/\delta$ was constant.

The census criterion for mulattoes was skin color. Since no degree of lightness was specified, the *average* criterion for mulatto was determined by the beliefs and perceptions of the enumerators. Since there were thousands of enumerators, and since they were drawn from the category of literate middle- and upper-class southern whites, the *de facto* or average criterion embodied in the census count would be the common conception of mulatto held by this category of whites. Moreover, since the enumerators were drawn from the same category of persons in 1850 and 1860, the law of large numbers may be relied upon to have produced the same *de facto* or average criterion in both years, provided (as seems likely) that perceptions of color among middle- and upper-class southern whites remained stable between 1850 and 1860.

While there was probably an undercount of slaves, as there was among free persons, there is no reason to suspect that the undercount of mulattoes (given the *de facto* census criterion for that designation) was significantly disproportionate, let alone that the bias fluctuated significantly between 1850 and 1860. Of course e would remain stable, even if there was a greater error in the count of mulattoes than of other slaves, as long as the degree of error was the same in both censuses. Indeed, a stable error is equivalent to a redefinition of the *de facto* criterion for the designation of mulattoes.

The conditions for $\hat{\delta}/\delta$ to have been stable are that color preferences for mating partners were stable and that the rate of white mating with slaves was stable, at least for the last several decades of the antebellum era.

Thus e is not a measure of tabulating or counting error in the census, but rather the ratio of the share of mulattoes in the slave population *according to "our" criterion for mulatto* to the share of mulattoes in the slave population *according to the* de facto *census criterion*. In other words, e is a correction factor for the disagreement by two observers (or collections of observers) over the way in which to divide slaves into two categories.

It is important to stress that our assumption that mulattoes were persons with $\beta \geqslant 1/8$ does not significantly affect the value of e. For the value of e depends on the ratio $\bar{\rho}/\rho$ and hence merely measures the extent to which our criterion led to a value of $\bar{\rho}$ which differed from the census value (ρ). To put the issue somewhat differently, in the cross tabulation shown in **4.6.1.2.**, only a is influenced by the particular β value that we specified. It can be seen from this tabulation that for any given value of e, ϵ_U and ϵ_L are quite insensitive to variations in the β value chosen to differentiate mulattoes from blacks. Thus if we accept the census criterion, then $e = 1$ and ϵ_U is bounded between 13.87 percent and 8.89 percent while ϵ_L is bounded between 6.05 and 0.61 percent (given, of course, the other assumptions under **4.6.1**).

Furthermore, the value of e does not depend on the particular *de facto* β value that the census chose as its criterion for mulatto but only on the extent of "our" agreement or disagreement with the criterion. Thus, e would equal 0.5 no matter what β level was chosen by the census as long as we specified a β level for mulatto that made $\bar{\rho}$ twice as large as ρ. The thrust of this point is that there is no such thing as a "right" or "true" β criterion for mulattoes and that in the attempt to estimate ϵ *from census data,* the appropriate value of e is 1. Where one sets the dividing line between mulatto and black has no effect on the actual distribution of gene admixtures. Slaves were what they were. Moreover, the particular gene used as the basis for measuring admixture (whether it is the one pertaining to skin color or any other gene) is also entirely arbitrary.

If the preceding arguments and assumptions are correct, the census data indicate that ϵ_U was bounded between 13.87 and 8.89 percent while ϵ_L was bounded between 6.05 and 0.61 percent.

4.6.2. The model considered in **4.6.1** takes no account of intergenerational effects. An intergenerational model is presented in table B.15. This model leads to the same conclusions as the model examined in **4.6.1**.

4.6.2.1. Table B.15 is computed with respect to a population of 100 males and 100 females. For convenience we assume that each couple gives birth to one boy and one girl, thus generating a population identical to the original one in size and sex distribution. The initial population is entirely black. To capture the effect of white interference we replace one black male by one white male at the beginning of each generation. Thus ϵ is set equal to 1 percent. To maximize the rate of growth of the mulatto population, we also assume that whites and mulattoes mate only with blacks. We

Table B.15
An Intergenerational Model for the Growth of the Mulatto Population among Slaves

	White	Mulatto			Black	Totals
Original population	$\beta = 1$				$\beta = 0$	
Males	1				99	100
Females	0				100	100
Total	1				199	200
First generation	$\beta = 1$	$\beta = 1/2$			$\beta = 0$	
Males	1	1			98	100
Females	0	1			99	100
Total	1	2			197	200
Second generation	$\beta = 1$	$[\beta = 1/2]$	$\beta = 1/4$		$\beta = 0$	
Males	1	1	2		96	100
Females	0	1	2		97	100
Total	1	2	4		193	200
Third generation	$\beta = 1$	$[\beta = 1/2]$	$\beta = 1/4$	$\beta = 1/8]$	$\beta = 0$	
Males	1	1	2	4	92	100
Females	0	1	2	4	93	100
Total	1	2	4	8	185	200

Fourth generation

	β = 1	[β = 1/2	β = 1/4	β = 1/8	[β = 1/16	β = 0]	Total
Males	1	1	2	4	8	84	100
Females	0	1	2	4	8	85	100
Total	1	2	4	8	16	169	200

Fifth generation

	β = 1	[β = 17/32	β = 9/32	β = 5/32	[β = 3/32	β = 1/32	β = 0]	Total
Males	1	1	2	4	8	1	83	100
Females	0	1	2	4	8	1	84	100
Total	1	2	4	8	16	2	167	200

Sixth generation

	β = 1	[β = 35/64	β = 20/64	β = 12/64	β = 8/64]	[β = 4/64	β = 1/64	β = 0]	Total
Males	1	1	2	4	8	1	1	82	100
Females	0	1	2	4	8	1	1	83	100
Total	1	2	4	8	16	2	2	165	200

Seventh generation

	β = 1	[β = 68/128	β = 39/128	β = 36/128	β = 21/128	β = 20/128]	[β = 12/128	β = 8/128	β = 0]	Total
Males	1	1	1	1	1	3	8	16	68	100
Females	0	1	1	1	1	3	8	16	69	100
Total	1	2	2	2	2	6	16	32	137	200

Eighth generation

	β = 1	[β = 140/256	β = 80/256	β = 51/256	β = 48/256	β = 33/256	β = 32/256]	[β = 20/256	β = 16/256	β = 8/256	β = 0]	Total
Males	1	1	2	2	2	2	6	1	1	15	67	100
Females	0	1	2	2	2	2	6	1	1	15	68	100
Total	1	2	4	4	4	4	12	2	2	30	135	200

also assume that mulattoes with the greatest β always mate with blacks having the greatest β. Mulattoes are again defined as $1 > \beta \geqslant 1/8$. A model based on these assumptions has little bearing, of course, on feasible values for an upper limit on ϵ. However, it does illuminate the lower range of feasible values of ϵ.

4.6.2.2. The eight generations described in table B.15 fill about 240 years, or the number of years which elapsed between 1620 and 1860. Table B.15 shows that the share of the slave population which is mulatto behaves as follows:

Generation	Percent mulatto
1	1
2	3
3	7
4	7
5	7
6	15
7	7
8	15

It can be shown that regardless of the value of ϵ, the mulatto share of the population will oscillate after the fifth generation. As is indicated by table B.16, the bounds between which it will oscillate depend on ϵ and will be equal to 7ϵ and 15ϵ. A value of $\epsilon = 0.01$ nicely bounds the observed shares of the slave population that were mulatto in 1850 (7.7 percent) and 1860 (10.4 percent). Thus, both the intergenerational and the one-decade models imply that the observed sizes of the mulatto population are consistent with low levels of white interference.

4.6.3. The work of geneticists on gene flows between whites and Negroes is described by Morris [234, pp. 409–426] and Reed [275].

Table B.17 gives the values of $\bar{M}$ (the accumulated admixture coefficient = the share of "Caucasian" genes presently found in U.S. Negro populations) computed for the gene Fy^a. It also gives the value of m (the average annual rate of transmission of this gene from whites to Negroes = the average percentage of white parents of Negro children in a given generation) and ϵ. The value of m is computed from equation 4.5 (see [145]),

Table B.16

Bounds of the Mulatto Share of the Slave Population for Various Values of ϵ (percent)

ϵ	Share of mulattoes in the total population oscillates between
0.694	4.86 and 10.41
0.823	5.76 and 12.35
1.00	7.00 and 15.00
1.10	7.70 and 16.50
5.00	35.00 and 75.00

Table B.17

Estimates of $\bar{M}$, m, and ϵ Derived from the Fy^a Gene Frequencies for American Negroes in Five Areas

Region and locality of the Negro population sample	Values of		
	$\bar{M}$	m	ϵ
Northern populations			
New York City	0.189	0.018	0.036
Detroit	0.260	0.026	0.052
Oakland, California	0.2195	0.021	0.042
Southern populations			
Charleston, South Carolina	0.0366	0.003	0.006
Evans and Bullock counties, Georgia	0.106	0.010	0.020

Sources: Values of $\bar{M}$ are from [275, p. 436]. The values of m and ϵ were computed from equation 4.5 by Jorge Marquez-Ruarte.

$$(4.5) \quad (1 - m)^k = 1 - \bar{M}$$

and ϵ is assumed to be equal to $2m$.

Since m is the percentage of Caucasian parents in a given generation, the condition for $\epsilon = 2m$ is that men were the only white parents of mulattoes. Because some white parents of mulattoes, especially in recent decades, were women, m should be multiplied by a number less than 2 to get ϵ. In other words, even if the estimates of m are unbiased, the values ϵ given in table B.17 are biased upward.

Table B.17 shows that the highest rates of admixture of Caucasian genes were found among Negro populations in northern cities. Even at these high values of $\bar{M}$, the maximum estimated value of ϵ is 5.2 percent. Moreover, this is the average rate of ϵ over 11.5 generations (roughly, over the years from 1640 to 1965) of which three generations are since the Civil War. This is important since the movement of the Negro population both from the South to the North and from rural to urban areas has probably caused the rate of gene transmission since the Civil War to be higher than before the Civil War.

For the estimation of the antebellum rate of gene transmission, values of $\bar{M}$ computed from two rural counties in Georgia (Evans and Bullock) are more appropriate than the values of $\bar{M}$ for northern cities. The value of ϵ indicated by these two counties is just 2 percent.

That even the last figure may be too high is suggested by the values of $\bar{M}$ (0.0366), m (0.003), and ϵ (0.006) computed for the Gullah Negroes of South Carolina. Gullahs have been culturally isolated from whites since the Civil War, and prior to the Civil War they lived on plantations in counties which were overwhelmingly Negro. Thus the only sustained contact of Gullahs with whites prior to the Civil War was the contact they had with their white overseers or masters. If we assume that there has been a zero rate of gene transmission between Gullahs and whites since the Civil War (which is equivalent to setting $k = 8.5$ in equation **4.5**), the computed values of m and ϵ for the antebellum era are 0.5 and 1.0 percent. For this group of slaves, it appears that masters and white overseers were, at most, the fathers of 1 out of every 100 Negro children.

The genetic evidence, thus, indicates that miscegenation was inversely correlated with the degree to which masters were able to keep their slaves isolated from whites. In the cities where, by all accounts, slaveowners were least successful in effecting a separation between the races, miscegenation rates were highest. In rural areas, where separation was more complete, miscegenation rates were quite low. Among the Gullah slaves, whose contacts with whites were limited almost exclusively to those they had with the families of their masters and overseers, the rate of white gene transmission was lowest. Masters apparently used their control over slaves not primarily for sexual objectives but for economic objectives.

This inverse correlation also throws into doubt the theory that the high level of $\bar{M}$ found in cities today is to be explained by a pattern of migration since the Civil War in which rural mulattoes were overrepresented. For the geographic distribution of mulatto slaves in 1850 and 1860 closely resembles current distributions of $\bar{M}$, although the migration decisions of slaves were controlled by their masters.

4.6.4. The share of white fathers among ex-slaves was computed by Jones [197, p. 188]. Jones's sample covered roughly 30 percent of the biographies in the slave narratives. A complete count of white parentage for all ex-slaves in the narratives is now under way. This is part of a systematic content analysis of the material in the narratives.

4.7. (p. 135). Figure B.5 presents a possible economic explanation for the failure of Nashville slaveowners to supply slaves as prostitutes (see [198]). In that diagram $\bar{w}$ is the wage rate for unskilled females. The curve labeled D is the demand for prostitutes. The curve labeled S gives the number of free women (H) who will enter the occupation at a money wage of w.

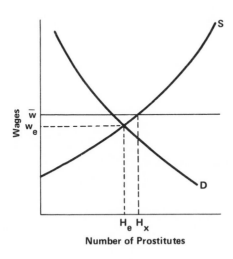

Figure B.5

While S is initially below $\bar{w}$, the two curves cross at H_x, after which S is above $\bar{w}$. This means that some free women, H_x in number, get positive nonpecuniary income from prostitution, while all others get negative nonpecuniary income. The amount of nonpecuniary income is equal to $\bar{w} - w$.

In figure B.5, H_e is the equilibrium number of prostitutes. At that level the total wage (pecuniary plus nonpecuniary) received by prostitutes is equal to $\bar{w}$. However, the pecuniary component of the wage is only w_e, while $\bar{w} - w_e$ is the nonpecuniary component.

If we assume that slaveowners are indifferent to the source of the income (i.e., attach zero nonpecuniary value to the nature of any job) but merely place slave women in the activity which yields the highest pecuniary income, and if the total labor force of unskilled females is large relative to the usual number of prostitutes, the supply curve of slave women for prostitution will be perfectly elastic at a money wage of $\bar{w}$. Consequently slaveowners offer no slave women as prostitutes in this market because at the prevailing equilibrium the money wage received by prostitutes (w_e) is below the supply price of slave women.

It should be emphasized that this is not the only economic rationalization for the absence of slave prostitutes in Nashville. Our basic point is that in this occupation there was probably a wedge of some sort between the supply curve of free women and that of slave women. We have portrayed the wedge as arising out of a positive nonpecuniary income which existed for some free women in the potential supply. The wedge could have arisen because owners of slave women were confronted with certain costs (special taxes, legal barriers, etc.) that were not imposed, or were imposed more lightly, on free women.

4.8. (pp. 136–144). Analysis of the demographic characteristics of the slave family and of the effects of slavery on family formation is still at a preliminary stage. Steckel [307] is investigating the effects of economic incentives for childbearing, slaveowner financing of child-rearing costs, and the economic independence of the aged from their children, on the age of marriage, on child spacing, and on the size of completed families.

4.8.1. Data obtained from the plantation records indicates an average age of mothers at first birth which is approximately one year less than that indicated by the data in the larger sample from the probate records. We have not yet been able to determine whether this difference is due to some statistical artifact or whether it reflects a behavioral difference, such as a lower age of marriage on large plantations.

4.8.2. The text discussion of figure 37 stressed that most women did not have their first child until after their twentieth birthday. Some readers might be inclined to stress that 40 percent of all first births took place before the mothers were 20. Obviously, both statements are true.

We put our stress on the "shortage" of births before age 20 in order to emphasize that a significant degree of sexual abstinence among unmarried persons was probably a feature of slave behavior. For in a well-fed, relatively healthy, noncontraceptive population, one would expect to have discovered a much larger percentage of first births occurring before age 20 if sexual intercourse had been ubiquitous at early ages.

The same conclusion is, of course, suggested by the difference between the seasonal patterns of first and subsequent births.

4.8.3. If it is assumed that the marriage breakup rate was the same in all slave sales as in the interregional trade, the New Orleans data can be used to provide a tentative estimate of the proportion of slave marriages destroyed through all slave sales. Calderhead [34, p. 51] estimates that 1.92 percent of slaves were sold each year in Maryland. If, as in the interregional trade, 13 percent of these sales involved the destruction of marriages (see 2.5.4), approximately 0.25 percent ($1.92 \times 0.13 = 0.25$) of slave marriages were broken through trade each year.

Given that the average age of a woman at first marriage was 20 and that the average age of her groom was 24, Evans's survivor table [105, p. 212] implies that the expected duration of a marriage broken only by death was 24 years. If the probability of marriage breakup through sale was random and independent of whether a family had been broken previously (these are the assumptions which maximize the extent of breakups), the probability that a marriage would be broken by trade rather than by death is given by equation 4.6:

$$(4.6) \quad D = 1 - z^{24}.$$

Since $z = 1 - 0.0025 = 0.9975$, D is equal to 5.8 percent.

We have not yet taken into account those slave marriages that were forcibly broken through nonmarket transactions. Estates divided among heirs also resulted in the breakup of some slave marriages, as did gifts of slaves from parents to children. Based on Maryland data, Calderhead estimates (privately communicated) that approximately one half as many exchanges of slaves took place in this way as through market sales. If we assume that the propensity to destroy marriages was the same through inheritance as through market sales, an additional 2.8 percent of marriages were destroyed in this manner.

These figures suggest that roughly 8.6 percent of all slave marriages were destroyed through economic transactions in slaves.

Since no account has been taken of gifts of slaves, other than through inheritance, the last figure may be too low. On the other hand, we assumed that no marriages ended in voluntary divorce. If we had taken account of voluntary dissolutions of marriages, the expected life of marriages would have been less than 24 years, and D would have been lower.

4.9. (pp. 144-147). An adequate social history of whipping remains to be written.[13] The fragmentary evidence which is available in secondary sources [22; 106; 235; 264; 394] suggests that whipping was a common means of enforcing discipline on members of the laboring classes through the middle of the eighteenth century in both Europe and America. Not only did American courts routinely order whipping as a form of punishment, but those who held the contracts of indentured laborers were generally presumed to have the right to use whipping, in moderate degree, to achieve normal levels of effort in production.

The shift away from whipping appears to have been accomplished in the North and in most of Europe largely between 1750 and 1850, although it lingered on longer in some areas than in others. Whipping remained an acceptable instrument of punishment for criminals throughout the nineteenth century. It was not until 1850 that flogging was forbidden by the U.S. Navy, a tightening of earlier (1835) legislation which permitted flogging only for "justifiable cause." Pollard [264, p. 186] points out that "[u]nsatisfactory work was punished by corporal punishment, by fines or by dismissal" in English factories. Commenting on an 1833 Factory Commission report which pointed to the use of corporal punishment to enforce obedience among factory children, he claims that "[b]eatings clearly belonged to the older, personal relationships and were common with apprentices, against whom few other sanctions were possible, but they survived because of the large-scale employment of children." The major method of enforcing discipline was, by this time, dismissal or the threat of dismissal. In Russia, a reform move in the 1830s and 1840s "ordered that the master could not sentence his serf to more than 40 blows with the rod, or 15 with the cudgel" [22, p. 429]. The extreme form of punishment in Russia was, of course, banishment to Siberia.

4.10. (pp. 147-151). Much work remains to be done before we have an adequate picture of the nature of the incentive system under slavery, the

---

[13] The data reported in fig. 40 are from [72].

size distribution of slave incomes, or the degree of variation among planters in the combination of force with positive incentives (cf. **6.7**).

In focusing on the magnitude of the "extra" earnings of top field hands or other favored groups relative to "basic income," we did not mean to suggest that all, or that even a majority, of slaves necessarily received such additional income. Our aim was rather to reveal the range of variation in slave incomes. In this respect, the measure we employed, the ratio of "top incomes" to basic income, might understate the degree of variation. For basic income was probably fairly close to average income. A measure such as the interdecile range, if we could construct it, might reveal a greater range of variation than the measure we employed.

4.10.1. Basic income was computed by first valuing the slave "market basket" of food shown in table B.13 at farm prices. An allowance was made for the omitted foods on the assumption that these entered into the slave diet in proportion to their caloric value in the 1879 diet. Housing and fuel per slave was estimated at 32.7 percent of expenditures on food. Clothing was estimated at 13.8 percent of food expenditures. These ratios are the ones which prevailed in the two lowest budgets of Massachusetts laborers in 1875 (after an adjustment for the lower fuel requirements of the South), the earliest budget study for workers that is available [350, p. 35]. Three dollars per year was added for medical care. This yielded an average annual income per slave of $34.13. Average income per slave was converted to average income per adult male by weighting each of Atwater's age-specific food consumption factors [366, pp. 52–53] by the share of the slave population in each age-sex group. The resulting adjustment factor (1.41) multiplied by $34.13 yielded a figure of $48.12 as the "basic income" of an adult male. No allowance was made for such other consumption expenditures as transportation, certain consumer durables, education, tobacco, religious activities, or recreational activities.

4.10.2. Table B.18 compares the age distribution of males age 15 or over with the age distribution of the artisans as obtained from the probate records. Craton's [59] analysis of slaves on the Worthy Park plantation in Jamaica also shows that artisans and slave managers were disproportionately represented in the older age groups. Some evidence that the skewed age distribution of artisans was the consequence of deliberate decisions by planters to award these jobs as prizes for performance is contained in a plantation guide [283, p. 87] published in 1823 which advised slaveowners to choose artisans on the basis of previous performance:

Other head men, such as carpenters, coopers, masons, coopersmiths,

Table B.18

A Comparison of the Age Distribution of Adult Males with the Age Distribution of Male Artisans

Age group	*(1)* Percentage of males age 15 and over in age group	*(2)* Percentage of artisans in age group
15–19	20	2
20–29	33	23
30–39	20	33
40–49	13	23
50 or more	13	19

Sources: Column 1: [338, pp. 594–595]; Column 2: computed from the probate records.

and watchmen, are next in succession as principal slaves on an estate. They generally arrive at their headship, from being distinguished either by the proprietor, overseer, or some superintending mechanic, as good workmen. . . .

Insofar as it precluded slaves from certain occupations, or greatly reduced the entry of slaves into certain occupations, slave society was more closed than free society. On the other hand, slave society appears to have been more open to the entry of any individual into the preferred occupations that were allowed to slaves; entry into these occupations appears to have depended less on kinship and more on performance than was the case in many free societies.

To say that kinship played a weaker role in occupational mobility does not imply that it played no role. While a systematic count has not yet been undertaken, it appears that those who held preferred occupations were, to a disproportionate extent, the offspring of slaves who held such occupations.

4.10.3. That slavery weighed most heavily on the talented and that they were the most likely to run away or buy themselves out of bondage is suggested by Hershberg's [174; 175] analysis of survey data pertaining to free Negroes living in Philadelphia during the years 1838, 1847, and 1856. For 1838 and 1847 Hershberg found that ex-slaves had more wealth than did the freeborn. Those slaves who purchased their own freedom tended not only to have more wealth, but also a better distribution of occupations than did other ex-slaves or the freeborn. The 1856 survey revealed that ex-slaves had a less favorable occupational distribution than the freeborn, but the data in this survey do not permit comparisons among categories of ex-slaves. Hershberg concludes that "the condition of the great majority of the ex-slaves was not *markedly* inferior to that of the free-born," and that "the consistently superior position of the ex-slave males who 'bought their own freedom and often that of their nearest relations,' confirms the belief that the adverse conditions could be molded by some to their advantage."

4.11. (pp. 153–157 and fig. 41). Neither the Marxian nor the Robinsonian definitions of exploitation are cast in such a manner as to take account of variations in the rate of exploitation over time. Marx, for example, carried on his discussion with respect to the rate of exploitation per day.

Slaves, however, were a long-term investment. During many years the difference between the value of the product of slaves and their income was large and positive. During other years, however, it was large and negative. Not only was there variation in the amount taken from an individual slave over the years of his life, but there was also variation from slave to slave. Some slaves lived long, productive lives. For these slaves, the amount expropriated was quite high. Other slaves, however, died when they were quite young and never earned enough income to cover the cost of rearing them. Still other slaves lived many years, but because they were sickly or handicapped, also failed to earn enough income to cover their maintenance costs.

What is needed, then, is a measure which takes account of these variations, both over the years of the lifetime of a particular individual and over individuals. Such a measure is given by equation 4.7,

$$(4.7) \quad B = \sum_{t=0}^{n} \frac{\lambda_t(\alpha_1 P_{ct} Q_t L_t^{-1} - M_t)}{(1 + i)^t}$$

which was previously set forth in slightly different form as equation 3.27 (see **3.5**).

The expression in parentheses in the numerator is, of course, Robinson's measure of exploitation during the year t (see **4.1**). Since λ_t is the probability that a slave will live through year t (or the share of a cohort which survives through year t), the right-hand term of equation 4.7 is the expected present value of the income expropriated from a slave over the course of his lifetime and hence is equal to B, the value of a "birthright."

4.11.1. The various points of the curve in figure 41 are the values of the right-hand term of equation 4.7 for each value of t from 0 to 75. The values of the variables entering equation 4.7 were estimated in the manner described in **3.4.1** and **4.10.1**, except that an allowance of 26 percent was added to basic income to cover the average amount of "extra" income received by slaves (see **6.7.1.2**). The resulting figure ($42.99) was the average value of M. Atwater's weights [366, pp. 52–53] were used to convert the average value of M into age and sex specific values.

4.11.2. Figure B.6 illustrates why countries in which slaves had high mortality rates discouraged child rearing. This figure may be taken as a very rough approximation to the Jamaican case. The life table used [335, p. 81] is probably a fair description of the demographic experience of Jamaican slaves [cf. 278]. And the discount rate employed (11 percent) is of the magnitude suggested by Sheridan [294, p. 305; 295, pp. 54–56]. However, we have used U.S. values for R_{gt}.

In figure B.6. curve C gives the present value of the accumulated expropriation through age t for a cohort born at time 0. Curve I gives the present value of the accumulated "expropriation" for a slave born at time zero who survived to age 75. The life expectation at birth is 18 years.

In the "Jamaican" case the break-even point on a slave who lived a full life (curve I) is age 26. However, since the life expectation at birth is 8 years *less* than the break-even point of curve I, the present value of the accumulated expropriation for the cohort (curve C) never becomes positive.

It should be stressed that the condition set forth in the text for slave rearing to be profitable (a life expectation at birth greater than the break-even age of survivors) is not an invariant condition. Whether or not it holds depends on the rate of discount. At sufficiently low discount rates, child rearing may be profitable even when the life expectation is less than the break-even age of survivors.

4.11.2.1. In suggesting that figure B.6 might be an appropriate interpretation of the "Jamaican" case, we are, of course, assuming the validity of the traditional representation of the "facts" of the slave experience in Jamaica and certain other parts of the Caribbean and South America during the late seventeenth century and most of the eighteenth century. It should be noted, however, that recent research has uncovered data which, while not yet sufficient to warrant the rejection of the traditional interpretation, do raise questions which require further exploration. Craton [59]

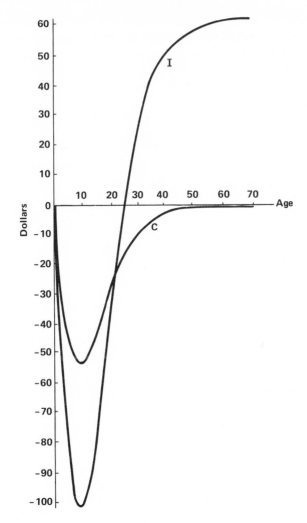

Figure B.6

reports finding positive prices for infants and young children at Worthy Park about 1793 and Roberts [278, pp. 236-237] reports planter payments to female slaves upon childbirth at about the same time. There is also fragmentary evidence of positive prices for infants in Barbados as early as the 1770s. While the findings for both Jamaica and Barbados apply to the period after which planters switched to the policies identified as amelioration, the dates in question still precede the closing of international slave trade. Under these circumstances, a careful exploration of the demographic evidence for Jamaica and other colonies which are thought to have discouraged child rearing, needs to be undertaken before firm conclusions are drawn.

4.11.3. The difference in behavior between the I curve and the C curve brings to the fore an issue which has confused some scholars [216; 296]. Not all of the difference between $\alpha_1 P_{ct} Q_t / L_t$ $(=R_{gt})$ and M_t in later years was expropriated by the ruling class. Indeed, most of it was an intergenerational transfer in which prime-aged (and other older) surviving slaves were either repaying for income received during their youth or supporting the children who never lived long enough to become productive (in the "Jamaican" case 60 percent of all slave children died before their tenth birthday) as well as the handicapped and the aged.

The fact that most of the gap between R_{gt} and M_t during the productive years was not expropriation but an intergenerational transfer explains why it is that the C curve never becomes positive, even though the I is positive at age 26. In this society the surviving slaves simply did not earn enough to support the nonsurvivors and the unproductive and still leave slaveowners with a normal rate of profit on the capital invested in child rearing.

In the "Jamaican" society (figure B.6) the birthright is negative. Thus on the basis of the "Robinsonian" definition, there is negative exploitation of slaves over the lifetime of a slave. In the U.S. case (figure 41), by contrast, the birthright is positive, having a value of approximately $30 at birth.

It is to be noted that a $30 birthright (zero-age price) goes along with a difference between R_g and M at age 35 of over $100 and a price of male slaves at age 26 of about $800 (see figures 18 and 19).

4.11.3.1. The primary difference between slave and free societies with respect to intergenerational transfers is that the amount and the pattern of these transfers was determined not primarily by the slaves themselves, but by the slaveowners. Thus in this area, as in so many others, the latitude for personal choice was much less for slaves than for free men.

The point should not be exaggerated, however. Free society also places many restrictions on the choices of parents with respect to intergenerational transfers. Minimum educational requirements and minimum ages for working are examples of such restrictions. In some free societies the state interferes even more heavily in restricting the freedom of choice in inter-generational transfers. Moreover, the substitution of slaveowners for parents as decision makers may, for reasons indicated in **4.10.2**, have led to a more egalitarian pattern of intergenerational transfers than would have prevailed if parents were unrestricted in their choice.

4.11.4. Under the "Robinsonian" definition, exploitation arose because the market for slave labor is not in long-term equilibrium (see **3.1.3.1**) and quasi-rents existed. Indeed, the birthright is the present value of the quasi-rents. These quasi-rents are always captured by the owner of the asset in short supply. Under slavery, the owner of the human capital is not the slave but the master. Hence exploitation takes the form of the expropria-tion of quasi-rents.

A full analysis of the course of the value of the birthright is still to be performed. Our tentative investigations suggest that the zero age price of a child was probably about $5 in 1810 and rose to about $30 in 1850. These prices, however, are not quite equivalent to the birthright as defined by equation 4.7, since they are not necessarily net of pregnancy costs and they reflect the expected future expropriation rather than the actual ex-propriation. Nevertheless, it seems quite probable that the value of the birthright was rising in the U.S. over time, thus indicating that after 1810 the demand for slaves was increasing more rapidly than their supply.

4.11.5. The existence of a positive birthright on a newborn slave means that the slave was expected to produce an output over his lifetime with a greater value than the maintenance provided to him by his owner. It is important to note, however, that the owner may not have made more than normal profits from slave ownership. This is because when the owner pur-chased the mother of the newborn slave, the price included the value of these future positive birthrights. If, for example, there was perfect fore-sight about the course of slave prices at the time of the closing of the inter-national slave trade, no subsequent owner could have made anything but normal profits, since the price paid for a slave at the time of closing would have included the present value of these future gains. Only if foresight were imperfect could subsequent owners (as a group) have made excess profits, for then the price paid for a slave at the time that the slave trade was closed would not have reflected actual, future changes in slave values.

4.11.5.1. Who captured the rent on slaves before 1807? To answer this question we need to know the elasticity of supply of slaves in Africa. (The nature of the rivalries among nations and the disputes among traders of each nation indicate that the actual carrying trade was competitive, and could not have been a source of abnormal profits.) If the supply had been inelastic, any increased demand for slaves would have accrued to the provider of the scarce resource (in this case, the slave). This presumably would have been the capturers of African slaves. If the supply of slaves had been perfectly elastic, then the increased demand for slaves would have led to a greater supply of slaves at a constant price (either because of more slaves provided by traditional suppliers or due to the entrance of new suppliers), and, because the industry using slaves to produce consumer goods in the Western Hemisphere was perfectly competitive, the ultimate beneficiaries would have been the consumers of the products and/or the owners of the complementary factor (land).

Since the increased labor supply due to slavery may have increased land values by raising the labor-land ratio, a more complete analysis of the nature of land distribution in the Western Hemisphere, and the pattern of changes in the value of land, is needed before one can determine the distribution of gains from the international slave trade with any degree of confidence. But it seems probable that the main beneficiaries of that trade were either the African suppliers of slaves or the European consumers of slave-produced products, depending upon the elasticity of the supply of slaves in Africa [17; 103; 154, p. 371].

4.11.6. The birthright can be converted into a rate of exploitation by making use of equation 4.8:

$$(4.8) \quad E_x = \frac{B}{\displaystyle\sum_{t=0}^{n} \frac{\lambda_t (\alpha_1 P_{ct} Q_t L_t^{-1})}{(1+i)^t}} \ .$$

This was the equation used to determine the 12 percent rate of exploitation reported in chapter 4.

4.11.6.1. It should be noted that E_x is the "inherent" or "potential" rather than the "actual" rate of exploitation. It is the rate that would have prevailed if all economic variables had remained constant. Since the break-even age was 26 (see fig. 41), the "actual" exploitation rate was negative on slaves born after 1839 – as a result of emancipation in 1865 (cf. **3.2.2.4** and **3.2.4**).

4.11.6.2. So far we have been measuring exploitation according to the "Robinsonian" definition, although, out of deference to Mrs. Robinson's current views, it might more appropriately be called the "neo-classical" definition. Equation 4.8 can be used to provide a "Marxian" definition of exploitation. According to Marx, only labor contributed to value. What is at issue here is not whether capital and land contribute to output but who ought to own the value of the marginal product of these factors. In the Marxian view profit and rents, whether or not they are measures of the productivity of capital and land, are nevertheless expropriations from labor.

The Marxian proposition, as applied to equation 4.8, can be interpreted to mean that E_x should be computed with a zero value for i. When this is done the rate of exploitation rises from 12 to 49 percent. To put it somewhat differently: If slaves had been free workers who directly or indirectly engaged in borrowing, the rate of expropriation would have been just 37 percent instead of 49 percent. If we express the rate of exploitation not as $B/\Sigma\lambda_t R_{gt}$ but as $B/\Sigma\lambda_t M_t$, which is more in the spirit of Marx's ratio (s/v), the rate of exploitation rises to 96 percent — not far from the 100 percent figure that Marx used to illustrate his examples of capitalist exploitation [218, p. 571].[14]

Which measure of exploitation one wishes to employ is a moral rather than an economic question. However, the strict Marxian analysis cannot explain the difference between "Jamaican" and U.S. behavior with respect to child rearing. To preserve the Marxian moral assumptions, while still explaining the causes of the differential behavior in the two cases, one would have to produce a hybrid analysis that merged the moral values of Marxians with some form of the neo-classical apparatus.

Both the Marxian and Robinsonian measures involve a narrow conception of exploitation. Both limit exploitation to the share of the value of output which is taken from labor (i.e., to expropriation). The two measures differ only because of different assumptions regarding what part of product "rightly" belongs to labor. Neither measure embraces the uncompensated "pain and suffering" imposed on slaves for being forced to live in bondage. An estimate of this aspect of exploitation is presented in chapter 6 and discussed in **6.8**. As one might suspect, the uncompensated pain and suffering is greater than the value of the product which was taken from slaves under any of the foregoing definitions of expropriation.

[14] Since B does not include all the income going to nonlaboring classes, still another, and greater, Marxian measure of exploitation could be constructed.

Notes to Chapter 6

6.1. (pp. 191–192). Economists generally use two categories of indexes to measure and compare efficiency in production. The first category consists of measures called "partial" productivity indexes. They are constructed by computing the ratio of output to one of the principal inputs. The most common of the partial productivity measures is the index of labor productivity (Q/L); but capital (Q/K) and land (Q/T) productivity indexes are also used.

The other category of measures consists of indexes of "total" factor productivity. These are computed by finding the ratio of output (or an index of output) to the average amount of inputs (or indexes of inputs). If the amounts of the various inputs are averaged arithmetically, as in equation 6.1,

$$(6.1) \quad C = \frac{Q}{\alpha_L L + \alpha_K K + \alpha_T T},$$

the index is called the "arithmetic index of total factor productivity." If the amounts of the various inputs are averaged geometrically, as in equation 6.2,

$$(6.2) \quad G = \frac{Q}{L^{\alpha_L} K^{\alpha_K} T^{\alpha_T}},$$

then the index is called the "geometric index of total factor productivity."

While both the arithmetic and geometric indexes usually give quite similar results, the geometric index has certain conceptual and mathematical advantages (see [78; 79]). Hence economists have, in recent years, preferred to work with the geometric index.

6.1.1. The relationship between the geometric index of total factor productivity and the partial indexes of productivity can be seen by rewriting equation 6.2 as

$$(6.3) \quad G = \left(\frac{Q}{L}\right)^{\alpha_L} \left(\frac{Q}{K}\right)^{\alpha_K} \left(\frac{Q}{T}\right)^{\alpha_T}.$$

Thus total factor productivity is a weighted average of the three partial productivity indexes, with the weights being the shares of each of the inputs in the value of output.

Table B.19

Definition of Symbols Used in Notes to Chapter 6

Q = output

L = input of labor

K = input of capital

T = input of land

$\alpha_L, \alpha_K, \alpha_T$ = shares in value of output of labor, capital and land

α_i = output elasticities of the inputs

A = the intercept of the production function

C = arithmetic index of total factor productivity

G = geometric index of total factor productivity

σ = the scale factor $(\alpha_1 + \alpha_2 + \alpha_3 - 1)$

Y = the age of land

V = an index of the quality of land

$\overline{Q}$ = the number of slaves demanded

D = the intercept of a demand function (all of the variables that cause the demand function to shift)

P = price

ϵ = elasticity of demand

w = wage rate

r = rental rate on land

m = rental rate on capital

I = Southern per capita income

I_i = the per capita income of the ith subregion

Π_i = the ith subregion's share of southern population

ψ_i = the ith subregion's share of southern income

* = an asterisk over a variable denotes the rate of change of that variable

$\wedge$ = a "hat" over a variable denotes the logarithm of that variable

s = a subscript denoting the South

n = a subscript denoting the North

i, j = subscripts identifying a member of a set

b = a subscript denoting slaves

c = a subscript denoting cotton

The relationship between G and the most common of the partial indexes (Q/L) can be seen by rewriting equation 6.2 as

$$(6.4) \quad \frac{Q}{L} = G \left(\frac{K}{L}\right)^{\alpha_K} \left(\frac{T}{L}\right)^{\alpha_T} .$$

The rate of growth transformation of equation 6.4 is

$$(6.5) \quad \overset{*}{Q} - \overset{*}{L} = \overset{*}{G} + \alpha_K (\overset{*}{K} - \overset{*}{L}) + \alpha_T (\overset{*}{T} - \overset{*}{L}).$$

Equation 6.5 reveals one of the limitations of the use of the labor productivity as a measure of efficiency. The index of labor productivity can increase even when there is no change in the efficiency of production merely because workers are being equipped with more (or better) capital $(\overset{*}{K} > \overset{*}{L})$ or land $(\overset{*}{T} > \overset{*}{L})$. Under the same circumstances, the geometric index of total factor productivity will not rise unless the increase in output is greater than the increase in capital and land multiplied by their respective shares. The index of total factor productivity, therefore, makes it possible to distinguish those changes in output which are due to an increase in the efficiency of the productive process *per se* from those changes which are due merely to the fact that labor has been equipped with more land and capital than was previously the case.

6.1.2. What explains changes over time (or differences between industries or sectors of industries at a moment of time) in the value of the total factor productivity index? The answer to this question depends on the nature of the production function which is used to describe the industry or industries in question. When it is appropriate to describe an industry with a Cobb-Douglas production function, it is possible to attribute changes (or differences) in the observed value of G to changes (or differences) in various aspects of the production function.

Since the equation for the Cobb-Douglas production function is

$$(6.6) \quad Q = AL^{\alpha_1} K^{\alpha_2} T^{\alpha_3},$$

if we solve equation 6.6 for A, we obtain

$$(6.7) \quad A = \frac{Q}{L^{\alpha_1} K^{\alpha_2} T^{\alpha_3}}.$$

Comparing equations 6.7 and 6.2, it can be seen that A, the intercept of the production function, will be equal to G, if the output elasticities of each of the inputs are equal to the shares of these inputs in the value of the total output (i.e., if $\alpha_1 = \alpha_L$, $\alpha_2 = \alpha_K$, and $\alpha_3 = \alpha_T$). That condition will be met if the industry in question is competitive and has constant returns to scale.

If there are increasing returns to scale, changes in the scale of operation will affect the value of G. It is possible to separate the influence of scale from other factors affecting the value of G by letting

$$(6.8) \quad \alpha_1 + \alpha_2 + \alpha_3 = 1 + \sigma.$$

Then equation 6.6 can be rewritten as

$$(6.9) \quad Q = A \left(\frac{Q}{A}\right)^{\frac{\sigma}{1+\sigma}} L^{\frac{\alpha_1}{1+\sigma}} K^{\frac{\alpha_2}{1+\sigma}} T^{\frac{\alpha_3}{1+\sigma}}.$$

If factors share in the value of output in proportion to the output elasticities, then

$$(6.10) \quad G = A \left(\frac{Q}{A}\right)^{\frac{\sigma}{1+\sigma}}.$$

Thus, when there are increasing returns to scale (i.e., the scale factor, σ, is greater than 0), total factor productivity depends on the level of output (Q) and increases with output.

To illustrate the way in which the scale of operations may affect the measure of total factor productivity, consider an industry in which each of the firms can be described by equation 6.9. Suppose there are two types of firms in the industry — small firms which have an output of Q_L each, and large firms which have an output of Q_B each. Suppose also that $\sigma = 0.1$ and that $Q_B = 5Q_L$. Then the ratio of measured efficiency of the large firms relative to the small firms will be:

$$\frac{G_B}{G_L} = \frac{A\left(\dfrac{5Q_L}{A}\right)^{\frac{0.1}{1.1}}}{A\left(\dfrac{Q_L}{A}\right)^{\frac{0.1}{1.1}}} = 5^{\frac{0.1}{1.1}} = 1.16.$$

In other words, even though the two types of firms are the same in all respects except size, the large firms will, in this hypothetical case, have a measure of efficiency which is 16 percent greater than the efficiency measure of the small firms.

6.1.3. Some economic developments make all inputs more efficient at the same rate. Other economic developments may affect efficiency through only one or the other of the inputs. To take account of these possibilities we rewrite equation 6.6 as

$$(6.11) \quad Q = A'(A_L L)^{\alpha 1}(A_K K)^{\alpha 2}(A_T T)^{\alpha 3}$$

or

$$(6.12) \quad Q = \left[A'A_L{}^{\alpha 1}A_K{}^{\alpha 2}A_T{}^{\alpha 3}\left(\frac{Q}{A}\right)^{\frac{\sigma}{1+\sigma}} \right] L^{\frac{\alpha_1}{1+\sigma}} K^{\frac{\alpha_2}{1+\sigma}} T^{\frac{\alpha_3}{1+\sigma}}$$

where

$$(6.13) \quad A = A'A_L{}^{\alpha 1}A_K{}^{\alpha 2}A_T{}^{\alpha 3}$$

and G is equal to the bracketed expression in equation 6.12; i.e.,

$$(6.14) \quad G = A'A_L{}^{\alpha 1}A_K{}^{\alpha 2}A_T{}^{\alpha 3}\left(\frac{Q}{A}\right)^{\frac{\sigma}{1+\sigma}} .$$

Equations 6.12 and 6.14 provide a flexible notation which can embrace the wide range of issues connected with the explanation of differences (or changes) in efficiency. A' represents all those influences which augment inputs (increase the efficiency of input utilization) at the same rate. A_L, A_K, A_T represent those specific influences which affect only labor, or only capital, or only land. Specific augmentation may be due to forms of technological advance which affect the efficiency of only specific inputs; it may also be due to the improvement in the quality of specific inputs or in the intensity of utilization of specific inputs.

6.2. (p. 192). A crude index of total factor productivity for southern agriculture relative to that of northern agriculture (G_s/G_n) was computed from published data in the U.S. census for the year 1860. Surprisingly, the computation showed that total factor productivity was 6.4 percent higher in the South than in the North (see table B.20). Since this unanticipated finding may be due to errors in the way in which either the output or input indexes were constructed, it is important to specify the procedures we followed.

6.2.1. The output index shown in table B.20 is derived from the estimate of income originating in agriculture for the year 1860 constructed by Towne and Rasmussen [329]. Their national totals for crops, meat and dairy, land improvements, and home manufactures were allocated between the North and South on the basis of regional shares which we derived from the 1860 census of agriculture [337]. The allocation of crops was based on census data regarding the physical product of each crop. Thus in the case of wheat, for example, the Towne-Rasmussen value of national wheat output in 1860 was $151.0 million. According to the 1860 census, the southern and northern shares of national wheat output were 22.4 and 73.2 percent, respectively. Therefore the value of southern wheat output in 1860 was measured as $33.8 million, while that of the North was $110.5 million. The procedure followed in computing the output index is equivalent to evaluating the outputs of each region by a set of uniform national prices. Our allocation of meat and dairy products between the regions was based on the shares of the regions in inventories of appropriate livestock. The value of land improvements was divided between the regions on the basis of shares constructed from Primack's estimates of the annual labor requirements for farm capital formation and Lebergott's data on farm wages by states [269; 207]. Regional shares in home manufactures were obtained from census data which reported such on-farm production by states [337].

The index of labor input was derived by applying to state census data the procedures devised by Lebergott in his recent reworking of the estimates of the U.S. labor force [338; 208]. Thus, the farm labor force of each region was taken to be equal to all free males aged 16 and over in

Table B.20

A Crude Index of the Relative Efficiency of Southern Agriculture, 1860

	South as a percentage of North
1. Output $\left(\dfrac{Q_s}{Q_n}\right)$	112.9
2. Labor $\left(\dfrac{L_s}{L_n}\right)$	120.7
3. Capital $\left(\dfrac{K_s}{K_n}\right)$	53.4
4. Land $\left(\dfrac{T_s}{T_n}\right)$	125.7
5. Index of inputs $\left[\left(\dfrac{L_s}{L_n}\right)^{\alpha_L}\left(\dfrac{K_s}{K_n}\right)^{\alpha_K}\left(\dfrac{T_s}{T_n}\right)^{\alpha_T}\right]$ where $\alpha_L = 0.58, \alpha_K = 0.17, \alpha_T = 0.25$	106.1
6. Index of relative total factor productivity $\left(\dfrac{G_s}{G_n}\right)$ (line 1 divided by line 5)	106.4

agricultural occupations, plus 17 percent of the free males in the ages 10–15 plus 82.8 percent of all slaves aged 10 and over [208, pp. 150-156]. The land input was measured by the total amount of land in farms (improved plus unimproved) in each region.

The capital stock was defined as the total value of livestock, machinery and implements, and buildings. The values of the first two items were obtained from the census. The value of buildings was obtained by applying Primack's ratio of the value of buildings to the cash value of farms [269; 337]. The capital input was measured by the annual rental value of the capital stock. This was taken to be equal to the value of the capital stock multiplied by the rate of return on farm capital plus the average rate of depreciation. The rate of return on farm capital was set at 10 percent (see **3.3.3**; cf. [117; 118]). Buildings were depreciated over 50 years, while implements and machinery were depreciated over 10 years.

The determination of factor shares is a difficult problem which is discussed in more detail in **6.2.2**. Several estimates exist for the antebellum period [29; 206], but their methods of calculation make them of limited usefulness. A large number of estimates have been derived for various postbellum years between 1870 and 1960. The labor share in these studies ranged from about 0.33 to 0.70 [29; 160; 161; 193; 200; 206; 213; 286]. The values which we employed for factor shares are those derived from our estimate of the southern agricultural production function. See **6.3.1**.

6.2.2. The value of the crude index of the relative efficiency of southern agriculture is affected by a series of measurement errors. It is our tentative hypothesis that the correction of these errors will increase the value of G_s/G_n. Our reasons for this belief will be set forth in this section. If we are correct, the problem of explaining why $G_s/G_n > 1$ reduces to the task of partitioning this ratio among the set of factors we have designated as "features of slavery."

There are three potentially important measurement errors in the construction of the output index. First, it is possible that on-the-farm manufactures may have been undercounted in the census (and thus underestimated by Towne and Rasmussen). Second, the assumption that the average weight of each category of livestock in the South equaled that of the corresponding type in the North is false. Third, we might have introduced a bias by using uniform national prices in constructing the regional indexes of total output. The main sources of measurement error with respect to inputs are the unsymmetrical way in which the labor of women and children are treated in the two regions, the failure to adjust for differences in the quality of land, and errors in the estimates of factor shares.

Available evidence suggests that the products omitted from the southern output index probably exceeded those omitted from the northern one. For example, manufacturing on-the-farm was much greater in the South than in the North. Manufacturing activities which had been extensively transferred to factories in the North — food processing, alcohol distillation, and various animal by-product industries — were still plantation industries in the South [102; 253]. Published census data are inadequate to make the required adjustment, although a partial adjustment is made in **6.2.3** on the basis of data in the Parker-Gallman sample and in probate records.

The average weight of farm animals was lower in the South [114; 115]. Hence the allocation of meat and dairy products between regions according to equally weighted livestock inventories would overstate southern and understate northern output (see **4.2.2.3** and **4.2.2.4**). The magnitude of the error depends upon the regional ratios of animals slaughtered to inventories on the census date, as well as upon the slaughter weights. On the other hand, the lower meat output due to lower quantity or quality of feed would be offset by higher crop output. This follows because, in determining the shares of crop output going into final consumption, the same percentages have implicitly been applied to all regions. If, for example, more corn went to human consumption in the South than in the North, southern crop output would have been understated. In table B.21 we correct the error for the overestimation of southern livestock weight by computing regional output shares for meat and dairy products from the census data on the value of livestock slaughtered, but not for the error on crops. This correction reduces the ratio of southern to northern output from 112.9 to 102.5.

The price-index problem is rather complex, since the appropriate income comparisons would involve the use of uniform prices for nontraded commodities and regional prices for traded goods. Once trade is allowed for, the relative values of regional income may not be reflected in relative shares of output valued at a uniform set of prices. For traded goods, allowance must be made for differences posed by transport costs. The relative income distortion in the procedure used depends upon the relative share of traded commodities and the regional price differentials. It should be noted that recent literature suggests that southern imports of agricultural commodities were small relative to total agricultural output (see **4.2**) while the cost of transporting southern agricultural exports was a relatively small percentage of delivered prices. Moreover Easterlin's computations for 1840 show about the same relative agricultural output for the South vis-à-vis the North using either nationally uniform prices or regional prices applied to regional physical production [93; 95; cf. 67]. While the evidence in Easterlin's study does not provide a conclusive answer to our problem, since his computation does not discriminate between traded and nontraded products, it suggests that the substitution of regional prices for uniform national prices in the case of traded goods will not markedly affect the North-South differential in the value of production. However, a definitive resolution of this issue will require a more detailed study.

The measurement errors in the input indexes are probably greater than those embodied in the output index. For example, in constructing the

Table B.21

A Partially Adjusted Index of the Relative Efficiency of Southern Agriculture, 1860

	South as a percentage of North
1. Output $\left(\dfrac{Q_s}{Q_n}\right)$ corrected for the quality of livestock	102.5
2. Labor $\left(\dfrac{L_s}{L_n}\right)$ corrected for southern age and sex composition and for domestics	93.3
3. Land $\left(\dfrac{T_s}{T_n}\right)$ all acres in farms corrected for quality	50.5
4. Capital $\left(\dfrac{K_s}{K_n}\right)$	53.4
5. Index of inputs $\left[\left(\dfrac{L_s}{L_n}\right)^{\alpha_L}\left(\dfrac{K_s}{K_n}\right)^{\alpha_K}\left(\dfrac{T_s}{T_n}\right)^{\alpha_T}\right]$ where $\alpha_L = 0.58, \alpha_K = 0.17, \alpha_T = 0.25$	72.8
6. Index of relative total factor productivity $\left(\dfrac{G_s}{G_n}\right)$ (line 1 divided by line 5)	140.8

labor index, all free females and most free children were excluded from the labor force. But in the case of slaves, nearly all females and children aged 10 or over who lived in rural areas were assumed to be fully employed in agriculture. These assumptions make the northern labor input too low and the southern labor input too high. While we cannot at this point correct for the northern omission, two adjustments can be made to the southern labor index. According to Gallman and Weiss [137], about 25 percent of rural slaves were employed not in agriculture, but as domestics. We can also adjust for the fact that the southern labor force had a larger proportion of females and children in it than in the North (cf. **6.2.3**). The adjustment for age and sex composition alone lowers L_s/L_n from 120.7 to 105.5. The adjustment for domestics reduces the ratio to 93.3.

The construction of the land input index employed in table B.20 is open to two criticisms. First, it was assumed that the productivity of an acre of unimproved land was equal to that of an acre of improved land. Second, the average quality of an acre of land was assumed to be the same in both regions. By using land prices to adjust for differences in land quality, one obtains an approximate correction for both errors. This adjustment lowers the figure for the relative land input from 125.7 shown in table B.20 to 50.5.

Table B.21 presents a recomputation of G_s/G_n, corrected (in the manner indicated) for the errors of measurement so far described. As this table shows, the net effect of these corrections is to increase the relative efficiency of southern agriculture. In table B.21 the value of G_s/G_n is 32 percent higher than the value of this ratio in table B.20.

It should be noted that the factor shares employed as weights in table B.21 are the same as those employed in table B.20. This should not be interpreted to mean that we consider these estimates sufficiently reliable to stand without further research. Quite the contrary; further investigation of factor shares in both the North and the South is one of the important objectives of our project. At issue is not only the particular values of the weights assigned to each input, but also the assumption that the southern weights are appropriate for the North.

Even with the output and input indexes of table B.20, the conclusion that the slave South was more efficient than the free North is not too sensitive to the assumed values of the northern factor shares. For the southern advantage to be converted to a northern one, the labor share would have to be increased from 0.58 to over 0.78 (while lowering the land and capital shares proportionally), or the capital share would have to be reduced to less than 10 percent (while raising the labor and land shares proportionally). However, given the more accurate output and input indexes of table B.21, there is no set of factor shares that could reverse the conclusion that the South was more efficient than the North.[15] This is because in table B.21

[15] In order to avoid making G_s/G_n the artifact of the units in which inputs are measured, northern and southern factor shares must be constrained to be equal. When the factor shares of the two regions differ, those of either one or the other region must be applied in both regions. If the differences in the factor shares of the two regions are sufficiently large, the usual type of index number problem may arise.

the average product of each factor is higher in the South than in the North. Still, the issue of northern factor shares is important in pinpointing the extent of the southern advantage.

6.2.3. It is possible to further refine the G_s on the basis of data in the Parker-Gallman sample and in the probate records (see **P.2.1** and **P.2.3**). Efforts to refine the estimate of G_n along similar lines are under way but are not expected to reach fruition for at least two years.

Table B.22 shows the effects of these corrections on the various partial productivity indexes that are averaged to obtain G_s. The new value of G_s/G_n is 134.7. It is this version of G_s/G_n which is shown in figure 42 and which was employed in constructing figure 45.

In order to make G_n comparable to the new index of G_s, as computed in table B.22, certain minor revisions were made in the computation of G_n. In table B.22 the value of land is measured by "value of land plus buildings" as obtained from the census, while in table B.21 an attempt was made to separate the value of buildings from that of land. In table B.22 the capital measure is the "value of equipment," while in table B.21 it was value of

Table B.22

A More Fully Adjusted Index of G_s and the Effect of These Adjustments on G_s/G_n

	Index computed from Parker-Gallman sample as a percentage of those computed from published census
1. Labor productivity (Q/L)	93.1
2. Capital productivity (Q/K)	119.7
3. Land productivity (Q/T)	87.4
4. Total factor productivity $\left[\left(\dfrac{Q}{L}\right)^{\alpha_L}\left(\dfrac{Q}{K}\right)^{\alpha_K}\left(\dfrac{Q}{T}\right)^{\alpha_T}\right]$ where $\alpha_L = 0.58, \alpha_K = 0.17, \alpha_T = 0.25$	95.6
5. Index of relative total factor productivity (G_s/G_n) $(140.8 \times 0.9564 = 134.7)$	134.7

equipment as obtained from the census plus our estimate of value of buildings. These changes, however, have a negligible effect on G_s/G_n.

More important is the new output index for the South which was computed from physical output data taken from the Parker-Gallman sample, weighted by prices taken from Towne and Rasmussen. For most crops we continued to follow the procedures described in the discussion of table B.21. In the cases of livestock and corn, however, we used the livestock weights and feed consumption estimates described in **4.2.2.2 – 4.2.2.4**. The output of dairy products was obtained in the manner indicated in **4.2.2.5**.

Use of the Parker-Gallman sample also permitted us to refine the index of labor input. The gross earnings profiles (see **3.4** and **4.10.1**) were applied to the ages of slaves and whites to obtain an index of equivalent hands on each farm (see **3.4** and **4.11.1**). The labor-force participation rate of 100 percent was assumed for all slaves over 10 and for white males over 15. On large plantations, the participation rate of white males between 10 and 15 and of white females 10 or over was assumed to be zero. On small farms, the participation rate for these two groups was assumed to be non-zero but to decline toward zero with farm size. These assumptions increase our estimate of the southern labor input relative to the northern labor input which, following the census and Lebergott, was computed on the assumption that the labor-force participation rate is zero for all white females. This adjustment in the southern labor input without a corresponding adjustment in the northern labor input biases the relative advantage of the South downward. How large the downward bias is depends on the extent to which women on northern farms participated in the production of measured output. However, the bias cannot exceed 19 percent and is probably substantially less than that.

Work is proceeding on the problem of the nonagricultural output of plantations. We hope eventually to have usable estimates of this component of production. For the present we deal with this problem by removing from the plantation labor force those males – primarily artisans – who were engaged in activities which are not covered by our current measure of output. The adjustment is not complete. Adult female slaves who performed services not included in the measured output of plantations, for example, are still included in the measure of labor input. As indicated in **6.2.4**, the failure to make an adequate adjustment for nonmeasured output probably distorts the pattern of relative efficiency by size of farm.

6.2.4. Total factor productivity indexes by farm size and subregion were computed from the Parker-Gallman sample in the manner indicated in **6.2.3**. The results are shown in tables B.23 and B.24.

Table B.23

Indexes of Total Factor Productivity on Southern Farms, by Subregion and Size of Farm (G_n = 100)

Size of farm as measured by the number of slaves per farm	Slave-exporting states (Old South)	Slave-importing states (New South)	All states in Parker-Gallman sample (Cotton South)
0	98.4	112.7	109.3
1–15	103.3	127.2	117.7
16–50	124.9	176.1	158.2
51 or more	135.1	154.7	145.9
All slave farms	118.9	153.1	140.4
All farms (slave and nonslave) in the subregion	116.2	144.7	134.7

Table B.24

The Relationship between Total Factor Productivity and Farm Size in Each Region (Index of free farms in each region = 100)

Size of farm as measured by the number of slaves per farm	Slave-exporting states (Old South)	Slave-importing states (New South)	All states in Parker-Gallman sample (Cotton South)
0	100.0	100.0	100.0
1–15	105.0	112.9	107.7
16–50	126.9	156.3	144.7
51 or more	137.3	137.3	133.5
All slave farms	120.8	135.8	128.5

6.2.4.1. Table B.23 reveals that with one exception, the average efficiency of southern farms in each size class and subregion exceeded the average efficiency of northern free farms. The one exception is free farms of the Old South which were, on average, 1.6 percent less efficient than free northern farms. However, since free farms in the New South were nearly 13 percent more efficient than northern farms, the Southwide average of the efficiency index for free farms exceeds that of northern farms by 9 percent.

6.2.4.2. Table B.24 shows that within each region efficiency increased with farm size. In the Old South small slave plantations (1–15 slaves) were just 5 percent more efficient than free farms. Large plantations (51 or more slaves), by contrast, were 37 percent more efficient than free farms. Medium plantations (16–50 slaves), were much closer in performance to large than to small farms, achieving a level of efficiency that was 27 percent greater than that of free farms.

The same basic pattern holds up in the New South, except that the efficiency index is higher for medium than for large plantations. While we cannot yet rule out the possibility that in the West this intermediate category of slave plantations was actually more efficient than large plantations, we suspect that the reversal is due to measurement errors. This conjecture is supported by an examination of the partial productivity indexes which shows that while labor productivity was higher on large plantations than those of intermediate size, land and capital productivity were quite low. Indeed, land productivity was lower on large plantations in the New South than on all other size categories in both the New and Old South. To put it another way, land per equivalent hand on large plantations of the New South was 60 percent higher than on medium plantations in the New South and 145 percent higher than on large and medium plantations of the Old South. Approximately the same ratios hold if the comparison is made in capital per hand.

All of this suggests that omitted product is greater for large western plantations than for the other categories of plantations. Regressions on land value by Wright [387, p. 95] indicate that in counties in which the value of land per acre was high, as in the Mississippi alluvial counties, improvements to land were as much as $100 per acre. But in areas where land values were relatively low, as in the Piedmont, improvements to land were below $10 per acre. Neither the annual investment in land improvement nor other forms of investment based on slave labor are included in measured output. The high level of equipment per hand also indicates that more manufacturing was carried out on large western plantations than on plantations of the other categories. Plantation manufacturing is another item omitted from measured output.

6.3. (pp. 193-209). Table B.24 indicates that efficiency generally increased with farm size. This suggests economies of scale. Not all aspects of efficiencies achieved by large plantations were intrinsic to the scale of operation. It is therefore useful to distinguish between what might be called "pure" scale effects and the "incidental" influence of scale. "Pure" scale effects are those increases in efficiency which can be achieved only by moving to a large scale of operation; such benefits cannot be achieved by firms (here farms) which operate on a small scale. "Incidental" scale effects are those which "happen" to be correlated with firm size, but large-scale operation is not a necessary condition for the achievement of such efficiencies.

The distinction we have in mind can be defined with respect to equation 6.10, which for convenience, will be rewritten as

$$(6.15) \quad G = A^{\frac{1}{1+\sigma}} Q^{\frac{\sigma}{1+\sigma}}.$$

Here the term $Q^{\sigma/(1+\sigma)}$ represents that part of measured efficiency which is due to pure scale effect, while the incidental influences of scale on the index of efficiency are captured by

$$A^{\frac{1}{1+\sigma}} \quad (A = A'A_L^{\alpha_1}A_K^{\alpha_2}A_T^{\alpha_3}).$$

In chapter 6 we argued that the benefits of the assembly-line type of operation epitomized by the gang system could only be achieved by relatively large plantations. We also suggested indivisibilities which led to pure scale effects in child rearing and in the utilization of the labor of the aged. These are the features of the plantation organization which are represented by $Q^{\sigma/(1+\sigma)}$.

"Incidental" scale effects might arise from a systematic mismeasurement of one or more of the inputs. For example, suppose that large planters tended to treat slaves more cruelly, as is frequently argued in the literature, and this took the form of working slaves more intensely — more hours per day or more days per year. Since we measured the labor input in man years, our failure to correct for hours per day or days per man year would show up as labor augmentation. Hence A_L would be positively correlated with Q.

Other variables which might be incidentally correlated with the level of output include the rate of land depletion, the rate of depreciation of equipment, the caliber of the management, and the difficulty of labor control. Obviously not all of these correlations are necessarily positive. If knowledge about, or experience with, the management of large slave labor forces was limited to a relatively small number of people, the efficiency of management might be related to Q by a function which reached a maximum and then declined. Thus $\partial A^{1/(1+\sigma)}/\partial Q$ could be positive or negative, or change from positive to negative as Q increased. If $\partial A^{1/(1+\sigma)}/\partial Q$ was negative, $A^{1/(1+\sigma)}Q^{\sigma/(1+\sigma)}$ might reach a maximum. This maximum would represent the optimum size slave plantation. Of course there could be different optimum sizes for different crops and the optimum size for any given type of plantation could be changing over time.

Table B.25

The Share of the Efficiency Indexes of Slave Plantations Explained by "Pure" Economies of Scale

Size of farm as measured by slaves per farm	*(1)* Index of total factor productivity (G_j)	*(2)* Value of G_j if the "incidental" scale effect had been zero	*(3)* Percentage of index of total factor productivity due to the "pure" scale effect
0	100.0	100.0	—
1–15	107.7	106.2	80.5
16–50	144.7	115.1	33.8
51 or more	133.5	123.4	70.0
All slave farms	128.5	115.1	53.0

6.3.1. Efforts to separate the "pure" and "incidental" influences on the correlation between G and plantation size have been impeded by the absence of satisfactory measures of some components of output on large plantations as well as by the paucity of information on A_L, A_K, and A_T.

Work on the problem thus far is, therefore, quite preliminary and the current findings are quite tentative.

We have attempted to isolate the pure scale effect by fitting

$$(6.16) \quad \hat{Q} = \hat{A} + \alpha_2(\hat{K} - \hat{L}) + \alpha_3(\hat{T} - \hat{L}) + (1 + \sigma)\hat{L}$$

to measures of inputs and outputs derived from the Parker-Gallman sample (see **6.2.3**). The resulting regression was

$$(6.17) \quad \hat{Q} = 2.898 + 0.1815(\hat{K} - \hat{L}) + 0.2606(\hat{T} - \hat{L}) + 1.0645\hat{L}.$$
$$\quad\quad\quad\quad\quad (0.0113) \quad\quad\quad\quad (0.0125) \quad\quad\quad (0.0124)$$

The contribution of pure scale to G_j (column 2 of table B.25) was computed from $(Q_j/Q_o)^{0.0606}$. In computing column 3 of table B.25, the term representing the interaction between the pure and incidental effects was distributed proportionally. It will be noted that table B.25 implies that $A^{1/(1+\sigma)}$ reaches a peak with medium plantations and then declines.

6.3.2. In a recent paper, Dickey and Wilson [76] attempt to determine the optimum size plantation in different regions by making use of the "survivor technique" (see [288; 313; 358]). After classifying plantations according to size, Dickey and Wilson used data from the 1850 and 1860 manuscript schedules to determine the minimum size of plantations in specified regions that increased their share in the total output of farms in these regions between the two censuses. Such plantations are designated as the "minimum efficient size" or the lower bound on the optimum size of plantations during the decade of the 1850s. Dickey and Wilson conclude that the optimum size of a plantation was at least 24 slaves in the Old South, 49 slaves in the black belt counties, and 212 slaves in the alluvial counties.

As with other studies of economies of scale on antebellum plantations, the findings of Dickey and Wilson are provisional. They used the production of cotton as a proxy for total output. And their calculations were limited to just a few counties in each of their 3 subregions.

Nevertheless, their findings suggest that the most efficient plantations in the New South had more than 50 slaves. If correct, this means either that the peak shown for G_s on medium plantations in tables B.23 and B.24 is, as we have argued, the consequence of mismeasurement, or else that there were substantial economies of scale on large plantations in marketing and finance which are not included in our measures.

6.3.3. Gray [154, pp. 529–544] is the author of an early, but still im-

Table B.26

Gray's Table on the Percent Distribution of Slaves by Size of Holdings, by States, 1850 and 1860

	1 and under 10		10 and under 20		20 and under 50		50 and under 100		100 and under 200		200 and under 300		300 and under 500		500 and under 1,000		1,000 and over		Median average	
	1850	1860	1850	1860	1850	1860	1850	1860	1850	1860	1850	1860	1850	1860	1850	1860	1850	1860	1850	1860
Alabama	19.6	18.4	19.8	18.1	32.2	30.2	18.7	20.8	8.4	10.3	1.0	1.3	.2	.9					29.9	33.4
Arkansas	31.6	26.1	22.0	20.9	24.9	26.7	15.2	16.8	5.3	7.6	.9	1.3				.6			18.4	23.4
Delaware	88.1	79.6	11.9	20.4															5.7	6.3
Florida	21.2	20.1	20.7	21.5	28.7	30.0	18.3	16.8	10.2	10.8		.8	.9						28.5	28.4
Georgia	21.1	22.2	21.2	21.9	38.5	32.5	12.5	15.8	4.8	5.7	1.2	1.2	.3	.6	.3	.2			26.0	26.4
Kentucky	49.0	48.9	31.5	30.7	17.5	18.1	1.7	1.8	.3	.4		.1							10.3	10.4
Louisiana	20.2	15.8	15.0	13.0	23.4	21.7	20.5	21.5	15.5	20.2	3.4	4.6	.9	2.3	1.1	.9			38.9	49.3
Maryland	43.9	39.8	26.8	25.7	22.5	24.4	5.3	7.2	1.0	2.5	.4	.4	.4						12.2	14.0
Mississippi	17.9	16.8	18.4	17.8	31.7	30.8	20.8	22.2	8.7	9.8	1.4	1.6	1.0	.8	.2	.2			33.0	35.0
Missouri	58.5	60.1	27.5	25.9	12.2	11.6	1.4	1.8		.5	.3								8.6	8.3
North Carolina	26.7	27.4	27.1	24.4	30.3	29.7	11.1	12.1	3.5	5.2	.9	.8	.4	.5					18.6	19.3
South Carolina	15.9	15.8	17.8	17.1	26.9	27.1	17.8	20.0	13.7	13.0	4.1	3.3	2.8	2.1	.4	1.3	.5	.3	38.2	38.9
Tennessee	36.1	36.8	26.7	26.1	28.2	26.4	7.6	8.0	1.0	2.1	.2	.5	.1	.1					15.2	15.1
Texas	35.8	31.0	28.7	25.0	22.3	29.5	10.5	10.2	2.3	4.1	.4	.3							14.9	17.6
Virginia	28.4	27.2	26.7	26.0	32.2	31.9	9.1	11.0	3.0	3.4	.4	.4	.1	.1					18.1	18.8
Total South	26.6	25.6	22.8	21.6	29.0	27.9	13.1	14.9	6.3	7.6	1.3	1.4	.6	.7	.2	.3	.1		20.6	23.0
Border States	35.5	35.4	27.5	26.3	27.0	26.4	7.4	8.4	2.0	2.8	.4	.4	.2	.2					15.3	15.6
Lower South	19.8	19.4	19.1	18.6	30.5	28.8	17.5	19.0	9.6	10.6	2.1	2.1	1.0	1.1	.3	.4	.1		30.9	32.5

portant, discussion of economies of scale in slave agriculture. Four of his tables are condensed into three and reproduced here as tables B.26, B.27, and B.28. In these tables Gray used a measure which he described as "the median average." By this he meant not the median of an array of plantations, but a plantation of such size that half of all slaves were resident on plantations of that size or greater.

6.3.3.1. Table B.26 is, of course, a "survivor" table. Although Gray did not label it as such, he emphasized the striking "tendency in the seventh decade toward concentration in slave ownership." For the South as a whole, the median rose by 12 percent. Since the Southwide increase was greater than the increase in either of the two subregions, part of the rise in the median size of a slave holding is due to the increase in the relative importance of states with larger than average plantations. The three states which showed the most rapid increase in size (Louisiana, Texas, and Arkansas) were all in the west south central region.

6.3.3.2. Plantations with less than 50 slaves generally reduced their share of the slave population. On the other hand, plantations with between 50 and 200 slaves increased their share by 16 percent, while those with between 200 and 1,000 slaves increased their share by 14 percent. Among large plantations, only the category of 1,000 or more slaves exhibited a relative decline.

6.3.3.3. The highly aggregative nature of table B.26 cloaks many shifts that were under way in particular regions and with respect to particular crops. Tables B.27 and B.28 suggest that the optimum size of a slave plantation was generally greater in sugar than in rice; in rice than in cotton, with the exception of the alluvial regions; in cotton than in tobacco; and in tobacco than in general farming.

6.3.4. Various observers and historians have offered suggestions regarding the explanation for economies of scale and the nature of the constraint which determined the optimum size of a plantation.

Russell [285, pp. 180, 285-286] emphasized that economies of scale were the cause of large plantations without attempting to identify the reasons for economies of scale. However, he stressed the role of discipline in plantation life which he characterized as "almost as strict as that of our military system." As a result of this discipline, he said, slaves "worked as methodically as machines." Stampp [303, pp. 39-42] suggested that the main constraints on the size of plantations were the availability of managers and the walking distance from the slave cabins to the fields. Phillips [263, p. 136] also stressed walking distance as the ultimate constraint:

Table B.27

Gray's Table on the Median Holdings of Slaves by Size of Holdings, 1860: The Minor Staples, Tobacco Regions, and Alluvial Regions Growing Short-Staple Cotton

Name of region	Median
Regions of the minor staples:	
Entire sea-island cotton and rice region of Georgia and South Carolina	64
Sea-island cotton and rice, South Carolina	70
Colleton County, South Carolina	92
Georgetown County, South Carolina	135
Brunswick County, North Carolina	42
Sugar region, Louisiana	81
Ascension Parish, Louisiana	175
Brazoria County, Texas	52
Western Shore tobacco region, Maryland	21
Selected tobacco regions	
Middle Virginia tobacco region	24
South central Virginia tobacco region	28
North Carolina tobacco region	25
Clarksville-Hopkinsville tobacco region, Kentucky	14
Entire tobacco region of western Kentucky	14
Christian County, Kentucky	19
Short-staple cotton—alluvial regions	
Issaquena County, Mississippi	118
Yazoo Delta, Mississippi	55
Yazoo and Warren counties, Mississippi	56
Madison and Hinds counties, Mississippi	39
River counties of southwestern Mississippi	70
Mississippi River counties, Louisiana and Mississippi	87
Concordia Parish, Louisiana	117
Alluvial counties, southeastern Arkansas	52

Table B.27 (continued)

Name of region	Median
Crittenden County, Arkansas	31
Rapides Parish, Louisiana	125
Upper Red River counties, Louisiana	44
Tennessee River valley, Alabama	32

Table B.28

Gray's Table on the Median Holdings of Slaves by Size of Holdings, 1860: Upland Cotton Regions East and West of the Mississippi River and Regions of General Farming Based Mainly on Slave Labor

Name of region	Median
Older upland cotton regions, east of Alabama	
Northeastern cotton region, North Carolina	26
Southwestern cotton region, North Carolina	17
Middle and upper coastal plain, South Carolina	37
Southern piedmont regions, South Carolina	30
Williamsburg County, South Carolina	47
Upper coastal plain, Georgia	33
Southern piedmont region, Georgia	26
Older counties of the same region	36
Upland cotton regions in Alabama and Mississippi	
Black prairie, Alabama	49
Wilcox and Sumter counties, Alabama	47
Eastern piedmont region, Alabama	17
Upper coastal plain, southern Alabama	17
Clay hills region, Alabama	18
Northwestern Alabama	10
Northeastern black prairie, Mississippi	44

Name of region	Median
Central and lower coastal plain, southern Mississippi	15
North central Mississippi	11
Northwestern Mississippi	28
Central Gulf coastal plain, Mississippi	19

Upland cotton regions west of the Mississippi river

Claiborne Parish, Louisiana	18
Ouachita Valley, Louisiana	29
Ouachita Valley, Arkansas	18
Dallas County, Arkansas	19
Northeastern Texas cotton counties	20
Polk County, Texas	26
East Texas cotton counties	23
Southern part of the black prairie, Texas	16
New Madrid County, Missouri	16
Fayette County, Tennessee	26

Regions of general farming based mainly on slave labor

Eastern Shore, Maryland	11
Tidewater counties, Virginia	19
Bluegrass region, Kentucky	14
Central farming counties, Kentucky	11
River counties, Missouri	13
Middle Tennessee	13
Valley of east Tennessee	9
Central farming counties, North Carolina	15
Tidewater farming counties, North Carolina	20
Pickens County, South Carolina	14
North Georgia farming counties	16

When the trudge of a gang, morning and evening, reached a half-hour's length it would cost more in time and energy than could be offset by economies of quantity production. A two-mile radius was perhaps an extreme limit, and except in sugar it is probable that one mile was not often exceeded. This would have more or less meaning as to the volume of labor and of tilled acreage, according to whether the headquarters were near or far from the center of the estate and whether the fields were of solid spread or broken by woods and waste land. Alluvial districts offered the greatest continuous fields, but the steadings were generally at an edge rather than in the middle – on the river front along the Mississippi, and on the high land behind the riparian strips of the rice coast. In the Piedmont at large the ruggedness of surface, together with the practice of clearing new grounds and abandoning old, often restricted the tilled portion of a property to a small fraction of its total area.

Gray [154, pp. 529-544] argued that the optimum size depended on the nature of the crop, the quality of soil, nearness to market, and other marketing conditions including access to financial markets. Wright [387, p. 122] and Dickey and Wilson [76] emphasized the quality of management.

6.4. (pp. 195-196). To test the hypothesis that soils were being depleted in the selling states, we examined the relationship of land yields and land values to length of settlement in these states (cf. Wright [387, chap. IV]). The effect of length of settlement on land yields was estimated from equation 6.17.[16]

$$(6.18) \quad \hat{Q} - \hat{T} = \beta_0 + \beta_1(\hat{L} - \hat{T}) + \beta_2(\hat{K} - \hat{T}) + \beta_3 Y.$$

This equation was fitted to output and input measures constructed from the Parker-Gallman sample (see **6.2.3**). When T was measured by total acres, the resulting regression was

$$(6.19) \quad \hat{Q} - \hat{T} = 3.988 + 0.6073(\hat{L} - \hat{T}) + 0.2682(\hat{K} - \hat{T}) - 0.00570Y.$$
$$(0.0243) \qquad (0.0174) \qquad (0.00077)$$

[16] β_1 and β_2 are not to be treated as estimates of α_1 and α_2. T^σ has been omitted from the equation to emphasize that equation 6.18 is not the Old South production function. Omission of an adjustment for land quality biases the estimates of the output elasticities since the ratio of improved to unimproved acres varied with the output mix and with the size of the farm.

When T was measured by improved acres, the resulting regression was

$$(6.20) \quad \hat{Q} - \hat{T} = 3.336 + 0.3736(\hat{L} - \hat{T}) + 0.1786(\hat{K} - \hat{T}) - 0.00558Y.$$
$$\quad\quad\quad\quad (0.0241) \quad\quad\quad (0.0167) \quad\quad\quad (0.00071)$$

In both regressions β_3, which we interpret as the rate at which land yields changed with the length of settlement, is statistically significant, negative, and small. The value of β_3 implies that land fertility in the selling states was declining at 5 percent *per decade*. Whether this rate of decline was more or less than in the North remains to be determined. However, even if the decline in fertility could not have been retarded or reversed by the application of fertilizers or other improved practices, it would still have taken about 125 years for the fertility of the land to have fallen to one half of its original level.

To test the effect of the length of settlement on land values, we followed Wright [387, p. 132] in constructing an index of land quality from the residuals of a regression of the value of land (plus improvements) on acres of improved land and on acres of unimproved land. These residuals were then regressed on the length of settlement to obtain equation 6.21:

$$(6.21) \quad \hat{V} = 0.2871 + 0.00233Y.$$
$$\quad\quad\quad\quad\quad (0.00083)$$

Once again the coefficient of Y, here the rate of change in the index of land quality, is statistically significant and small. But this time it's positive – an odd result, if our interpretation of β_3 in equation 6.19 and 6.20 was correct. For that interpretation implies that the marginal product of land was declining with age. Hence, land values should also have declined with age.

That land values were higher on older lands than on newer lands, suggests the existence of a wedge between the *physical* and the *economic* productivity of land. That wedge could have been due to transport costs which made lands with high physical yields less valuable than lands with low physical yields, because they were more remote or in more impenetrable terrain. Under these circumstances, β_3 would be a measure of the rate of reduction in the wedge – i.e., the rate at which transportation improvements made it possible to bring into production one-time submarginal lands with high physical yields. This is precisely the process that took place in the North as transport improvements led to a switch from the relatively low-yield lands of the Northeast to the high-yield lands of the north central states.

6.4.1. If we accept β_3 as a measure of the rate of soil depletion, it is possible to estimate the circumstances under which it would have been economically warranted for farmers of the Old South to have increased expenditures on fertilizers to a level which would have reduced the depletion rate to zero.

Estimates derived from the Parker-Gallman sample indicate that the average value of output per improved acre was $10.92. At a depletion rate of 0.00558 per annum, output per acre declined at 6 cents per year. It follows that an increase in the use of fertilizers to the level required to halt land depletion was warranted only if the cost of the additional fertilizer (including the labor time) was not greater than 6 cents per acre.

Genovese [139, p. 94], estimates that the cost of fertilizing an acre of land with guano was between $2.00 and $5.00 per acre. Hence it probably was sound business judgment, rather than indifference or backwardness, which led most southern farmers to eschew such an undertaking.

6.5. (pp. 200, 210–212 and fig. 46). Some scholars have overestimated the number of free overseers employed in the slave sector because they assumed that all whites listed in the census as overseers worked on slave plantations. However, since the word "overseer' is a synonym for "supervisor," it was used to describe managers in industry as well as in agriculture, on free farms as well as on slave farms, in the North as well as in the South.

Scholars have also been misled by the fact that the number of free southern overseers in 1850 was not much larger than the number of plantations with over 50 slaves. This fact led easily to the assumption that virtually all of the large plantations had white overseers, that very few of the medium plantations had such overseers, and that small plantations virtually never had such overseers. Thus Scarborough wrote [289, p. 10]: "Assuming that each of these upper-class planters had at least one overseer in 1850, only 11 percent of the 84,328 middle-class planters — those owning from ten to fifty slaves — could have been utilizing overseers."

Analysis of the data in the Parker-Gallman sample shows that 14.5 percent of the medium plantations (16 to 50 slaves) had free overseers, that 3.0 percent of the small plantations (1–15 slaves) had free overseers. While these figures may seem only slightly different from Scarborough's 11 and zero percent, if they are applied to the size distribution of slave holdings for 1850, they account for 13,739 overseers out of the national total of 18,859. Another 1,887 overseers were employed in the North. Thus the residual number of overseers left for large slave plantations could not exceed 3,233. Some part of the last number were engaged on the free farms, and in the factories of the South. But even if we assume they were all on plantations of 50 or more slaves, only 40 percent of these large estates would have had white overseers.

Table B.29

Goldin's Estimates of Demand Elasticities for Slaves in Ten Cities, Three Urban Aggregates, and the United States

	ϵ		ϵ
United States	.10	Richmond	.47
Baltimore	.54	St. Louis	1.64
Charleston	.53	Savannah	.12
Louisville	1.64	Washington, D.C.	1.15
Mobile	.09	Old South Cities	.95
New Orleans	.75	New South Cities	.54
Norfolk	.78	Border Cities	1.23

6.6. (pp. 234–235). Goldin [146; cf. 148] has estimated that the elasticity of demand for slaves in rural areas was about 0.1, while the demand elasticity in urban areas was about 1.0. Her demand equations were fitted to data for the period from 1820 to 1860. As she notes, omitted variables probably bias the estimates of the elasticities in both sectors downward, but the downward bias is probably larger for the estimates of the urban elasticities than for the estimate of the rural elasticity. Goldin's estimates of the elasticities of demand for 10 southern cities and 4 aggregates are shown in table B.29.

6.6.1. Goldin used equation 6.22,

$$(6.22) \; \overset{*}{Q}_{bi} - \overset{*}{Q}_{bj} = (\overset{*}{D}_{bi} - \overset{*}{D}_{bj}) - \epsilon_{bj}(\overset{*}{P}_{bi} - \overset{*}{P}_{bj}) - \overset{*}{P}_{bi}(\epsilon_{bi} - \epsilon_{bj}),$$

to account for the decline in the slave population of cities relative to that of the countryside, to account for the more marked cycles in the urban slave population than in the total slave population, and to account for differences among southern cities in the rates of growth of their slave populations. She found that the elasticity term (the third right-hand term) of equation 6.22 largely accounts for both the decline in the urban slave population relative to rural slave population and for the more marked cycles in the urban than the rural slave population. However, both the first and the third right-hand terms are important in explaining differences among southern cities in the rate of growth of the slave population. In this connection, Goldin stressed that there were differences not only among the three groups into which southern cities are frequently grouped (Border, Old South, and New South), but also in the behavior of the various cities within each group [146, pp. 94-99] :

The classification of the South into the three categories, Old South, New South and Border States is used in this dissertation. But the characteristics which I attribute to these urban divisions are slightly different from those given to them in the traditional literature. The Border State cities, Baltimore, Louisville, St. Louis and Washington, D.C. all experienced rapid increases in their economic activity during the period 1820 to 1860. Louisville expanded greatly during these years and although the results in table [B.30] show that the demand for her slaves increased rapidly during all decades, much of this was due to market size factors. Baltimore also grew during these decades, but despite this, the growth in demand for her slave services was weak, and in fact, was negative for the last decade. What can explain these differences?

Baltimore's slaves were basically female domestics, whereas Louisville had a larger percentage of male slaves. It is possible that although the elasticity of demand for Baltimore slave services was less than that for Louisville, Baltimore received more immigrants during the period. Therefore, the price of substitute labor was declining, relative to that for slaves, and Baltimore residents shifted away from slave labor. Because of the lower elasticity, Baltimore cycles are smaller than those for Louisville or St. Louis. Baltimore, in fact, became progressively female, in its slave population. This shows that as slave prices rose, Baltimore slave owners sold their male slaves, whose skills were less specific, but retained their female domestics. Washington, D.C. also gained female slaves, but her demand was not declining during the period. In fact, the demand for her slaves increased at a rather steady pace. It is possible that persons who came to the District of Columbia were complementary to, and not substitutes for, slaves. Therefore, the alternative price for slaves did not decline, and in fact, the demand for their services increased as persons entered this city. Thus, the Border State cities were similar, for each did not have a large fraction of their labor force which was slave, and all had many more female slaves than male. But, they each reacted differently to the cycles in slave prices. Louisville and St. Louis experienced huge cycles, due to the large

Goldin's Estimates of the Average Annual Rate of Growth in the Demand for Slaves ($\overset{*}{D}$) by Decade, in Ten Cities, Three Urban Aggregates, and the United States

	1820–30	1830–40	1840–50	1850–60
United States	+.023	+.027	+.029	+.026
Baltimore	+.004	+.001	+.001	−.005
Charleston	+.002	+.020	+.042	−.019
Louisville	+.071	+.060	+.084	+.043
Mobile	+.035	+.124	+.064	+.003
New Orleans	+.001	+.111	−.013	+.001
Norfolk	+.014	+.032	+.026	+.017
Richmond	+.044	+.045	+.037	+.041
St. Louis	+.018	−.024	+.085	+.001
Savannah	+.025	+.021	+.034	+.019
Washington, D.C.	+.026	+.020	+.035	+.020
Old South Cities	+.024	+.049	+.044	+.034
New South Cities	+.009	+.109	+.001	.000
Border Cities	+.032	+.034	+.046	+.021

elasticity of demand for their slaves; Washington, and Baltimore had lower elasticities, and experienced smaller oscillations in their slave labor forces. Baltimore seemed much more subject to influxes of immigrants who were substitutes for slaves. St. Louis' and Louisville's dramatic growth in demand for slaves was due primarily to their overall increase in economic activity.

The two New South cities, Mobile and New Orleans were also very different. Mobile sustained slightly more rapid growth in the demand for slaves than did New Orleans although both were subject to extreme fluctuations. The two cities experienced great booms during the 1830 to 1840 period, and the growth in both the demand for slaves and the realized quantities was substantial during that decade. New Orleans, being a large port, was like Baltimore during the latter period, that is, subject to large increases in free labor. These laborers competed with slaves for the lesser skilled jobs, and displaced them in many areas.

What have traditionally been grouped together as Old South cities, include an even more diverse group than the other classifications. Richmond stands out as the city with the most stable and large increases in demand for slaves. It is also the city with one of the smaller elasticities of demand.

Richmond was the most industrial of all the urban areas, and it was also not subject to much immigration. Therefore, Richmond's slaves had few substitutes and they were, on average, a more skilled group than was found in the other cities. These facts can account for the, on average, low elasticity value for Richmond slaves. Charleston, on the other hand, decreased in importance as a port during the 1850's. This accounts for the decrease in demand for her slaves during that period. Her slaves were employed in all forms of production and are less easy to classify than are Richmond's. Savannah grew at the steady pace that characterizes Richmond, and this is reflected in the growth of the demand for her slaves.

6.7. (pp. 236-239). Discussions of slavery are frequently carried on as if the use of force to obtain labor is unique to that form of society. Slave societies are presumed to rely exclusively, or almost exclusively, on force to *compel* labor, making no, or little, use of wages and other forms of positive inducement. Free societies are presumed to rely exclusively on wages (or other payments) to *elicit* labor, making no, or virtually no, use of force. This oversimplified but widely held conception is not only an inaccurate description of slave societies but also of free societies. Both slave and free societies rely on the combination of force and positive inducement to bring forth labor. What distinguishes them is the proportions in which these methods of extracting labor are combined.

As with all other choices in the production process, the exact combination of force and wages that will prevail depends on both the relative productivity of two forms of labor inducement and the relative costs of the two forms of inducement. The problem can be formalized with the usual production-isoquant mapping, as done in figure B.7.

In this figure the line designated *PP* is the unit isoquant for the "production" of labor. It shows all of the various combinations of force and "wages" (positive inducements) that will yield one unit of labor (measured, say, in man years). The shape and the position of this curve is determined not by technology but by culture. The level at which workers respond to a given amount of force or "wages" and the rate of substitution between the two are determined by attitudes, mores, expectations with respect to income levels, opportunities to spend wages, tastes for consumer goods, the value attached to leisure, etc.

Over time culture will change and such changes lead to shifts in isoquants. If, for example, workers become less responsive to force and more responsive to "wages" the isoquant will shift from *PP* to *P'P'*. Such a shift could come about by a revulsion against force which makes workers less responsive to it. Or it could come about because of an increased desire for

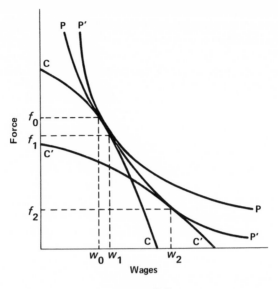

Figure B.7

consumer goods — because workers become "hooked" on "mass consumption." Of course, both types of influence could be at work simultaneously.

The curve designated *CC* in figure B.7 is the isocost curve. It describes all of the different combinations of force and "wages" which can be "purchased" for a given total expenditure. We have drawn this curve as concave to the origin, rather than as a straight line, to emphasize that the price of a unit of force (or "wages") does not remain constant (is not independent of the level of utilization) when it is measured in efficiency units. The more force that is used, the greater the cost of an additional unit of force of a given "quality."

The position (intercepts) of the isocost curve and the ratio of relative prices (slope) are to some extent influenced by the personal attributes of a manager (or of the managerial class). The more skillful a slaveowner or a factory manager, the farther out will be a given isocost curve for his firm as compared with some other firm. Historically, however, the legal codes and the political and social institutions of societies have been the basic determinants of the shape and position of the isocost curve. Under the legal codes and institutions of slavery, force was relatively cheap and "wages" were relatively expensive. Slave society gave masters a high degree of discretion both with respect to the amount of force they could apply to labor and the forms that force could take. At the same time slave and similar societies held masters (or lords) responsible for the behavior of their laborers, to the point of being subject to suits for damages caused by their laborers. They were also required to protect their chattel (or vassals) from marauders, to the point of risking both fortune and life. Moreover, either by custom or law, or both, they were required to feed, clothe, and shelter their laborers at some minimum level, regardless of market conditions — and to guarantee their support regardless of age or health. This is the core of the "paternalism" of slave societies that Genovese [139; 140; 141] and others have stressed.

Over time, legal codes and institutions have changed in such a manner as to raise the cost of force and to reduce the cost of "wages." The discretion allowed to members of the managerial class in the application of force has been greatly reduced. Indeed, in many societies they are prohibited from the personal exercise of various forms of force altogether and must appeal to the state to bring force to bear — a very costly procedure. At the same time, the cost of "wages" has been greatly reduced. The liability of managers for the behavior of their employees has been greatly decreased. While a minimum payment per hour or day may still be required, there is no effective minimum obligation with respect to the annual (or longer term) payment. The level of "wages" is permitted to fluctuate with market conditions. Employees of below average ability, or poor health, may be dismissed without further obligation, except as determined by prior contract. The effect of these changes is shown in figure B.7 by the shift of the isocost curve from CC to $C'C'$.

Figure B.7 can be used to show how social, political, and economic forces interacted to change societies from "high-force" to "low-force" civilizations. If a society is initially characterized by high force, its situation can be represented by curves CC and PP. Profit maximization will lead to an equilibrium in which labor is obtained with f_0 amount of force and w_0 amount of "wages." A popular revulsion against force, or a shift in the taste of workers for market-produced goods, will be reflected in a shift of the isoquant from PP to $P'P'$. The new position of the isoquant indicates that workers have become less responsive to compulsion and more responsive to "wages." Thus, even without a legal and institutional response to the new morality, profit maximization would lead slaveowners or managers to reduce the use of force from f_0 to f_1 and to increase "wage" payments from w_0 to w_1. If legal codes and institutions respond to the new morality by limiting the discretion of managers in using force and also lightening their paternal obligations, the isocost curve will shift from CC to $C'C'$. Once

157

again economic forces will then lead managers to reduce force, this time from f_1 to f_2, and to increase "wage" payments, from w_1 to w_2. Thus moral, political, and economic forces interacted to transform society from "high-force" and "low-wages" to "low-force" and "high-wages."

In the foregoing example, we initiated the process of change with a shift in attitude on the part of workers. We do not mean to imply that this was necessarily the actual chronology. There is evidence to suggest that in many societies the initial shift was in the isocost curve — a shift brought about by the protests of antislavery and other critics who became powerful enough to alter either legal or institutional arrangements. Changed attitudes of workers may have lagged and, indeed, have been a delayed response to the new legal and institutional milieu.

While we have identified "high-force" with slavery, it should be stressed that many nominally free societies are also "high-force." This is not only true of such one-time slave societies as the postbellum South (see 82; cf. 236; 385]) or postslavery British Guiana (see [1; 231]) which used debt peonage, vagrancy laws, as well as legal and extralegal corporal punishment to compel labor. It was also true of the antebellum North in which indentured labor, corporal punishment, and other forms of force continued to exist after slavery was illegalized. Of course, many free countries today are still high-force societies, when measured by standards currently prevailing in nations such as England or the United States.

6.7.1. The estimates of output by farm size and of factor shares developed from the Parker-Gallman sample make it possible to compute the labor income of free farmers and to compare it with the income earned by slaves. According to these estimates there was an average of 6.48 persons on a free southern farm in the cotton belt. The annual value of the output of such a farm was $418.13, of which 58 percent or $242.52 was labor income. The average income of a slave family of exactly the same size and age-sex composition, living on a large plantation, was $279.18. In other words, the labor income of the slave family was 15 percent larger than the labor income of the corresponding free family. (See **6.7.1.2** for the method of estimating the average annual income of slaves.)

6.7.1.1. This surprising finding can be explained by referring to figure B.8. In that diagram, w represents the "wage" of a slave family on a large plantation and w' is the "wage" that the same family would have received on a free farm. Masters are able to elicit a unit of labor (here defined as the labor input of one slave family of average size during the course of a year) by combining a "wage" payment of w with an amount of force equal to f. If they chose to do so, masters could have extracted the same amount of

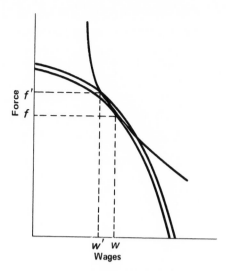

Figure B.8

labor with a wage payment of only w' provided that they increased the amount of force from f to f'. However, figure B.8 shows that the substitution of $f' - f$ force for $w - w'$ wages, would have raised rather than lowered the cost of a unit of labor, since the point (w', f') lies on a higher isocost curve than the point (w, f).

6.7.1.2. We estimate that annual per capita income of slaves on large plantations was $42.99. This figure was computed by adding to our previous estimate of $34.13 for "basic" income (see **4.10.1**) an allowance of $8.86 per capita for "extra" income. Average per capita income multiplied by 1.41 (the ratio of adult male to average income) yields $60.62 as the estimated average income of adult males.

Extra income was estimated from the Parker-Gallman sample on the following assumptions: 1, the only source of extra income was production on slave patches; 2, only males worked on such patches; 3, on average only half of one day per week was devoted to such labor; 4, the land in these patches was of average quality; 5, slaves were permitted to use the implements which they normally employed in field labor. While the $8.86 figure derived from these assumptions falls well within the $5.00 to $10.00 range that is conventionally suggested for "extra" income, we believe that this figure is probably too low. It contains no allowance for Christmas and other gifts made by planters; it also omits the extra earnings of artisans and women.

To obtain the estimate of the income that would have been paid to a slave family of the same size and age-sex composition as the average free household in the Parker-Gallman sample, $42.99 was multiplied by 1.00218. This standardized for differences in the age-sex structure. The resulting figure, $43.08, multiplied by 6.48, equals $279.16.

6.7.2. The "pure" gains from scale on large plantations was 23.4 percent and the labor share was 0.58 (see **6.3.1** and table B.25). Hence the maximum bribe that could be offered to free farmers whose only income was labor income (farmer operators who rented land and equipment) was 44 percent ($1.234^{1/0.58} = 1.44$). Of course farmers who already owned land could only increase their total income by 23.4 percent by freely merging their holdings and combining into gangs. However, their labor income could be increased by 44 percent.

6.7.3. Seagrave [292] has collected data on the wages paid to freedmen in Louisiana for gang labor. He finds that in 1865 wages of gang workers were 2.42 times as large as the earnings of sharecroppers. In 1866 the ratio was 2.11. Seagrave also compares the real wages of gang laborers in 1866 and 1867 with income of slaves in 1850 by constructing a consumer price index. He finds that gang wages were between 2.39 and 2.75 times as high as slave income in 1850.[17]

6.8. (pp. 244–246 and table 3). In computing the gains and losses shown in table 3 there is a difficult index number problem. Seagrave's figures [292] indicate that slaves would have required a bribe in excess of $75 to accept gang labor. That is the figure we used to compute the nonpecuniary disadvantage. Seagrave's samples of the wages of gang workers and of the annual earnings of sharecroppers are small, with the latter limited to data from just four plantations. While the sample of gang wages is drawn from a larger number of plantations (15), these were all located in Louisiana. Consequently, the estimate of an average Southwide nonpecuniary disadvantage of $75 must be treated as a tentative approximation. Work to expand both the size and coverage of the relevant samples is now under way.

One could also argue that the nonpecuniary disadvantage of gang labor was less than or equal to the amount of the wages that slaves would have foregone if they attempted self-purchase. A slave could have bought him-

---

[17]Seagrave's estimate of slave maintenance is too low. But this is offset by his omission of the extra earnings of gang laborers after the war and his assumption that gang laborers drew rations and made use of the cabins provided to them for only 10 months out of the year.

self out (compensated his master) by reducing his "wages" by an amount equal to the master's gain from the pure scale effect, i.e., by $23 [($61 ÷ 1.15) × 0.44 ≈ $23] per annum, of which $15 must be paid to the master and $8 represents the difference between slave "wages" and free "wages."[18] Since few slaves chose self-purchase, it appears that to most slaves freedom was not worth $23 per annum.

The anomaly arises because the sums involve a large part of slave income. Hence the marginal utility of the income of slaves cannot be assumed to have been constant over such a range. Reduction of income by $23 per annum would have pushed slaves below the level of subsistence. At an income of $53 (the average income of adult males on free farms), slaves would have rejected an offer of $128 (53 + 75) for gang labor. But most slaves would also have rejected an offer of freedom if it meant that they would have had an annual income of only $38 (61 – 23). In other words, the utility of a loss of $23 was greater than the utility of a gain of $75.

6.8.1. The other entries in table 3 were computed on the following assumptions:

    1. The long-run supply of cotton is given by

$$(6.23) \quad P_c = A^{-1} w^{\alpha_1} r^{\alpha_2} m^{\alpha_3}.$$

    2. The demand for cotton was perfectly inelastic.
    3. Only slaves on large plantations received "wage" benefits from gang labor.

Assumptions 1 and 2 imply that, in the long run, the effect of a 25 percent increase in A was to reduce the revenue from cotton by roughly $30,000,000 (using the 1850 value and output of cotton [329, p. 308]). Since there were roughly 1,000,000 slaves on large plantations and their average income was $43.00 per person, of which 0.15/1.15 was their share in the gain from scale, assumption 3 implies that slaves benefited by $6,000,000 (1,000,000 × [0.15/1.15] × 43 ≈ 6,000,000).

Because the demand for cotton increased more rapidly than the supply, slaveowners earned a quasi-rent. The quasi-rent per slave was equal to the birthright multiplied by the rate of return. Since there were 3,200,000 slaves, slaveowners received roughly $10,000,000 per year in quasi-rents (30 × 0.1 × 3,200,000 ≈ 10,000,000).

---

[18]If all the gain from scale went to labor, "wages" would rise to 1.44 of the free level. Since slaves' "wages" were 15 per cent greater than free "wages," the gain to masters was 1.44 ÷ 1.15 ≈ 1.25.

The balance of the income gain brought about by the rise in A was $14,000,000 (30,000,000 - 6,000,000 - 10,000,000). And this accrued to consumers of cotton.

6.9. (pp. 247–249 and table 4). The basic estimates of relative regional per capita income were developed by Easterlin [93; 94]. We have made certain modifications in Easterlin's estimates, the most important of which is described in **6.9.1**. The regional relatives were then applied to Gallman's constant dollars estimates of national income for 1840 and 1860 [133] to obtain the entries shown in table 4.

6.9.1. The most important of our revisions of Easterlin's computations was the estimation of income for Texas in 1840, so that Texas could be brought into the southern region in both years (it was excluded from Easterlin's computations). To insure that this revision introduced no upward biases into the estimates of the rate of growth, Texas per capita income in 1840 was assumed equal to the 1860 level. The 1840 population was interpolated between the 1836 and 1846 estimates presented in Newton and Gambrell [242, p. 280]. Thus the regional breakdown in table 4 differs from Easterlin's in including Texas in the South, but accords with his placement of Delaware and Maryland in the Northeast. The Mountain and Pacific states were excluded from the national and regional totals in both years.

6.9.2. A recent paper by Gunderson [164] has questioned the plausibility of Easterlin's southern per capita income estimates for 1840 by using a residual method based upon "crediting known slave populations with their reported earnings [based upon Evans's hire rate data] and then arguing that the remainder of total income (as reported by Easterlin) attributable to the free population is (for certain areas) much too low to be plausible." He argues, in particular, that the reported incomes for the states in the South Atlantic and east south central retions are too low, and that the differences between these regions and the west south central are overstated. Gunderson's suggested revisions would raise the relative southern per capita income for 1840. Until similar calculations are performed for 1860, the effect upon measured southern income growth is uncertain. Moreover, Evans's hire rates are too high to be applicable to slaves in rural areas for reasons indicated in **3.2.4.2** and **3.4.2.2**. Gunderson's applications of Louisiana hire rates to east south central states also imparts an upward bias to his proffered correction. Pending further investigation we consider Easterlin's estimates still to be the best currently available.

Easterlin has recently reworked his estimate of income originating in northern and southern agriculture [95]. These new estimates are not significantly different from his earlier ones.

6.10. International comparisons of per capita income can never be precise, because of various index number problems (see [143; 144; 203, pp. 216-252]) arising out of currency exchange rates, differences in commodity mixes, and differences in the relative prices of various nations. The ranking shown in table 5 represents what we believe to be the most reasonable resolution of these problems, given the available data. Alternative weighting systems led to a ranking of the South as high as second and as low as ninth. Thus, under all the alternative systems of weights permitted by available data, the South was clearly one of the most developed "nations" of the period, although its exact position within the top group is open to debate. Under any system of weights the per capita income of the South was at least 7 or 8 times as great as such truly underdeveloped nations as Mexico or India.

Table 5 rests mainly on estimates presented by Kuznets [204, p. 24] of "approximate product per capita at the beginning of modern growth." Kuznets's estimates were prepared in 1965 prices by: 1, computing GNP per capita for each country shown in 1965 U.S. dollars; and 2, extrapolating the GNP per capita back to the date of the onset by modern growth on the basis of the rate of change of per capita income computed from the income estimates of each country shown. Those countries for which we used Kuznets's estimates and the specific decade to which the estimates apply are: Belgium (1865), Netherlands (1865), Switzerland (1865), Denmark (1865-69), Norway (1865-69), Sweden (1861-69), Italy (1861-69), Japan (1874-79), Canada (1870-74), and Australia (1861-69).

For France, we used Kuznets's estimated per capita income for 1831-1840, carried forward on the basis of the estimated rate of growth of per capita income from that decade to 1861-1870 [204, p. 11]. For Germany, Kuznets's estimate for 1850-59 was carried forward to 1860-69 on the basis of the average rate of increase per decade from 1850-1859 to 1880-1889 [204, p. 38]. For India, Kuznets's estimate for 1861-1869 was used. For the United States, the Kuznets estimate for 1834-1843 was extrapolated forward to 1859 on the basis of the rate of growth of per capita income computed by Kuznets from 1834-1843 to 1859 [204, p. 13]. The allocation in the United States between North and South was on the basis of regional relatives underlying table 4.

For Austria, we carried forward an estimate of national product per capita in 1841 by Gross [162, p. 101] on the basis of the rate of growth of industrial output per capita between 1841 and 1865, converted into U.S.

dollars of 1860 [163, p. 909]. The estimate for Ireland was from Deane and Cole [73, p. 335] for 1861, converted at the par exchange rate. For Great Britain we used the ratio of British to American per capita income for 1840 (in 1840 prices) computed by Gallman [133, p. 5], carried forward to 1860 on the basis of growth rates of per capita income in each country. The estimate for Mexico was derived by applying Maddison's ratio of the income relative for Mexico and India [214, p. 18] to Kuznets's estimate of per capita income in India.

6.11. The relationship between the rate of growth of per capita income in the South and in its subregions is given by the following: By definition

(6.24) $I = \Sigma \pi_i I_i; \quad i = 1, 2, 3.$

It can be shown that the rate-of-growth transformation of equation 6.24 is

(6.25) $\overset{*}{I} \approx \Sigma \psi_i (\overset{*}{\pi_i} + \overset{*}{I_i}); \quad i = 1, 2, 3.$

Substituting the following values for the variables in equation 6.25 (the ψ_i are the estimated regional shares for the midyear of the period) we obtain

	ψ_i	$\overset{*}{\pi_i}$	$\overset{*}{I_i}$
South Atlantic	0.41	-0.8	1.2
East south central	0.38	0.0	1.3
West south central	0.21	3.8	1.0

Hence

$$\overset{*}{I} \approx 0.41 \, (-0.8 + 1.2) + 0.38 \, (0.0 + 1.3) + 0.21 \, (3.8 + 1.0)$$

$$\overset{*}{I} \approx 1.67.$$

Thus, about 30 percent of the annual growth in southern per capita income was due to the redistribution of population among subregions and the balance to the growth of per capita income within the subregions.

Of course, equation 6.25 can also be applied to the relationship between the North and its subregions or to the relationship between national and regional rates of growth.

6.11.1. Because of difficulties in allocating the output of the service sector among regions, we have calculated the contribution of the shift from agriculture to manufacturing to the growth of commodity output per worker in the northern states from 1840 to 1860 and multiplied this by the share of national income originating in commodity production for 1859 [136, p. 27]. This calculation omits the contribution of the shift towards the service sector, and thus underestimates the contribution of intersectoral shifts to the overall northern growth rate.

6.11.2. The large contribution of interindustry shifts to the growth of per capita income was not merely a phenomenon of the early period of industrialization. Massell's study [219] of U.S. manufacturing since World War II indicates that interindustry shifts explain 30 percent of the measured increase in total factor productivity. Denison [75] found that the shift of labor from agriculture to manufacturing explained about the same proportion of the growth of per capita income in Europe after World War II.

6.12. (pp. 253–254). Analyses of census data on the distribution of wealth by Wright [387; 388], Soltow [299; 300; 301], and Gallman [134] indicate that in 1860:

1. The distribution of wealth was much more unequal in urban than in rural areas.
2. The distribution of wealth was slightly more unequal in the rural South than in the rural North.
3. The overall inequality of the wealth distribution was roughly the same in the South as in the North since the greater weight of the urban population in the North offset the higher level of inequality in the rural South.

These comparisons, which include slaves as part of wealth, apply only to the inequality of the distribution of the wealth of the free population. This, of course, is appropriate for the issue raised by Olmsted and Cairnes. What remains to be done is to construct the wealth distribution of the entire population, slave as well as free.

For Wisconsin in 1860, Soltow estimated that the top 2 percent of adult males over the age of 20 held 31 percent of total wealth. In Milwaukee county the top 2 percent held over 50 percent of wealth, a figure below that which Soltow has found for ten large northern cities in 1860 [299; 301]. Wisconsin, as an area of relatively recent settlement and one which was not heavily urbanized, can be considered to have been representative of the northern wealth distribution. If anything, Wisconsin probably had a more equal distribution than the North as a whole.

Gallman has presented wealth distributions within several subregions of the South, but he has not presented an all-South measure. The top 2 percent of white families had 25.4 percent of gross wealth in the cotton counties; 37.3 percent in Louisiana (outside of New Orleans), and 59.6 percent in New Orleans. Gallman also presents the shares for Maryland, and uses the rural areas of Maryland as an estimate for noncotton and nonsugar farming throughout the nation in his national measures. The top 2 percent of white families in Maryland (outside of Baltimore) owned 25.8 percent of total wealth.

We have used Gallman's figures to compute a rough estimate of the all-South wealth distribution. We assumed that the distribution in New Orleans was typical of the urban South, and that Louisiana was typical of the rice and sugar areas. The cotton counties were taken to represent the rest of the South. (Use of the Maryland estimates for areas outside of the cotton, rice, and sugar counties of the South would not affect the result.) The computation indicated that the top 2 percent of southern white families owned about 28 percent of total wealth.

There are, of course, difficulties in measuring the inequality of wealth and in comparing estimates based on different sampling procedures. The share going to the top 1, 2, or 5 percent is a standard measure, and it generally provides the same picture as alternative measures, such as Gini coefficients. We doubt that the differences in sampling procedure or in the allocation by adult males, as opposed to families, will significantly affect the basic conclusion that many scholars have greatly overstated the extent of differences in the distribution of wealth among the white population in the northern and southern states during the antebellum period.

6.13. (p. 255 and table 6). The estimated railroad mileage for European countries in 1860 is taken from a table in Mitchell [228, pp. 56–57]. Data for other countries (except the U.S.) are taken from a table in Woodruff [375, p. 253]. The U.S. data are taken from [340, p. 333]. These sources sometimes give a number of alternative estimates for several countries, but in all cases the measures are only slightly different from those used and have no effect upon the implications of the table.

The estimates of cotton production for all countries (except the U.S. and Great Britain) are based upon the statistics of cotton consumption in

1860 compiled by Mulhall [238, p. 156]. For Great Britain we used the estimate shown in Mitchell and Deane [229, p. 179]. For the North and South we used data from [339, p. xxi]. Here again alternative estimates (see [228, pp. 47-48]) present only slightly different results from those shown in table 6.

The estimates of pig iron production for European countries are the average of the quinquennia 1855-59 and 1860-64 as given by Mitchell [228, pp. 40-41]. The estimates for the North and South in 1860 are from [339, p. clxxx].

To convert to a per capita basis we used population estimates in Mitchell [228, pp. 14-15] for European countries, in [338, pp. 598-599] for the North and South, in [215, p. 164] for India, and in [375, pp. 110-111] for Canada and Australia.

6.14. (p. 257). The parameters which must be estimated, and the issues resolved, to determine the effect of productivity changes on the level of southern income and the share of manufacturing in total output, are discussed by Pope [265] and Passell and Wright [254].

Appendix C.

Notes on the Evolution of the Traditional Interpretation of the Slave Economy, 1865-1956

In this appendix we comment briefly on various books and articles published between 1865 and 1956 that we found to be useful in understanding the evolution of thought about the economics of slavery. The limited nature of our objectives here should be emphasized. We have eschewed any attempt at a full-scale evaluation of the literature as a whole or of individual writers. No special significance should be attached to the relative length of our comments on various works and writers. The extent of some comments are more of an index of what we believe we can add to previous appraisals by other historians than an index of importance. Our desire not to repeat points already made in the main text or in appendix B also contributes to the unevenness of our treatment of various writers, essays, and issues.

Citations of particular studies are made directly in the text of the appendix as follows: [1, pp. 23-32]. The first number within the brackets refers to a book or paper given in the list of references at the end of appendix C. The numbers following the comma refer to the relevant pages in the cited study. When several citations are made within one pair of brackets, the citations are separated by semicolons.

The bold-faced numbers at the beginning of each note are the *note index*. The note index is used for making cross-references within appendix

C. Cross-references to material in appendix B are identified by adding the letter "B" to the note index. Thus "See **B.1.3.2**" means "See section 2 to note 3 of chapter 1 in appendix B." Cross-references to material in the primary volume (main text) begin with the letter "T" and include both chapter and page references. For example, "See T.2, pp. 39–43" means "See pages 39 through 43 of chapter 2 in the main text."

1. The origin of the "economic indictment" of slavery is described in chapter 5, and some aspects of its evolution into a "traditional interpretation" are discussed in chapter 6. As we define it, the traditional interpretation of the slave economy involves five main propositions. These are:

1. that slavery was generally an unprofitable investment, or depended on trade in slaves to be profitable, except on new, highly fertile land;
2. that slavery was economically moribund;
3. that slave labor, and agricultural production based on slave labor was economically inefficient;
4. that slavery caused the economy of the South to stagnate, or at least retarded its growth, during the antebellum era;
5. that slavery provided extremely harsh material conditions of life for the typical slave.

1.1. In chapter 5 we emphasized the works of three writers — Helper [172], Olmsted [244; 245; 246; 247], and Cairnes [33] — as central to the original formulation of the economic indictment of slavery. Nearly as important as these works is Fanny Kemble's *Journal* [199]. In this volume, Kemble described her experience during one year of residence on a Georgia plantation owned by her former husband. Although her sojourn in Georgia ended in 1839, Kemble did not publish her journal until 1863. Like Cairnes's book, Kemble's *Journal* was a polemic aimed at rallying British support to the northern cause. The *Journal* has been particularly influential in shaping historians' views of the material and psychological conditions of slave life. Kemble painted a grim picture, emphasizing the poor food and clothing given to slaves, the inadequate health care, the perversion of the slave family, and the deformation of slave personalities. Among the historians who have leaned heavily on Kemble's *Journal* are Rhodes [277], Stampp [303], and Elkins [101].

2. During the first half of the period between the Civil War and the ascendancy of Phillips, historians writing on the slave economy strongly echoed the themes that were formulated in the course of the ideological struggles of the War and immediate pre-War years. Northern historians condemned slavery as an inefficient, cruel, and moribund economic system that thwarted the development of the South; they hailed the Civil War as a moral crusade which served to advance mankind [184; 277; 291; cf. 16; 268]. Southern writers stressed the positive features of the slave and plantation systems and portrayed the Civil War as an act of aggression which devastated both the economy and society of their region (cf. [16; 38; 268]).

As the memory of the War receded, however, these themes evolved in subtle but important ways. Racist elements, which had always been part of the antislavery ideology, became increasingly prominent in the work of northern historians. This, together with a revulsion against Reconstruction, led to changes in the northern view of the "Negro problem" and shifted the interpretation of the slave experience somewhat closer to southern positions. Stress on the immorality of slavery was somewhat diminished and the role of slavery as an obstacle to the development of both the South and the nation began to receive somewhat more emphasis [30; 222; 277]. A more sympathetic attitude was expressed for the view that the "backwardness" of the Negro race posed special and difficult problems to southern whites [30; 39; 168; 277]. The error of the South was, therefore, not in the belief that blacks should be kept subordinate to whites, but in choosing slavery as the means to accomplish such subordination [30; 277].

The views of southern historians also underwent a significant metamorphosis. While continuing to find much that was admirable about the antebellum South, southern historians became critical of many aspects of the slave system and of the slavocracy. They began to emphasize that slavery stifled the growth of cities, confined production to agriculture, and, because it was unprofitable, kept the South poor [28; 330; 370]. A distinction was drawn between the "cotton magnates" and the yeomanry. The big planters, reared in a feudal environment, it was said, had become arrogant and reactionary, while the small farmers, who were seen as true bearers of progress, had been inhibited by the domination of the slavocrats [77; 330; 370; cf. 310; 311].

Another new element of post-War historiography was the emergence of a "school" of Negro historians with interests substantially different from those of white scholars of both regions. These black historians concentrated on two main topics: the reconstruction of the black experience in America and the establishment of the cultural connections of

American blacks to their African origins. Because these "Negro" issues were of little interest to those who dominated the historical profession during this era, the Negro "school" remained apart from, and, in some respects, an oddity to, the mainstream of the profession.

The zenith of the Negro school came after the formation of the Association for the Study of Negro Life and History in 1915. The basis for later developments, however, was laid during the years between 1875 and 1915 with the publications of George Washington Williams [367; 368], Booker T. Washington [353], and W.E.B. Du Bois [86; 87; 90; 91]. Despite the many differences in ideology and emphasis among these scholars, and although it is probably more appropriate to classify Du Bois as a pioneer in the development of sociological approaches to black history (see 5.3) than as a member of the Negro school, all three men shared a common determination to establish the cultural heritage of American Negroes and to reveal the record of black accomplishments.

2.1. Assessments of the early Negro historians sometimes stress their parochial interests and their amateurish methodology. In retrospect, the preoccupations of the early Negro historians are not difficult to rationalize. Except for this handful of scholars, little of the talent or research effort of the rapidly expanding historical profession was directed toward illuminating the Negro experience in America. And what little attention was paid to the Negro past by the mainstream of the historical profession was not only one-sided and inaccurate in many respects, but often deeply distorted by an adherence to racist doctrines (cf. [63]).

Thus it fell on the Negro school to serve as the principal center of opposition to the myth of the incompetence of blacks. Until quite far into the twentieth century, only in this school was there a sustained effort to define and portray either the cultural evolution of Negroes or their contribution to the general American culture (see 5.2).

In methodology, also, the Negro school proved to be quite innovative. The paucity of materials on blacks in usual sources led Negro historians to explore hitherto neglected documents. They were, for example, among the first American scholars to exploit and make use of numeric information in the manuscript schedules of the U.S. census [123; 188; 380; 381]. They also pioneered in the use of the oral history technique [32; 274] (see 5.2).

3. U. B. Phillips dominated historiographic writing on the antebellum South during the first half of the twentieth century. As the author or editor of 8 books and 55 articles, Phillips dealt with a wide range of social, political, and economic issues.

While Phillips is sometimes referred to as an economic historian [92; 155], his principal interests were social and political. Above all, Phillips sought to rescue the slaveowning aristocracy (and its civilization) from the damnation to which it had been assigned not only by northern historians such as Rhodes [277] and McMaster [222], but also, to an increasing degree, by southern historians such as Trent [330] and Dodd [77]. The "dominant class" of the antebellum South was, in Phillips's view, neither the "immoral," "impoverished," "inhospitable," "dilettantish" class of Olmsted, nor the "cruel," "licentious" product of youthful contact with Negroes as claimed by Rhodes, nor the collection of "illiterate," "arrogant," "feudal" overlords portrayed by Trent, nor the ruthless "cotton magnates" of Dodd. Phillips conceived of those who led antebellum society as "talented," "benevolent," and "well bred" men, who were "ruled by a sense of dignity, duty and moderation," who "schooled multitudes white and black to the acceptance of higher standards," and who "wrought more sanely and more wisely than the world yet knows" [261, pp. 97, 328, 343; 259, p. v].

To prove that his was the right view, Phillips set out to uncover evidence that would reveal the true nature of antebellum civilization. Believing that the great plantations were the centers of this civilization, he sought to collect evidence bearing on the operation of these institutions both as business enterprises and as communities of government. It was in the course of his efforts to interpret the evidence that Phillips became involved in such central economic issues as the profitability and viability of slavery, the efficiency of slave labor, and the effect of slavery on the economic development of the South. As we have stressed elsewhere, Phillips's treatment of these issues, despite its influence on others, was neither original nor profound (see T.3, pp. 59-61; T.6, pp. 225-227; **B.3.2.1**; **B.6.3.4**). He did, however, add much to knowledge about the business routine and organization of cotton, rice, sugar, and tobacco plantations as well as about the material conditions of the lives of slaves who lived and worked on these plantations.

3.1. Whatever his motives, it was Phillips who launched the collection of systematic evidence bearing on the operation of the slave system. In so doing, he made a major contribution to the advance of American historiography in general and of southern historiography in particular. The data which Phillips collected came from three main sources: records of large plantations, probate records, and bills of sale.

The plantation documents pertained to some 60-odd plantations ranging in size from 23 to several hundred slaves, although most of them had

in excess of 100 slaves [181, pp. 112, 116]. In addition to cotton plantations in both the Old and New South, Phillips's sample included farms
specializing in sugar, rice, tobacco, and general farming. Phillips did not
compute fertility rates, death rates, or other key demographic variables.
Nor did he systematically relate demographic characteristics to economic
or social variables. He employed slave lists, mortality lists, clothing lists,
and morbidity records in a rather informal manner, using them largely
as ancillary support for impressions of plantation operations and life
formed mainly from his reading of such plantation documents as diaries,
letters, and instructions to overseers. It was on the basis of these varied
sources of evidence that Phillips formulated his views of the annual
work routine on large cotton, rice, and sugar plantations. Phillips also
used this evidence as the basis for his characterization of the central
features of plantation management and of the conditions of life for slaves.

Phillips's exploitation of the probate and sales records was much
more limited than his exploitation of the plantation documents. The
evidence in these records was primarily numerical, and while Phillips
had a greater appreciation of numerical evidence than most historians
of his day, he does not appear to have been as comfortable with it as he
was with literary evidence. Consequently his use of the probate and sales
records was limited almost exclusively to the construction of indexes of
slave prices over the period from 1795 to 1860. Phillips constructed such
indexes for four areas: New Orleans, central Georgia, Charleston, and
Virginia.

3.1.1. It is difficult to appraise Phillips's handling of numerical data,
since he provided very little information on his procedures. In the case
of probate and sales records, for example, we have only the following cryp-
tic comments [261, pp. 368–370]:

The materials extant comprise occasional travellers' notes, fairly numerous newspaper items, and quite voluminous manuscript collections of
appraisals and bills of sale, all of which require cautious discrimination in
their analysis. The appraisals fall mainly into two groups: the valuation
of estates in probate, and those for the purpose of public compensation
to the owners of slaves legally condemned for capital crimes. The former were oftentimes purely perfunctory, and they are generally serviceable
only as aids in ascertaining the ratios of value between slaves of the diverse
ages and sexes. The appraisals of criminals, however, since they prescribed
actual payments on the basis of the market value each slave would have
had if his crime had not been committed, may be assumed under such
laws as Virginia maintained in the premises to be fairly accurate. A file

of more than a thousand such appraisals, with vouchers of payment attached, which is preserved among the Virginia archives in the State Library at Richmond, is particularly copious in regard to prices as well as in regard to crimes and punishments.

The bills of sale recording actual market transactions remain as the chief and central source of information upon prices. Some thousands of these, originating in the city of Charleston, are preserved in a single file among the state archives of South Carolina at Columbia; other thousands are scattered through the myriad miscellaneous notarial records in the court house at New Orleans; many smaller accumulations are to be found in county court houses far and wide, particularly in the cotton belt; and considerable numbers are in private possession, along with plantation journals and letters which sometimes contain similar data.

Now these documents more often than otherwise record the sale of slaves in groups. . . . But group sales give slight information upon individual prices; and even the bills of individual sale yield much less than a statistician could wish. The sex is always presumable from the slave's name, the color is usually stated or implied, and occasionally deleterious proclivities are specified, as of a confirmed drunkard or a persistent runaway; but specifications of age, strength and talents are very often, one and all, omitted. The problem is how may these bare quotations of price be utilized. To strike an average of all prices in any year at any place would be fruitless, since an even distribution of slave grades cannot be assumed when quotations are not in great volume: the prices of young children are rarely ascertainable from the bills, since they were hardly ever sold separately; the prices of women likewise are too seldom segregated from those of their children to permit anything to be established beyond a ratio to some ascertained standard; and the prices of artizans varied too greatly with their skill to permit definite schedules of them. The only market grade, in fact, for which basic price tabulations can be made with any confidence is that of young male prime field hands, for these alone may usually be discriminated even when ages and qualities are not specified. The method here is to select in the group of bills for any time and place such maximum quotations for males as occur with any notable degree of frequency. Artizans, foremen and the like are thereby generally excluded by the infrequency of their sales, while the middle-aged, the old and the defective are eliminated by leaving aside the quotations of lower range. . . .

The foregoing quotation suggests that Phillips inadvertently adopted sampling procedures which introduced certain biases. His exclusion of relatively low prices, for example, on the ground that they represented aged or crippled slaves, appears to have biased his estimate of the level of slave prices upward. Our analysis of the data in the New Orleans notarial records, presumably Phillips's major source for his New Orleans index, indicates that his procedures led to an overestimation of the average level of the prices for prime-age males by about 15 percent. However, his index appears, by and large, to be unbiased in portraying year-to-year movements in slave prices. (For a more complete evaluation of Phillips's price indexes, see [119; cf. 105].)

Phillips's treatment of hire rates was much less satisfactory than his handling of slave prices. For Phillips concluded that there was a secular rise in the price-hire ratio, due to a persistent lag of hire rates behind slave prices [257, p. 269]. However, both Evans's sample [105, pp. 227–238] and our own show no secular trend in the price-hire ratio, although there were, of course, substantial cyclical fluctuations (see T.3, pp. 103–106). In the case of hire rates, Phillips's penchant for choosing "maximum quotations" [257, p. 269], clearly biased his results. A further difficulty arose from his failure to confine temporal comparisons of hire rates, and of the price-hire ratio, to similar phases of the business cycle.

Phillips may be criticized not only for mishandling the data that he secured but also for inadequacies in his pursuit of some classes of evidence. His failure to exploit certain types of data is, in some instances, attributable to technical difficulties. But in other instances the failure was related to his preoccupation with what he believed to be the calumny of the slaveholding class (see 3.2).

Phillips neglected information in the probate and sales records other than slave prices and hire rates. He did little, for example, to retrieve the evidence in these records bearing on the sexual behavior and family life of slaves or on the forceful destruction of slave marriages through sales. Still, Phillips was far from oblivious to these possibilities. He did note the infrequency of separate child sales. He also made the following insightful comment on the frequency of group sales [261, p. 369]:

One of the considerations involved was that a gang already organized would save its purchaser time and trouble in establishing a new plantation as a going concern, and therefore would probably bring a higher gross price than if its members were sold singly. Another motive was that of keeping slave families together, which served doubly in comporting with scruples of conscience and inducing to the greater contentment of slaves in their new employ. The documents of the time demonstrate repeatedly the appreciation of equanimity as affecting value. . . .

3.2. Phillips's priorities in the collection of data appear to have been related to his attitude toward evidence bequeathed to him by his predecessors. While he embraced the first four of the five propositions in the economic indictment of slavery (see 1), he did not embrace the inferences which the authors of the indictment drew from these propositions. The indictment asserted that slaveholders had failed in a ruthless and immoral attempt to increase their wealth and income at the expense of those kept in bondage. But the first four propositions could also be used to support the hypothesis which Phillips favored. Phillips held that the main purpose of plantation slavery was not economic but social. In this view slave plantations were inefficient and unprofitable, not because planters had failed, but because efficiency and profit were not their central objectives − were not the criteria by which they evaluated the performance of the "peculiar institution."

To Phillips the fifth point was the crux of the resolution of the conflicting interpretations. If it could be shown that the material treatment of slaves had been good by the standards of the day, if it could be shown that slaveholders had been paternalistic rather than ruthless, his interpretation would prevail. This appears to have been the line of thought that shaped his research strategy. In any event, his main efforts were directed toward documents capable of casting light on the relationship between masters and slaves. He found these in the records of large plantations. With the exception of the data on slave prices, Phillips's most noteworthy contributions to the fund of knowledge regarding the operation of the slave system came from plantation records.

These revealed that the food, clothing, shelter, and medical care provided to slaves were relatively good for the working class by the standards of the antebellum era. Methods of managing slaves turned out to be more complex and less harsh than suggested by most abolitionist tracts and by historians who based themselves on these tracts. Phillips also discovered more scope for an independent black role than the abolitionists had allowed. He conceded that masters had much power. But slaves, he argued, "were by no means devoid of influence." The regime that emerged was to a considerable extent "shaped by mutual requirements, concessions and understandings, producing reciprocal codes of conventional morality" [261, p. 327]. Phillips summed up his findings on slave treatment as follows [261, pp. 327–328]:

Masters of the standard type promoted Christianity and the customs of marriage and parental care, and they instructed as much by example as by precept; they gave occasional holidays, rewards and indulgences, and permitted as large a degree of liberty as they thought the slaves could be trusted not to abuse; they refrained from selling slaves except under the stress of circumstances; they avoided cruel, vindictive and captious punishments, and endeavored to inspire effort through affection rather than through fear; and they were content with achieving quite moderate industrial results. In short their despotism, so far as it might properly be so called, was benevolent in intent and on the whole beneficial in effect.

These findings on treatment enabled Phillips to transform the meaning of the first four points of the economic indictment of slavery. The evidence showed, he could now declare, that the primary role of the plantation system was not the organization of business, but racial control. "Plantation slavery . . . was less a business than a life; it made fewer fortunes than it made men" [261, p. 401]. Indeed, the fact that slavery had been unprofitable, Phillips insisted, meant that the cost of racial control — which benefited the entire nation — had been borne by slaveholders [262].

Thus, by embracing most of the *economic* indictment of slavery fashioned by antebellum critics, Phillips was able to blunt the edge of the *moral* and *social* indictment of slavery and of the slaveholding class. The objective of the slaveholding class was transformed by Phillips from self-aggrandizement to self-sacrifice. Plantations were transformed from business organizations into schools — "the best schools yet invented for the mass training of that sort of inert and backward people which the bulk of the American negroes represented" [261, p. 343]. Slaveholders were transformed from a cruel, mean, backward, and corrupted class into a highly civilized and highly moral class.

4. During the four decades following the publication of *American Negro Slavery,* historical debate and investigation of the economy of the antebellum South was dominated by the approach and interpretations of Phillips. The substantial advance in scholarship that he represented was widely recognized [24; 101; 181; 303; 310; 351; 373; 377]. Even those most conscious of the deficiencies in *American Negro Slavery,* such as Du Bois and Woodson, remarked on the scope of the "labor and research" embodied in the book [92, p. 725] and characterized it as a study which "far transcends the limits of most histories dealing with slavery" [378, p. 480]. The fruitfulness of Phillips's methodological innovations, particularly his use of data in plantation and associated records, were also widely recognized. As Woodson put it, "No one has hitherto given the public

so much information about the management, labor, social aspects, and tendencies of the plantation" [378, p. 480].

It is not surprising, then, that much of the historiography of the South during the twenties, thirties, forties, and fifties strongly exhibited the mark of Phillips's intellectual influence. Many of the monographs published during these years were so similar in content, organization, sources, and interpretation as to give the impression that they came out of a single department. While actually written at several different universities, these books were clearly the products of a common "school," the "Phillips school." Phillips's influence ramified in two directions: one might best be characterized as "institutional"; the other might be called "political" or "sociopolitical." Of course these two tendencies were never completely separate, but the distinction is nevertheless useful.

4.1. The institutional wing of the Phillips school is best exemplified by a series of 12-odd state studies of slavery which were published between 1924 and 1963. The Phillips school did not initiate the study of slavery on a state-by-state basis. That distinction belongs to Herbert Baxter Adams, whose students at Johns Hopkins (cf. [24; 311; 351]), beginning with Brackett in 1889, published a series of monographs that examined the legal codes and judicial decisions which governed slavery in both northern [56; 308] and southern states [10; 12; 26]. While useful in describing the legal context of slavery, these studies did little to reveal the actual operation of the slave system. The principal economic issues regarding slavery were never joined and little was revealed about material or psychological conditions of the lives of slaves. This one-sided attention to legal issues was, in certain respects, quite misleading. It sometimes led to inferences regarding behavior that were unwarranted.

A number of state studies published between 1911 and 1922 reflected both the influence of the Adams school and the Phillips school [173; 221; 255; 331; 332]. Henry's monograph on the control of slaves in South Carolina [173], for example, while still focused primarily on statutes and judicial decisions, did attempt to use newspapers, pamphlets, interviews of "ante-bellum people still living," and secondary sources to deal with the relationship between legal authorization and actual practices (see, for example, [173, pp. 29, 39, 94-95, 99-102]). Often, however, Henry merely presumed that the existence of statutes, cases, or newspaper editorials implied that the authorized behavior was actually widespread (see, for example, [173, pp. 27-28, 43, 48]). He did little to relate the various aspects of the control of slaves that he studied to economic issues.

Trexler's book on slavery in Missouri [331] represented another step toward discovering actual economic conditions. In his first chapter, "Missouri Slavery as an Economic System," Trexler drew on the manuscript schedules of the 1850 and 1860 censuses and on tax rolls to compute size distributions of slave plantations. He searched probate records to obtain slave prices and hire rates by age and sex. Trexler also sought to assail the question of the profitability of an investment in slaves, but had to abandon the effort. "No matter what contemporaries or present-day authorities conclude," wrote Trexler, "the problem is not one to be mathematically settled. The amount of data is so enormous and at the same time so incomplete and so contradictory that one is not justified in drawing conclusions" [331, p. 56]. After the first chapter, Trexler turned to the legal issues that were the central concern of the earlier Hopkins dissertations. Matters such as the treatment of slaves and master-slave relationships received scant consideration.

The transition from concentration on legal codes and judicial decisions to concentration on the actual operation of the slave system was completed with two short doctoral dissertations written under Phillips at Michigan in the 1920s. Both Moody's study of Louisiana [230] and R. H. Taylor's study of North Carolina [326] focused primarily on large plantations, made limited use of plantation documents, and specifically probed the issues of profitability, slave treatment, and master-slave relationships. Compared to the later state studies, however, these volumes were quite sketchy.

It was only with the publication of Flanders's study of Georgia [112] and Sydnor's of Mississippi [320], both of which appeared in 1933, that the standard which was to distinguish the institutional wing of the Phillips school was finally realized: the exhaustive search for both literary and quantitative evidence regarding the actual operation of the slave system in court records, tax records, manuscript schedules of the census, plantation papers, and antebellum newspapers and journals. The evidence culled from these sources provided detailed information about the production routine of various types of plantations, the commercial aspects of slave plantations, the conditions under which slaves worked, the quality of the food, clothing, and shelter provided to slaves, the health of slaves and the nature of the medical care provided to them, the method of operation of slave sale and hire markets, the system of punishment and rewards, the nature of the family life of slaves, the skill composition of the slave labor force, and certain aspects of the social and cultural lives of slaves. By and large, the findings of Sydnor and Flanders on these issues coincided with those of Phillips.

The Sydnor and Flanders volumes set a pattern that was extended to North Carolina by Johnson [196], to Alabama by Davis [68] and Sellers [293], to Louisiana by Sitterson [297] and J. G. Taylor [324], to Texas by Curlee [64] and Sitterson [297], to Arkansas by O. W. Taylor [325], to Tennessee by Mooney [232], and to Kentucky by Coleman [48]. For the most part these studies concentrated on the set of issues that were singled out by Phillips and were pursued by Sydnor and Flanders. In each case — except, perhaps, Coleman, who published neither footnotes nor a bibliography — the authors were resourceful in uncovering important plantation records and were meticulous in their search of these records. As a group, the scholars in the institutional wing increased the sample of records pertaining to large plantations from the 60 or so collections retrieved by Phillips to about 200.

While the topics considered in these state studies were generally quite similar, there were some notable discussions that distinguished one or another of them. Sydnor, for example, has an excellent analysis of newspaper notices regarding runaway slaves. The most frequent reason that slaves ran away, Sydnor concluded, was "for the purpose of rejoining severed ties of family or of friendship" [320, p. 103]. Johnson has, perhaps, the best chapter on the social life of slaves. Although dated in certain respects, it represents one of the few attempts by scholars of the Phillips school to probe into the reactions of slaves to their circumstances. "No matter how hard he had labored during the day as his master's property," said Johnson of the typical slave hand, "he shed his chattel state as he left the field behind, and he entered his own cabin as a person. This life which he led with his own people, apart from the ever-watchful eye of his master, was the life that made slavery endurable" [196, p. 522; cf. 195].

Two of the most useful works in the canon of the institutional wing are Curlee's (now Mrs. Holbrook) dissertation on slavery in Texas [64] and Postell's book on the health and medical care of slaves [266]. Completed a year before the publication of either the Flanders or Sydnor volumes, but not yet published, Mrs. Holbrook's study of Texas may well be the most important of all the state studies. She contributed more additions to the sample of plantation documents which can be used as a basis for systematic analysis than any other scholar except for Phillips. Her Texas sample is particularly valuable since it provides evidence bearing on the contentions of Cairnes (see T.2, pp. 47–48) and Sutch [317] that treatment of slaves in the West was far more severe than in the East and that western slaveowners were less interested in child rearing than those of the East. Mrs. Holbrook's findings fail to sustain these assumptions. Among the many contributions of her study is an illuminating discussion of the incentive system on Texas plantations.

Postell's book has frequently drawn criticism because of the author's unabashed nostalgia for the antebellum South (cf. [25; 351]), the implication being that Postell's sympathies biased his treatment of the evidence. Yet Postell's discussions of the frequency of various diseases and injuries, of the quality of health care, of the care of pregnant women and infants, of conditions of childbirth, of morbidity rates, and of infant death rates are all carefully drawn. They are based on thorough research and systematic analysis of substantial bodies of data. Prior to recent cliometric work, Postell's samples of plantation data bearing on morbidity rates and infant death rates, for example, were the largest available. Both inspection of the sources which he employed and statistical tests of his samples against those which we have collected fail to sustain the fear that Postell's sympathies biased his treatment of evidence (see **4.1.2** and **6.3**).

4.1.1. Despite their resourcefulness in retrieving data, the contribution of the institutional wing of the Phillips school to the resolution of the principal economic issues connected with slavery was rather uneven. The members of the institutional wing were at their best in describing the economic organization and routine of plantations and other institutions which utilized, or facilitated the use of, slave labor. They also provided much information on the material conditions of slave lives, including very useful demographic information.

Testimony to the high quality of their research on these questions was indirectly paid by Stampp. In his second chapter [303], for example, which deals with the routine of slave plantations and the conditions of slave labor, Stampp cited members of the Phillips school no less than 39 times. Of course, Stampp also studied the primary sources carefully. His second chapter contains 47 citations to manuscript collections. That the material which Stampp retrieved from the cited documents added virtually no factual information not already contained in the state studies, indicates the thoroughness of those who preceded him. Stampp's principal use of plantation documents, in his second chapter, was as a source of quotations which made more vivid one or another matter which he was explicating.

Except for Sellers, Mooney, and Johnson, all the authors of the post-Phillips state studies explicitly dealt with the issue of profitability. Most of the discussions, however, were poorly formulated. Many of the basic theoretical issues in the calculation of the profit rate were overlooked. The representativeness of various estimates of income and cost were not carefully considered. In some cases conclusions were based on data for a single year, without taking account of cyclical or random fluctuations. Some of the discussions of profitability degenerated merely into the cataloguing of individuals who complained about financial difficulties or proclaimed financial successes without considering whether such experiences were more or less frequent for slave plantations than for other enterprises. Only Sydnor attempted to calculate an average rate of profit for a typical plantation based on estimates of the average normal prices of slaves, land, equipment, and cotton, of normal output per slave hand, and of normal expenses (cf. [167, pp. 319-320]). Unfortunately this attempt was marred, as Govan [150] pointed out, by various omissions and a theoretical blunder (see **5.1.2**). On the substance of the issue, the members of the institutional wing were divided. The authors of four of the state studies found that slavery was generally profitable [64; 297; 324; 325]; five found that it was generally unprofitable [48; 112; 230; 320; 326]; one was ambiguous [68].

While the state studies provide a great deal of information relevant to the evaluation of the economic efficiency of the slave plantation (such as the role of gangs, the skill structure of the labor force, the production routine, and the change in the size distribution of plantations), they rarely confronted the issue directly. Occasional references to the efficiency of labor were merely paraphrases of Phillips or other expositors of the traditional viewpoint (cf. [112, pp. 227-228]), and did not constitute hard evidence.

On the economic viability of the slave system and the effect of slavery on economic growth, neglect by the state studies was almost complete. Taylor stressed that "slavery was a vital and growing institution during its existence in Arkansas" [325, p. 47]. He based that statement not on an analysis of economic data but on the rapid rate of growth of the slave population in Arkansas. The fact that Arkansas was a slave-importing state was, of course, an insufficient basis for resolving the issue of viability posed by Cairnes and others. Davis, on the other hand, asserted that "forces which would have made" the "downfall" of slavery "inevitable had long been at work" [68, p. 189]. But he offered no new evidence to support that contention.

4.1.2. In the analysis of the quantitative data which they unearthed, the members of the institutional wing did not go far beyond Phillips. Except for the extensive use of manuscript schedules to compute the size distributions of the holdings of slaves, land, and wealth [43; 49; 232; 250; 251; 356], no quantitative project undertaken by the institutionalists matched in ambition Phillips's work on the construction of time series of slave prices. In most instances these scholars simply reported what they found without attempting to compute statistics such as means or variances. Explicit consideration was rarely given to biases that might exist in attempting to make inferences about parameters of overall populations from the samples of data that were uncovered. More complicated statistical procedures such as regression analysis, chi-square tests, and simulation techniques were never employed. Of course, some currently used statistical techniques were just being developed when the earliest of the institutionalists began their inquiries. But others were already well-known. In any case, the last of the institutionalists were writing in an era when modern statistical techniques were being employed fairly widely in historical research.

Perhaps the most important contributions of the institutionalists to the systematic analysis of available data occurred in the study of the demographic characteristics of the slave population. Postell, as previously noted, computed the average infant death rate in a sample of 14 plantations and the average morbidity rate in another sample of 15 plantations. These samples were based primarily on the plantation records available in the collections of the Southern Historical Collection at the University of North Carolina and of the Department of Archives at Louisiana State University. Postell did not investigate the properties of these samples, the populations to which they pertained, or the possibility that the infant death rate, in particular, was biased downward by underenumeration. Nor did he attempt to relate death and morbidity rates to variables such as plantation size, geographic location, and principal crop. These questions are now under investigation by cliometricians (see **B.4.5**). Preliminary findings indicate that errors arising out of the unrepresentativeness of Postell's samples do not appear to be great, although it is likely that his estimate of the infant death rate is biased downward because of underenumeration by those who kept the plantation records (cf. [307]).

Sydnor attempted to estimate the life expectancy of a Mississippi slave at age twenty from the death statistics published in the census of 1850. His main computation yielded a figure of 22.3 years, which was 6 percent less than his estimate of the corresponding statistic for Mississippi whites [319, p. 572]. Interestingly enough, Sydnor presumed that his procedures probably biased his result upward. Actually, he underestimated life expectation for both slaves and free men by about 17 years (see **6.3**). The principal reason for this large bias was his erroneous assumption that it was possible to estimate the probability of death at a given age from the observed ratio of deaths at that age in 1850 to total deaths of persons aged 20 or more in 1850. In other words, what Sydnor computed was not the life expectation of a twenty-year-old slave but, as Evans [105, pp. 209-210] pointed out, "the average number of years lived beyond age twenty by all those twenty and older who died in that year [1850] ."

Flanders, following Phillips [258] , used tax records to construct tables giving the size distribution of slaveholdings over the period from 1802 to 1864 for two counties [112, pp. 69-75] . These, like Phillips's tables, showed a marked tendency toward concentration over time. Flanders appears to have recognized that this tendency was related to the efficiency of large-scale methods, but he did not pursue the issue. Mooney, using a sample of data drawn from the census manuscripts for 1850 and 1860 analyzed the tendency toward concentration of slaveholding in Tennessee. He argued that at least 30 slaves were needed to "operate a plantation in the then existing state of technological advance" [232, p. 125] . Yet, as indicated in appendix B (see **B.6.2.4** and **B.6.3**), economies of large-scale organization appear to have been substantial for plantations with as few as 16 slaves.

Perhaps the most serious error in the analysis of quantitative data by a member of the institutional wing was committed by Sydnor. Discovering that there were nearly as many plantations in Mississippi with 30 or more slaves as there were overseers in the state, Sydnor jumped to the false conclusion that virtually every plantation with 30 or more slaves employed a white overseer to manage production [320, pp. 67-69] . This false inference was subsequently picked up by Stampp, who made it a central assumption for his contention that cruel treatment for slaves was widespread [303, pp. 38, 82] (cf. **6.3**). The same mistaken inference regarding the ubiquity of white overseers on large plantations was also made by Scarborough (see **B.6.5**), Gray [154, pp. 498-499] , and Eaton [97, pp. 25-26] . This error in the analysis of census data on overseers appears to be a principal factor in the explanation for the failure of historians to have discovered the major role played by blacks in the management of the production side of large slave plantations.

That we have been more critical of Sydnor's errors in data analysis than those of other members of the institutional wing should not be taken to imply that he was a lesser scholar than his colleagues. The greater frequency of such errors by Sydnor appears to be due to a greater effort on his part to elicit information from the data that he collected. Unfortunately, Sydnor lacked the training needed for success in such an undertaking. His inexperience with mathematical methods is most clearly revealed in his essay on life expectation in Mississippi (cf. **6.3**). Sydnor misinterpreted the equations in the demographic handbooks that he cited and that he was attempting to follow in making his computations.

4.2. The political wing of the Phillips school did not contribute significantly to the retrieval of new bodies of evidence bearing on any of the five basic issues raised in the economic indictment of slavery. The central interests of the scholars in this wing were social, political, and moral. They sought to revise prevailing interpretations of antebellum society and to reassess the causes of the Civil War. In this effort at historical revisionism, however, they leaned quite heavily on a number of economic propositions. In so doing, the revisionists once again propelled economic issues to the center of political and social debates. Ironically, the principal weapons of the revisionists were, with one exception, the same economic propositions that abolitionist critics had fashioned in their ideological onslaught against slavery.

It was Phillips, of course, who first perceived the possibilities for converting the economic indictment from an attack on slave society into a justification of it (see **3.2**). Phillips had not, however, extended the argument to the interpretation of the Civil War. That task was undertaken by Ramsdell, who renewed Cairnes's contention that economic forces were inexorably militating toward the dissolution of slavery [270]. Phillips had acknowledged that slavery tended to be economically moribund and had incorporated that proposition into his revision of the traditional interpretation. But compared to the other economic issues, it was practically shunted aside in *American Negro Slavery* (cf. [391]). Ramsdell revitalized the question by combining Cairnes's emphasis on the need of slavery for unlimited quantities of virgin territory with Phillips's contention that the failure of cotton prices to keep pace with slave prices had made slavery unprofitable. By the end of the 1850s, said Ramsdell, the doom of the slave system had been sealed. The natural geographic limits for the extension of the cotton culture had already been reached and the decline of cotton prices (and of the profits of cotton producers) was accelerating rapidly (see T.3, pp. 61-63, 90-97). It was therefore evident, Ramsdell concluded [270, p. 171], that those who "dreaded" the expansion of slavery

had nothing to fear. Even those who wished it destroyed had only to wait a little while — perhaps a generation, probably less. It was summarily destroyed at a frightful cost to the whole country and one third of the nation was impoverished for forty years. One is tempted at this point to reflections upon what has long passed for statesmanship on both sides of that long dead issue. But I have not the heart to indulge them.

Two other strands of Phillips's version of the traditional interpretation were taken up by Owsley. Building on Phillips's contention that the antebellum economy was designed not to make profit but to make men (see 3.2) Owsley contended that the fundamental conflict of the era was between an uncommercial southern agrarianism and a profit-seeking northern industrial capitalism [248; 249]. Antebellum southern society, then, extolled nature, self-sufficiency, leisure, human relationships, and family — all of which were preferred to profit. That slavery was maintained even though it was unprofitable, and that urban industry was shunned even though it was profitable, proved that life-style rather than commercial gain provided the motive force of the antebellum South. In this way, the abolitionists' charge (and Phillips's admission) that the South was made economically stagnant by slavery was converted into a decision by Southerners to resist the evils of industrialization and to preserve the simplicity, democracy, and warmth of agrarian life. Other than the collection of census data, which showed a more equal distribution of land holdings than had been acknowledged by critics of the slave South, Owsley and his students contributed little new evidence about economic characteristics.

The proposition that slavery was moribund (would soon have expired of internal economic contradictions) brought into question, if not the moral justification for the Civil War, at least its expediency. Was a brief advance in the date of emancipation worth more than half a million lives, and hundreds of thousands of wounded, maimed, and impoverished? Was the Civil War a blunder committed by inept politicians on both sides? Ramsdell had raised these questions at the end of his famous 1929 paper, but did not have "the heart to indulge them." Other historians were not so reluctant. Craven [60; 61; 62] and Randall [271; 272] took up the proffered theme of a "blundering generation" and produced revisionist histories of the politics of the last decades of the antebellum era. In basing their political argument on the traditional economic interpretation of slavery (Phillips's version), they helped raise this economic view to the level of an axiomatic truth.

Interestingly enough, the manner of the rebuttal to Craven and Randall also served to buttress the impression that the traditional interpretation of the slave economy was indeed true. When Schlesinger censured the revisionists for "historical sentimentalism" [290], it was not for their economic position. Slavery, he agreed, "was on the skids economically. It was overcapitalized and inefficient; it immobilized both capital and labor; its one crop system was draining the soil of fertility; it stood in the way of industrialization." The error of the revisionists was rather in the assumption

that southerners would have recognized the causes of their economic predicament and taken the appropriate measures. Yet such an assumption would be plainly contrary to history and to experience. From the beginning the South has always blamed its economic shortcomings, not on its own economic ruling class and its own inefficient use of resources, but on northern exploitation. . . . Nothing in the historical record suggests that the southern ruling class was preparing to deviate from its traditional pattern of self-exculpation long enough to take such a drastic step as the abolition of slavery [290, p. 974].

5. It was not until after the publication of Stampp's *The Peculiar Institution* in 1956 that the domination of the Phillips school over the interpretation of the slave economy was broken. The basis for this powerful assault on Phillips's intellectual dominion, however, was laid when his school was at the summit of its reign. In this connection, four developments between 1918 and 1956 should be singled out. These are the rise of economic history, the expansion and professionalization of Negro history, the development of the sociological and anthropological approach to history in general and to black history in particular, and the resurgence of neoabolitionism.

5.1. The emergence of a discipline of economic history within the United States introduced an important new element into the debate on the economics of slavery. While scholars such as von Holst, Rhodes, Dodd, Phillips, and Ramsdell dealt with economic questions in their studies of southern society, their primary concern was with political and social issues. As a consequence, their treatment of many issues vital to understanding the economic operation of the slave system was quite superficial. Prior to the appearance of Gray's massive two-volume history of southern agriculture [154], few examinations of the slave states had pushed economic questions to the center of attention.

Agriculture in the Southern United States to 1860 was the seventh of a series of historical studies of the U.S. economy published by the Carnegie Institution of Washington under the general title "Contributions to Economic History." The topics of the first six studies were the history of America's domestic and foreign commerce [194], manufacturing from

1607 to 1860 [44], transportation before 1860 [226], the history of labor [52], agriculture in the North from 1620 to 1860 [20], and manufacturing from 1860 to 1914 [44]. The project as a whole was initiated shortly after the turn of the twentieth century with the objective of producing, for the first time, a multivolume general economic history of the United States.

A description of the origin of the Carnegie project is contained in [386]. Progress reports on the project are to be found in [20; 51; 106; 194; 226]. In addition to the seven volumes in this particular series, the Carnegie Institution stimulated such other important efforts as Commons's eleven-volume collection of source materials on industrial history [51], Hasse's sixteen-volume index to economic information in state documents [170], Catterall's five-volume collection of judicial documents on slavery [37], and Donnan's four-volume collection of documents bearing on the international slave trade [80]. While the movement for the establishment of economic history as a formal discipline within the United States had many sources, the work initiated by the Carnegie Institution was perhaps the most important of these streams. Certainly few studies in American economic history have proved to be as enduring as those published under the Carnegie aegis.

An adequate treatment of the development of the field of economic history is yet to be undertaken. Sketches of some aspects of the evolution of the discipline in the United States are contained in [8; 41; 42; 46; 47; 111; 116; 132; 149; 152; 153; 171].

5.1.1. Gray's study, which was published in 1933, dealt with virtually all of the major issues and problems which affected the course of agricultural production in the South prior to the Civil War. The book is, as Henry C. Taylor noted, remarkable for its "richness of detail on innumerable subjects that have been passed over by other writers in general terms" [154, p. v]. Among the topics pertaining to antebellum agriculture – for which Gray, after 40 years, is still an indispensable source – are: the properties of various southern soils, technical characteristics of varieties of plants and breeds of livestock, methods of animal husbandry, systems of crop rotation, the effectiveness of various types of agricultural implements, properties of different fertilizers, the quality of entrepreneurship, problems of marketing, the relative efficiency of various types of farm organization, credit systems, the effectiveness of various government programs aimed at encouraging the development of particular crops or practices, the scope of education and research, the determinants of land values, the consequences of alternative land policies, the advantages and disadvantages of the plantation system, the quality of slave labor, determinants of the prices of various commodities, factors affecting both long- and short-term movements of commodity prices, and factors affecting the overall level of prosperity of farmers located in different subregions and specializing in different crops.

Not only did Gray go far beyond the range of economic issues entertained by Phillips, but he was far more thorough than Phillips on most of the issues central to the economic indictment of slavery. On the issue of efficiency, for example, Phillips confined himself largely to paraphrasing Olmsted and Cairnes. His entire treatment of the question is contained in a few paragraphs. Gray, by contrast, devoted all of chapter XX and substantial parts of several other chapters to discussing criteria for the determination of economic efficiency in both production and distribution as well as to the presentation of evidence bearing on the performance of slave plantations with respect to these criteria.

Gray also went far beyond Phillips in his analysis of the questions of economies of scale and in the determinants of the supply of slave labor. Gray's discussion of the issue of scale reflected a considerable command of economic analysis and in certain respects is yet to be superseded. (See **5.1.1.1**, **B.6.3.3**, and **B.6.3.4**.) His discussion of the preference for slave over indentured labor during the colonial period was far more solidly based in both economic theory and fact than the work of Phillips and most other subsequent writers. And although Gray overestimated the scope of the interregional slave trade (because he relied on Collins's [50] estimates) and was too ready to accept racist depictions of slave mores [154, pp. 521–522, 658, 663], his economic argument for rejecting the myth of breeding slaves for sale was cogent [154, p. 473].

In short, Gray's volume constituted a rejection of most of the economic indictment of slavery and of the traditional interpretation into which it had evolved. Of the five main propositions of the traditional interpretation listed in **1**, Gray rejected all but the fourth. He accepted the contention that slavery had retarded southern economic growth by diverting capital from investment in nonagricultural enterprise. Determination of the validity of this contention, of course, would have required an analysis of investment opportunities in southern industry, and that task was beyond the scope of Gray's assignment.

5.1.1.1. Gray was far more skillful than Phillips in his analysis of quantitative evidence. Gray's command of economic theory gave him a clear edge in the interpretation of such data as slave and cotton prices. This edge is particularly evident in his critique of Phillips's attempt to infer unprofitability from data on slave and cotton prices [154, pp. 475-477, 665-667] (cf. **B.3.2.1**). It is also evident in Gray's penetrating discussion of the advantages of slave over free labor in agriculture [154, pp. 370-371, 478-480]. Equally impressive was the extent of the new information that Gray was able to extract from such well-worked sources as the published census. By properly classifying the available data on size of slaveholdings by state, he was able to demonstrate the tendency toward the increase in the average size of slaveholdings. By analyzing data at the county level, he was able to associate the average size of slaveholdings with the type of crop in which particular plantations specialized (see **B.6.3.3** and **B.6.3.4**).

On the other hand, Gray fell short of the achievement of Phillips in the collection of data from manuscript sources. Gray's bibliography lists neither probate records nor the manuscript schedules of the U.S. census. His use of plantation papers was confined to documents on deposit in the Library of Congress. This gap in Gray's research is reflected in the limited nature of his contribution to the issue of slave treatment.

In the absence of systematic data bearing on slave food consumption, medical care, and demographic experience — such as those contained in the manuscript schedules, probate records, and plantation records — Gray lacked the hard evidence needed to discriminate among the conflicting claims of the antislavery critics and the slaveholders. That his conclusions on the issue of treatment were much closer to those reached by Phillips than by neoabolitionist writers is attributable largely to his belief that "the rapid rise in [the] value of slaves" provided the necessary economic incentive for slaves to have been "in general well provided for as to physical needs." "[T]he influence of the economic motive," he wrote, "is shown in the tendency to employ Irish laborers in ditching and other unhealthful employments rather than to risk the lives of highly valuable field hands" [154, pp. 517-522].

5.1.1.2. Despite the high quality of the scholarship and the cogency of his critique of the main elements of the traditional interpretation of slavery, Gray's work was largely neglected by most historians of the South during the quarter century that followed its publication. When it was used, as Wall and Moore have pointed out [351; 233], it was more often for its data than for its interpretation. Occasionally Gray was cited by scholars taking issue with the Phillips version of the traditional interpretation (see **6.1**). However, leading members of the Phillips school took little notice of such attacks. Scholars such as Ramsdell, Sydnor, and Craven did not feel called upon to reply to Gray's attacks on their positions with respect to the issues of profitability, viability, and efficiency.

5.1.2. Two other economic historians who made significant contributions to the economic analysis of slavery were Russel [284] and Govan [150]. Russel focused on the relationship between slavery and the growth of the southern economy. Conceding that slavery may have retarded the diversification of industry, he argued that such retardation was the consequence of the development of large-scale farming which made southern agriculture highly profitable. The concentration on cotton and other staples was, therefore, from an economic standpoint, "beneficial to the South on the whole" [284, pp. 45, 53]. Russel saw very little merit in most of the other criticisms regarding the alleged negative effects of slavery on southern economic growth. "'[S]kinning' the soil," he pointed out, was "practiced in all sections of the country" and was not special to slave agriculture [284, p. 35]. The severe problem of land erosion in the South was due to the characteristics of the soils, lack of native grasses, and heavy rains – not to slavery. Russel also rejected the contention that the slave trade absorbed capital. Trade in slaves, he wrote, only redistributed capital from one person or region to another.

As for the deleterious effects of slavery on white labor, Russel challenged the view that "slavery inspired a contempt for physical labor among the white people of the South." Slavery, he argued, created an attitude that certain tasks typically performed by Negroes were "menial." These were primarily "such personal services for others as cooking, washing, scrubbing, and attendance as maids or valets." But there "was no stigma attached in the South in slavery days to the performance of manual labor, as distinguished from menial, or of any other sort of labor not considered menial" [284, p. 38].

Russel's contribution, it should be noted, was purely on the level of interpretation. He offered no new evidence, relying upon the familiar travelers' reports and secondary literature.

Govan's article was more limited in scope than Russel's. He focused on the issue of the profitability of an investment in slaves, criticizing those who argued that slavery was unprofitable. His main contribution was the disclosure of an error in Sydnor's attempt to calculate the profit rate on a typical plantation (see **4.1.1**). Sydnor's principal error, he pointed out, lay in the subtraction of an imputed interest charge from the net earnings of planters. Sydnor had also excluded from his calculation, said Govan, such important items of income as the personal services of slaves, improvements to land, additions to structures, and the increased value of slaves. Govan went on to calculate the rates of return on three plantations. These records indicated "that year after year, during periods of financial crisis or prosperity, some plantations were making profits in the ordinary business sense of the term, and were increasing, not decreasing in value" [150, p. 535]. To show that this situation was general, Govan turned to the published census, citing data for 1850 and 1860, which showed a substantial increase in the value of farms throughout the slaveholding states.

5.2. The historians of the Negro school never became deeply involved in the debate over the economics of slavery. Their work, nevertheless, occupies a central role in the disenthronement of the traditional interpretation of the slave economy. In seeking to portray the development of Negro life in America and to define the Negro contribution to American culture, these scholars came into conflict with the assumption that blacks were inherently inferior to whites. Their attack on this assumption weakened the foundation on which the traditional interpretation of the slave economy had been erected (see T.5, pp. 177-181; T.6, pp. 215-232).

The organizational center of the Negro school was The Association for the Study of Negro Life and History. Carter Woodson, who founded the association in 1915 and served as its director until his death in 1950, was its preeminent figure. Woodson wrote or edited 18 books dealing with such diverse questions as the education of the Negro during the antebellum era [376], the development of the Negro church [379], and the history of the Negro wage earner [158]. Perhaps his most important book was *The Negro in Our History,* which aimed "to present to the average reader in succinct form the history of the United States as it has been influenced by the presence of the Negro in this country" [383, p. iv]. The significance of Woodson's general history of the American Negro is still not adequately appreciated. It is difficult to find a theme which today occupies scholars of black history that was not set forth in this pioneering book.

An energetic and effective entrepreneur, Woodson gathered around the association a number of young black and white scholars, including Wesley [360], Taylor [321; 322], Greene [156], Jackson [188], Aptheker [5; 7], and Franklin [123; 126]. He established the *Journal of Negro History,* which stimulated research into black history and in which appeared such important papers as those by Frazier on the Negro family [128], by Park on the development of Negro culture [252], by Aptheker [6] and Wish [371; 372] on Negro slave revolts, by Hofstadter attacking Phillips [181], by Bauer and Bauer on "day-to-day" resistance [15], by Linden criticizing the Owsley thesis [211], by Greene on runaways [157], by M. Williams comparing American and Brazilian slavery [369], by E. Williams on the slave trade [365], and the early publications of scholars who later attained such eminence as Franklin [124; 125], Davis [69; 70], and Genovese [138].

There is still no adequate history of the Negro school. Some aspects of its development are sketched in scattered articles [127; 241; 256; 328; 362; 363; 384] and in Thorpe [327].

5.2.1. The problem of uncovering the history of the common man has been an issue for all historians. Solutions to this problem have usually been inadequate. Until recently, political, social, and intellectual historians in the United States settled largely for mere recognition of the issue, continuing to devote their main effort to the great men and events of the particular epochs which occupied their attention. For the Negro historian such an easy solution was less feasible. Since one of the characteristics of slavery was its severe restriction on the opportunities of exceptional Negroes, there were far fewer prominent men and women on whom to focus.

While the discovery and celebration of those Negroes of exceptional accomplishment was one of central thrusts of the scholars of the Negro school, necessity turned them to a more intensive search for information on the common man than was true of most other historians. As a result they were pioneers or early users of a number of important sources of evidence that have since become standard materials. Among these were the manuscript schedules of the census, marriage registers, wills, birth and death registration certificates, deeds, court proceedings, and city directories.

In pursuing their emphasis on the achievements of the "common man," Woodson and his associates directed far more of their research effort to the study of free Negroes during the antebellum era than to slaves. Whether this was due to the greater difficulty of retrieving data on slaves than on free Negroes or because even they accepted too much of the abolitionist characterization of the nature of black life under slavery is difficult to know. Whatever the reason, the central thrust of the Negro school was aimed at ending the neglect of free Negroes, whose progress, said Woodson [381, p. xxxiv], could be reconstructed from "unexploited sources."

The master class could not be expected to speak of the economic success of the free Negroes, for that would be a direct argument against the policy of slavery. The active abolitionists were eliminated from the South by 1840 and could study the situation only from afar; and even if they had known of such instances, it would have been foreign to their plans and purposes to emphasize the progress of the Negroes in the land of slavery. The colonizationists deliberately tried to prove the impossibility of social and economic progress of the Negro in the United States to make a strong case for deportation. Yet, from all of these sources there may be obtained unconsciously given evidence to the effect that wherever free Negroes had a chance in the South they substantially grounded themselves in forming a permanent attachment to things economic so as to make their group more and more sufficient unto itself.

To demonstrate the magnitude of economic accomplishments by free Negroes, Woodson turned to the census manuscript schedules. In 1924 he published a list of free Negro owners of slaves culled from the records of the 1830 census [380]. A year later he published a list of Negro heads of families in 1830 [381]. Both lists, said Woodson, showed that "almost one-seventh of the Negroes of this country, were free prior to the emancipation in 1865," that many had accumulated substantial property, and that "a considerable number of Negroes were owners of slaves themselves, and in some cases controlled large plantations" [380, p. v]. The majority of Negro slaveholders, Woodson argued, purchased slaves for benevolent motives — to liberate husbands, wives, or other relatives, or to make it possible for slaves to obtain "their freedom for a nominal sum, or by permitting them to work it out on liberal terms" [380, p. vi]. In the introduction to the list of family heads Woodson included a long essay which sketched the history of free Negroes. In this essay he elaborated two main themes. One was the many accomplishments of free Negro labor. The other was the growth of racism which increasingly, especially after 1835, isolated black from white in education, religion, social life, and economic life.

The theme of the accomplishments of Negro workers was carried forward in two histories of Negro labor, one by Wesley [360], the other by Greene and Woodson [158]. Both books emphasized the substantial participation of Negroes in artisan crafts. Both stressed the hostility of white workers toward black craftsmen and the various efforts made by whites to limit competition from their rivals.

The most thorough investigation of Negro accumulation of property is contained in Jackson's study of Virginia [188]. Jackson devoted separate chapters to the accumulation of property by farmers, the city property owner, and property in slaves. He found that despite many obstacles and restrictions Negro property owners grew more rapidly than the free Negro population between 1830 and 1860. By the end of the period one out of every five free Negro families owned real estate.

The total value of the real estate in 1860 was less than one million dollars, but if the value of personal property is added, the total property holdings amounted to at least one and a half million dollars. To express these data in terms of the standing of the Negro race in a later day, the free class of the slavery period held property on a ratio equal to that of this group in Virginia in 1890 and in the entire South in 1910. The growth that came after the emancipation of the entire race is generally regarded as remarkable; if so, the advance made by the free Negroes of Virginia from 1830 to 1860 is likewise remarkable [188, p. 227–228].

The most outstanding of the various studies of the free Negro is Franklin's monograph on life in North Carolina [123]. This tightly written essay of just over 250 pages is based on a systematic search of tax records, court minutes, apprenticeship papers, manuscript schedules of the U.S. census, newspapers, and journals. From these and other sources Franklin was able to reconstruct to a remarkable extent the many facets of life in a deeply racist world — to detail the meaning of "quasi freedom." He sketched the pattern of growth and geographic distribution of the free Negro population between 1790 and 1860, assessed the contribution of manumission and miscegenation to that growth, described the legal restrictions under which free Negroes lived and worked, investigated the differing effects of urban and rural environments on Negro experience, constructed the distribution of occupational skills, and described the heartbreaking frustrations which caused some free Negroes to seek reenslavement in order "to escape the hardships which they were experiencing" [123, p. 219].

When they turned to the slave experience, scholars of the Negro school had a focus that was different from both the members of the Phillips school and the neoabolitionist writers. While giving the devil his due on such matters as the economics of slavery, Woodson criticized Phillips for "his inability to fathom the negro mind" [378, p. 480]. In one of his reviews of *American Negro Slavery*, Woodson said [377, pp. 102–103] that the book

lacks proportion in that it deals primarily with the slaves as property in the cold-blooded fashion that the southerners usually bartered them away. Very little is said about the blacks themselves, seemingly to give more space to the history of the whites, who profited by their labor, just as one would in writing a history of the New England fisheries say very little about the species figuring in the industry, but more about the life of the people participating in it. . . .

Woodson and other members of the Negro school generally accepted the economic indictment of slavery as it was set forth by abolitionist and neoabolitionist writers. Woodson even cited Rhodes's charge that "[s]ome planters" had "hit upon the seemingly more profitable scheme of working newly imported slaves to death during seven years" [376, p. 154]. But whereas abolitionist and neoabolitionist writers, for their own reasons, wrote of little other than the dehumanizing impact of slavery on blacks, members of the Negro school emphasized the struggles of slaves against the worst features of the system and their accomplishments in the face of adversity.

One neglected feature of black accomplishment brought to light by the Negro school was the persistent drive of slaves to acquire education and vocational skills. Toward the end of the eighteenth century, said Woodson, "Negroes were serving as salesmen, keeping accounts, managing plantations, teaching and preaching, and had intellectually advanced to the extent that fifteen or twenty per cent of their adults could then at least read" [376, p. 85]. The striving for education and vocational training continued, according to Woodson, even after 1830, when slavery became transformed "from a patriarchal to an economic institution" [376, p. 153] and the reactionary movement directed at repression of resistance to slavery took command. While "[a]bolitionists like May, Jay, and Garrison would make it seem that conditions in the South were such that it was almost impossible for a slave to develop intellectual power," Woodson estimated that even after 30 years of reactionary onslaught some "ten per cent of the adult Negroes [slave and free] had the rudiments of education in 1860, but the proportion was much less than it was near the close of the era of better beginnings about 1825" [376, pp. 227-228].

Wesley, supplementing Woodson's emphasis on formal education, focused on the large proportion of "skilled and semi-skilled" slaves engaged in the "mechanical pursuits of the plantations and of the towns" [360, pp. 5-6]. Contending that slaves and free blacks made up over 80 percent of the artisan class of the South [360, p. 142], he saw this "talented number" as "a necessity to a class of individuals who knew neither the value nor the process of labor" [360, p. 24]. Although he agreed that slavery and industrialism were incompatible, Wesley categorically rejected the contention that this was "because the slaves – being Negroes – were incapable of attaining the necessary skills" [360, p. 24]. That slaves and free Negroes had in fact attained the skills, Wesley was convinced, was well "demonstrated by the . . . facts" [360, p. 24].

The scholars of the Negro school were also distinguished from both the Phillips school and neoabolitionists in their depiction of black resistance to slavery. They neither treated slave insurrections as a form of crime, as Phillips did [261, pp. 464–488], nor elevated "lying," "cheating," and "stealing" to the level of revolutionary struggle, as did neoabolitionists (see [7; 302; 303]; cf. T.6, pp. 230–241; 6.1). Wesley considered the "indifferent" work of some slaves as "bad," but wrote that the "history of slavery and oppression reveals the same results in all groups" [360, p. 5]. In Woodson's textbook, slave insurrections are discussed in a chapter entitled "Self-Assertion." Without exaggerating either the numbers involved or the objectives, Woodson [383, p. 177] nevertheless celebrated the "bold attempts of the Negroes at insurrection." Because they were "[u]nwilling to undergo the persecutions entailed" by a "change of slavery from a patriarchal to an exploitation system," Woodson said, "a number of Negroes endeavored to secure relief by refreshing the tree of liberty with the blood of their oppressors."

Another issue on which the Negro school differed from neoabolitionist writers was that of racism. Woodson did not treat racism as exclusively a southern phenomenon, nor did he suggest that its worst manifestations were necessarily in the South. He pointed out that some of the bitterest experiences of free Negroes were encountered in the North. Because there "was, in fact, as much prejudice against the free Negroes in parts of the North as in the South," said Woodson, some free men "returned South early in the nineteenth century and reenslaved themselves rather than starve in the North" [381, p. xxxvii]. Greene and Woodson called attention to the fact that it was in the South rather than the North "where the Negroes developed highest in occupations" [158, p. 7]. The explanation for this phenomenon was provided by Wesley [360, p. 39]:

In New Orleans, racial barriers were not such obstacles as they were in New York. In matters of labor and service, the "color line" could be crossed often without the employer, the buyer, or the one seeking a service realizing the race of the worker with whom he was dealing. On the contrary, New York practiced wide discriminations against Negroes and these served to restrict the Negro occupations. Foreign workers also gave the colored worker a greater competition here so that the occupations which were carried on by Negroes in the South were often in the hands of other races in the North.

The pioneering innovations of the Negro school in many aspects of the historiographic craft, both substantive and methodological, have yet to receive their due recognition. On such issues as the reinterpretation of

Reconstruction [89; 321], slave resistance, northern racism, and the post-Reconstruction attack on Negro achievements, the Negro school was 30 to 50 years ahead of the mainstream of the historical profession. In its emphasis on the common man, it had no sustained rival anywhere in the American wing of the historiographic craft until well after World War II. In its integration of sociological and anthropological sciences into historical analysis [91; 353; 367; 381; 383], the Negro school was also a quarter to a half century ahead of the mainstream. In its emphasis on quantitative evidence and its identification and exploitation of obscure sources of such evidence, the Negro school was, prior to the computer revolution, matched (and perhaps exceeded) only by Phillips and his institutionalist followers.

5.2.2. The work of the Negro school was distinguished not only by the resourcefulness shown in the retrieval of numerical information but also by the care with which the recovered data were assembled and reported. The few mistakes that we have discovered (cf., for example, the last column of [360, p. 9] with data in [336, pp. 40, 179]) involve minor computational errors which have no effect on the interpretation of any issue.

Jackson's work [188] in assembling numerical information is particularly impressive. To obtain data on property accumulated by free Negroes in Virginia, Jackson scoured the manuscript schedules of the U.S. census and the tax books of each county and city of the state. These basic sources were supplemented by data in will books, birth and marriage registers, county deed registers, and land patents. Jackson, after carefully comparing state and federal sources, concluded that the state sources were more complete and more accurate. In his resourcefulness in identifying depositories of numerical information, in the thoroughness of his search, and in the care of his evaluation of the reliability of various bodies of data, Jackson has had few peers, even when the comparison is extended to include the recent achievements of cliometricians.

Very little was attempted in the way of the transformation of raw data into rigorously defined constructs that would shed light on economic or demographic behavior. Relationships between variables were not generally considered. Wesley, at one point, did present a table which, he argued, showed that "states with higher slave percentages have less per capita manufacturing wealth" [360, p. 8]. He attributed this inverse correlation to "the incompatibility of manufacturing and slavery" [360, p. 8]. What Wesley called "manufacturing wealth" was rather the annual value of the product of manufacturing firms evaluated at producer prices. Wesley did not actually compute a correlation coefficient but relied only on his eye. As it turns out, his eye did not deceive him. The coefficient of rank correlation between manufacturing output and the percentage of slaves in the population is negative and statistically significant.

Wesley was less fortunate in his explanation for this correlation. For, as Goldin has pointed out, such a correlation does not necessarily imply that slavery and manufacturing were incompatible. She shows that the demand for slaves in urban industrial areas was increasing more rapidly than in the countryside. The redistribution of slaves from urban to rural areas came about not because slaves were unwanted in urban areas or hampered the efficiency of manufacturing, but because the rural demand for slaves was less elastic than the urban demand (see T.3, pp. 97-102; T.6, pp. 234-235; **B.6.6**). In other words, the negative correlation which Wesley discovered merely reflected the fact that the forces of the market worked to locate slaves in those occupations in which it was most difficult (most costly) to substitute free for slave labor.

5.2.3. The long-run impact of the Negro school on the historical profession was much more important than its immediate one. During his lifetime the elders of the guild took little note of Woodson and his associates. Although scholars such as Hart and Turner provided formal encouragement, the work of the Negro school continued to be treated, generally, as something of a curiosa by the mainstream writers — overly enthusiastic, amateurish, parochial. Some measure of the worth attached to the school by the historical establishment is conveyed by the obituary for Woodson published in the *American Historical Review* [2, p. 1041]. This author of 18 books and gifted organizer of the movement for Negro history was alloted a total of 17 lines. On the facing page appeared an obituary for a minor historian of English medieval history whose magnum opus, and only volume, was a textbook. That notice ran 25 lines.

But the work of Woodson and other members of his school was read by and influenced such younger scholars as Hofstadter, Stampp, Woodward, Davis, Degler, and Genovese — men who were to become leaders of the historical establishment in the next generation. The school also spawned Franklin, the leading black historian of the present generation. Like Woodson, Franklin has been a prolific writer and an energetic promoter of Negro history and scholarship. But unlike Woodson, Franklin has affected thought on Negro history from the center rather than from the fringes — a fact symbolized by his election as a president of the Southern Historical Association.

5.3. Sociological and anthropological approaches were first introduced into historiographic work on slavery by black scholars. Williams, for example, began his two-volume *History of the Negro Race* with a discussion of monogenesis that formed the basis of an argument for the unity of mankind [367]. About a fourth of his first volume was devoted to the African origins of Negroes. Woodson opened his general history [383] with three chapters on the African heritage of American blacks, attacking prevailing myths about African civilization and describing the variety of African political organizations, family patterns, religions, occupations, music, and arts.

It was the pioneering work of Du Bois, however, which set the pattern for the sociological analysis of black life and history. Soon after he completed his doctoral dissertation on the slave trade [86], Du Bois turned from history to sociology. His second book, *The Philadelphia Negro,* was part of a "design of observation and research into the history and social condition of the transplanted Africans" [87, p. iii]. On the basis of a survey of 8,000 Negroes who lived in Philadelphia's seventh ward, Du Bois probed deeply into such issues as the sources of the Negro population, health, education and illiteracy, occupations and incomes, the family, and color prejudice. Current findings were placed in historical context in two chapters which sketched the experience of Philadelphia Negroes from 1638 to 1896. Briefer sections dealt with the history of Negro education, occupations, crime, suffrage, and religion.

Of particular note is Du Bois's discussion of the family. Examining statistics on size, he was struck by the preponderance of two-person families — a characteristic he attributed to "economic stress . . . so great that only the small family can survive" [87, p. 165]. At the same time Du Bois accused Philadelphia Negroes of spending too much on meat, clothing, "extravagantly furnished parlors," "amusements," and "miscellaneous ornaments and gewgaws" — all of which he saw as "a natural heritage of a slave system" [87, p. 178]. Du Bois attributed the marriage pattern and inner family life of Philadelphia Negroes to a combination of factors which included African polygamy, the "looseness of plantation life" under slavery, and "the strictness of Quaker teaching" [87, p. 192]. Among the lower classes "cohabitation" was "a direct offshoot of the plantation life and is practiced considerably" [87, pp. 192–193]. But in "the better class families there is a pleasant family life of distinctly Quaker characteristics" [87, p. 195].

Du Bois continued to carry out his "design of observation and research" when he moved to Atlanta University in 1897. During the next decade and a half he supervised a series of 16 monographs patterned after the topics and methodology of his Philadelphia study. In the most outstanding of these, *The Negro American Family,* Du Bois further elaborated themes that were later to become central in the work of others. Citing the travel reports of Olmsted [244] and Weld [359], Du Bois developed a sharp dichotomy between the family patterns attributed to slaves who were house servants and to those who were field hands. Of house servants he wrote [88, p. 47]:

Thus, gradually, the better class of slaves were brought closer into the bosom of the family as house-servants. Religion and marriage rites received more attention and the Negro monogamic family rose as a dependent off-shoot of the feudal slave regime. The first sign of this was the improvement in the Negro home; the house of the house-servants became larger, sometimes with two rooms; a more careful regard for outward decency was manifest, and the direct intercourse between the cabin and Big House brought better manners and ways of living.

Of the field hands, especially those who lived under the ruthless regime of the overseer, he wrote [88, p. 47]:

In its worst phase there was no Big House and cultivated master, only an unscrupulous, paid overseer, lawless and almost irresponsible if he only made crops large enough. The homes of the field hands were filthy hovels where they slept. There was no family life, no meals, no marriages, no decency, only an endless round of toil and a wild debauch at Christmas time. In the forests of Louisiana, the bottoms of Mississippi, and the Sea Islands of Georgia, where the Negro slave sank lowest in oppression and helplessness, the Negro home practically disappeared, and the house was simply rude, inadequate shelter.

One aspect of this degrading environment which Du Bois emphasized was [88, p. 49]

the absence of the father — that is, the lack of authority in the slave father to govern or protect his family. His wife could be made his master's concubine, his daughter could be outraged, his son whipped, or he himself sold away without his being able to protest or lift a preventing finger. Naturally, his authority in his own house was simply such as could rest upon brute force alone, and he easily sank to a position of male guest in the house, without respect or responsibility.

Du Bois also called attention to [88, p. 49]

the absence of the mother. The slave mother could spend little or no time at home. She was either a field-hand or a house-servant, and her children had little care or attention. She was often the concubine of the master or his sons, or, if unmolested in this quarter, was married to a husband who could not protect her, and from whom she could at any time be parted by her master's command or by his death or debts. Such a family was not an organism at best; and, in its worst aspect, it was a fortuitous agglomeration of atoms.

Du Bois's main concern in *The Negro American Family* was the explanation not of the slave experience but of what he believed to be the disorganization of the Negro family at the turn of the twentieth century — a disorganization that was symbolized, above all, by a black illegitimacy rate which he placed in the neighborhood of 25 percent. Du Bois turned to the slave experience to find an explanation for this disorganization. He concluded that slavery left Negroes with mixed mores. The majority had adopted "the monogamic sex *mores*," but a substantial minority had not [88, p. 152].

Du Bois's interest in the development of the Negro family was just one aspect of his broader concern with the determinants of Negro culture. Much of his writing was directed at the destruction of the belief that Negroes were merely imperfect copies of white men, that the slave personality and culture were totally explained by the compliant accommodation of submissive blacks to the conditions of slavery. As Williams had done before him and Woodson did after him, Du Bois rejected the view that the Negro meekly accommodated to the oppression of slavery. When the Cotton Kingdom took shape and slavery became harsher, there emerged "retaliation on the part of the Negroes" [91, p. 117]. Insurrections were one form of retaliation. "The real effective revolt of the Negro against slavery was not, however, by fighting, but by running away, usually to the North, which had been recently freed from slavery" [91, p. 118]. The "fugitives" combined with other free Negroes to carry on a war against slavery. Such struggles, said Du Bois, produced "hope and uplift for the Negro group, with clear evidences of distinct self-assertion and advance" [91, p. 120].

Sociological investigation of Negro life and history waned during the second decade of the twentieth century. When it intensified again, in the 1920s, the center of research had shifted from Atlanta to Chicago and the central figure was a white scholar, Robert E. Park. Park was a former journalist who, after receiving a Ph.D. from Heidelberg, spent several years at Tuskegee working on southern race problems and collaborating with Booker T. Washington. After joining the University of Chicago in 1914, at age 50, Park's research fell into three areas, the substance of which are suggested by the titles of the three volumes of his *Collected Papers.* Volume 1, *Race and Culture,* dealt with "such subjects as race relations, racial frontiers and attitudes, migrations, and the 'marginal man' — the name Park gave to the man who moves in more than one social world and is not completely at home in any" [186, p. 418]. Volume 2, *Human Communities,* presented his work on cities and human ecology. Volume 3, *Society,* was concerned with collective behavior.

Park attracted to his lectures and seminars a remarkable group of young men — black and white — who went on to dominate the sociological study of Negro life during the 1930s and 1940s. Among these were Johnson [191; 192], Doyle [84], and Cayton [85]. Park's most famous student in the area of black studies, however, was E. Franklin Frazier.

Frazier, like Du Bois, whose influence he acknowledged, was concerned with identifying the forces which had shaped, and were continuing to shape, the development of black culture. He dealt with such issues as effects of cultural contacts between blacks and whites on the "evolution, composition, and style of life of the Negro middle class" and of the way in which racial discrimination combined with incessant white pressures to "distort" the values of that class [100, pp. 553–554]. During the course of his career he wrote seven books and many articles dealing with the effects of racial experiences on the demographic, economic, and social behavior of Negroes. One of the most influential black scholars of his time, Frazier was elected president of the American Sociological Association in 1948 and served as chief of the Division of Applied Social Sciences of the United Nations Educational, Scientific and Cultural Organization from 1951 to 1953.

Frazier's main contribution to sociological thought is contained in his book on *The Negro Family in the United States.* His work on the Negro family started from the point at which Du Bois had ended — the extremely high illegitimacy rate among blacks, which averaged between 10 and 15 percent during the period from World War I to 1930. While Du Bois had merely attributed this phenomenon to the incomplete acceptance of the "monogamic sex mores," Frazier discovered the existence of a dual family structure among blacks. The male-headed nuclear family that typified white life was also found among blacks. But this family form coexisted with a female-headed family that "continued on a fairly large scale" and which was "tied up with . . . widespread illegitimacy" [129, p. 483].

In considering possible explanations for the dual family structure, Frazier rejected the possibility that it was a carryover of the African experience. "Except in rare instances," he wrote, "the few memories and traditions of African forebears that once stirred the imagination of the older generations have failed to take root in the minds of the present generation of Negro youth" [129, p. 19]. Nor was there "reliable evidence that African culture" had significant influence on the nature of family life among previous generations of American Negroes [129, p. 12]. There were only "scraps of memories" which formed "an insignificant part . . . of traditions in Negro families" [129, pp. 21-22].

Probably never before in history has a people been so nearly completely stripped of its social heritage as the Negroes who were brought to America. Other conquered races have continued to worship their household gods within the intimate circle of their kinsmen. But American slavery destroyed household gods and dissolved the bonds of sympathy and affection between men of the same blood and household. Old men and women might have brooded over memories of their African homeland, but they could not change the world about them. Through force of circumstances, they had to acquire a new language, adopt new habits of labor, and take over, however imperfectly, the folkways of the American environment. Their children, who knew only the American environment, soon forgot the few memories that had been passed on to them and developed motivations and modes of behavior in harmony with the New World. Their children's children have often recalled with skepticism the fragments of stories concerning Africa which have been preserved in their families. But, of the habits and customs as well as the hopes and fears that characterized the life of their forebearers in Africa, nothing remains. . . .

The dual family structure, Frazier argued, was entirely a product of the slave experience and subsequent developments. Among the features which shaped the sexual mores of slaves as well as their notions of family were "the disproportionate number of males in the slave population. It was not until about 1840 that the number of Negro women equaled that of men" [129, p. 23]. Mores were also affected by the "casualness" of sexual contacts. "There were masters who, without any regard for the preferences of their slaves, mated their human chattel as they did their stock" [129, pp. 24-25]. On the other hand the "plantation economy, which was more or less self-sufficient, gave numerous opportunities for the expression of individual talent" [129, p. 29]. Thus there arose "a divi-

sion of labor that became the basis of social distinctions among the slaves"
[129, p. 30].

Frazier sought to describe the way in which the operation of the slave
system affected the variety of black experiences and led to the development of dual sexual mores and dual family norms. He also set out to identify those groups of slaves who were the bearers of the alternative mores
and norms. Following Du Bois, Frazier drew a sharp distinction between
house servants, who he assumed were preponderantly mulattoes, and the
field hands. He also placed great emphasis on the crucial role of mothers,
who despite (or because of) the exigencies of the slave trade were, unlike
slave fathers, rarely torn apart from their children. "[T]he slave mother
and her children," he wrote, "especially those under ten, were treated as
a group" [129, p. 55].

Frazier summarized his findings on these matters in the following way
[129, pp. 480–482]:

The lives of the white master class became intertwined with the lives of
the black slaves. Social control was not simply a matter of force and
coercion but depended upon a system of etiquette based upon sentiments
of superordination, on the one hand, and sentiments of submission and
loyalty, on the other. Thus the humanization of the slave as well as his
assimilation of the ideals, meanings, and social definitions of the master
race depended upon the nature of his contacts with the master race.
Where the slave was introduced into the household of the master, the
process of assimilation was facilitated; but, where his contacts with whites
were limited to the poor white overseer, his behavior was likely to remain
impulsive and subject only to external control.

. . . Hence, on the large plantations, where the slaves were treated almost entirely as instruments of production and brute force was relied
upon as the chief means of control, sexual relations were likely to be
dissociated on the whole from human sentiments and feelings. Then, too,
the constant buying and selling of slaves prevented the development of
strong emotional ties between the mates. But, where slavery became a
settled way of life, the slaves were likely to show preferences in sexual
unions, and opportunity was afforded for the development of strong
attachments. The permanence of these attachments was conditioned by
the exigencies of the plantation system and the various types of social
control within the world of the plantation.

Within this world the slave mother held a strategic position and played
a dominant role in the family groupings. The tie between the mother and
her younger children had to be respected not only because of the depen-

dence of the child upon her for survival but often because of her fierce attachment to her brood. Some of the mothers undoubtedly were cold and indifferent to their offspring, but this appears to have been due to the attitude which the mother developed toward the unborn child during pregnancy as well as the burden of child care. On the whole, the slave family developed as a natural organization, based upon the spontaneous feelings of affection and natural sympathies which resulted from the association of the family members in the same household. Although the emotional interdependence between the mother and her children generally caused her to have a more permanent interest in the family than the father, there were fathers who developed an attachment for their wives and children.

But the Negro slave mother, as she is known through tradition at least, is represented as the protectress of the children of the master race. Thus tradition has symbolized in the relation of the black foster-parent and the white child the fundamental paradox in the slave system — maximum intimacy existing in conjunction with the most rigid caste system. Cohabitation of the men of the master race with women of the slave race occurred on every level and became so extensive that it nullified to some extent the monogamous mores. The class of mixed-bloods who were thus created formed the most important channel by which the ideals, customs, and mores of the whites were mediated to the servile race. Whether these mixed-bloods were taken into the master's house as servants, or given separate establishments, or educated by their white forebears, they were so situated as to assimilate the culture of the whites. Although a large number of this class were poor and degraded, fairly well-off communities of mixed-bloods who had assimilated the attitudes and culture of the whites to a high degree developed in various parts of the country. It was among this class that family traditions became firmly established before the Civil War.

Frazier, of course, was not an expert on the antebellum South. While he probed more deeply into the literature on slavery than did Du Bois, he still relied to a considerable extent on secondary sources and travelers' reports, especially Kemble's. Frazier did, however, make a very significant foray into primary materials. With the possible exception of Woodson, he was the first scholar to systematically examine the printed narratives of ex-slaves, and he drew heavily on them. Frazier reported the results of his examination of the narratives in a long article published in 1930 [128]. The influence of that review on his later work is clear. He apparently accepted the narratives as authentic reflections of slave family life, although he recognized that at least some had been influenced by the antislavery critics who edited them.

While many of the themes which appeared in Frazier's later work are set forth in the 1930 article, the article presents a picture of somewhat greater stability. He went so far as to state that on plantations "where a patriarchal relationship had grown up we often find a stable family life that compares favorably with the family life in peasant communities" [128, p. 257]. At one point he gave explicit recognition that so favorable a view might seem overdrawn [128, p. 251]:

In this account of the slave family it may appear that slavery in its most favorable aspects has been portrayed, although data which we have used have been drawn from all of the slave states. The object has not been to show up slavery either favorably or unfavorably but to discover those beginnings of the Negro family under the institution of slavery which gave stability to the family and built up a tradition that was handed down.

Frazier's approach to the Negro family involved not only sociological questions but anthropological ones as well. Shortly after the appearance of his book on the Negro family, conclusions that he reached began to be sharply disputed by some anthropologists. This challenge did not arise from advocates of old tenets of racial superiority but from a new group of scholars who were products of the revolution in anthropology which occurred during the last quarter of the nineteenth century and the first quarter of the twentieth century.

The central figure in the revolution was Franz Boas [314]. Trained in physics and possessing a greater command of mathematics than was characteristic of other anthropologists of his day, Boas pioneered in the application of statistical methods to anthropological problems. The results of his statistical research led him to a new view of the relationships between the concepts of race, language, and culture which had long been considered more or less "interchangeable terms" [210, p. 101]. In so doing he helped to redefine the domains of ethnology, anthropological linguistics, and physical anthropology and to establish them as distinct subdisciplines.

Boas's reformulation of anthropology revolved around his rejection of race as a valid paradigm and his questioning of the significance of the various biological criteria that had been used to establish racial categories. Arguing that "classifications based upon racial or biological criteria cannot be reconciled with those based upon linguistic or cultural criteria" [210, p.

101], Boas demonstrated that such measures as the cranial index exhibited more variation within given linguistic and cultural groups than between them, and hence had little operational significance. Instead of race, Boas put forward a new concept of culture: "All the various aspects of human life: bodily form, language . . . as well as the environment in which man is placed, are interrelated, and the form of culture is a result of this integration" [23, p. 98].

The influence of the new direction in anthropology was brought to bear on the study of American Negro history by one of Boas's students, Melville J. Herskovits. Herskovits's doctoral dissertation [176] involved the definition of cultural areas of Africa, while his first book reported on an attempt to study the racial characteristics of American blacks by combining physical measurements with information on the geneologies of several hundred Negroes [177]. Thereafter, Herskovits's research turned to the investigation of the "intensity of Africanisms" in "the cultures of New World Negro population" [227, pp. 43–44]. In addition to various field trips to Africa, Herskovits spent many years in the Caribbean studying the populations of Jamaica, Haiti, and Puerto Rico, among others.

The *Myth of the Negro Past* [178], published in 1941, has had more influence on Afro-American historiography than any of Herskovits's other works. In that volume he set out to demolish such myths about the Negro past as those which held that "Negroes are naturally of a childlike character," that "[o]nly the poorer stock of Africa was enslaved," that African tribal differences prevented American Negroes from having absorbed from their past a "common denominator of understanding or behavior," that African cultures were "so savage and relatively so low in the scale of human civilization" that American Negroes held on to few aspects of their African heritage [178, pp. 1–2, 292–299].

The heart of Herskovits's counterargument was set forth in five chapters. Chapter 2 presented data on the tribal origins of New World Negroes which indicated that most slaves were derived from a geographically concentrated part of Africa and from a relatively small number of tribes. Chapter 3 described the cultural characteristics and civilizations of the African regions from which most slaves were derived, covering such matters as economic and political organization, kinship systems, marriage patterns, religion, aesthetic expression, and languages. Chapters 6, 7, and 8 examined various aspects of the modern secular, religious, and artistic life of modern American Negroes, as well as their language, with the aim of demonstrating the existence of African survivals. Among the matters which Herskovits considered were certain features of family structure which he related to African polygamous patterns, certain supernatural beliefs which he compared with African concepts of magic, folk melodies and rhythms which he traced to African songs and dances, and peculiarities of dialect, especially of the Sea Island or Gullah Negroes, which he identified with the "syntax, inflections, sounds, and intonation" [178, p. 276] found in Africa.

Herskovits treated features of the slave experience throughout the book. But this question was dealt with most extensively in chapters 4 and 5, "Enslavement and the Reaction to Slave Status" and "The Acculturation Process." These chapters set forth the factors that determined the variety of ways in which slaves "accommodated themselves . . . to various aspects of the European culture they encountered" [178, p. 111], and hence, Herskovits believed, explained variations in the degree to which Africanisms manifested themselves in various parts of Negro culture.

Chapter 4 began with the following assertion [178, p. 86]:

Slaves who acquiesced in their status would be more prone to accept the culture of their masters than those who rebelled; hence, if the slaves were restless, as recent studies have indicated, and if this restlessness caused revolt to be endemic in the New World, then the reluctance to accept slave status might also have encouraged the slaves to retain what they could of African custom to a greater extent than would otherwise have been the case. . . .

The balance of chapter 4 was devoted to proving that American "slaves were restless" and that revolt was "endemic." By way of evidence Herskovits enumerated a total of 55 mutinies on ships carrying slaves from Africa over a period of 147 years. He also recounted the slave revolts in Jamaica, Brazil, Dutch Guiana, and Haiti, and he summarized the findings of Aptheker and Wish (see 5.4) on slave conspiracies and rebellions in the United States. Since there were very few actual rebellions in the United States — none that matched the scope or duration of the Caribbean uprisings — Herskovits introduced a new theme: indirect protest. This type of protest, said Herskovits, took the form "of slowing down work, and what seems to have been calculated misuse of implements" [178, p. 99]. Such behavior, while "almost never" previously "recognized as modes of slave protest," was, he insisted, "sabotage" [178, p. 99]. The evidence invoked by Herskovits consisted of seven quotations from Olmsted recounting either the dissatisfactions of masters with the work of their slaves or Olmsted's own jaundiced views of the quality of slave labor (cf. T.5, pp. 179–181; T.6, pp. 218–223).

209

The theme of indirect protest was elaborated by two students of Herskovits. In an article published in 1942, Bauer and Bauer gave this type of protest the name "day-to-day resistance" and extended the emphasis on such resistance beyond slowdowns and destruction of implements to arson, running away, feigning illness, self-mutilation, infanticide, and suicide [15]. Support for the newly discovered resistance came again largely from Olmsted, who was cited 27 times, but also from Phillips (cited 7 times), Kemble, and other familiar witnesses. Toward the end of their essay Bauer and Bauer raised the question of alternative interpretations of the alleged behavior of slaves. But motivations other than resistance were summarily dismissed. The extent of the cited behavior was not established. Comparisons with the incidence of similar behavior among nonprotesting, free men was not undertaken.

In applying his concept of African survivals to the Negro family, Herskovits made the theories of Frazier an explicit target. He attacked Frazier's contention that slaves had been "completely stripped" of their African heritage. He disputed the thesis that mulatto house servants had developed family mores superior to those possessed by field hands. He suggested that the matriarchal family had its origins in Africa rather than in the slave experience – that slavery merely reinforced an existing cultural pattern. He insisted that Frazier had underestimated the role of slave fathers as well as the degree to which the slave trade had torn children away from their mothers.

Frazier's response involved three main points. First, he said, Herskovits had confused the Caribbean, on which he was an expert, with the United States, on which he was not. There "were fewer African survivals in the United States than in other areas of the New World." While "large numbers of African slaves were concentrated on vast plantations" in the West Indies and Brazil, "in the United States the slaves were scattered in relatively small numbers on plantations and farms over a large area" [130, pp. 6-7]. Frazier conceded that the speech of the Gullah Negroes of South Carolina and Georgia contained many African words. But he held that this had come about because of their prolonged, relative isolation from whites and he considered them an exceptional case.

Frazier also argued that many characteristics which Herskovits attributed to African ancestry were found elsewhere in the world and could well have been the result "of spontaneous impulses in human behavior" [130, p. 19]. For such matters as the cooperation among Negroes, as reflected in their fraternal organizations, "the needs of an isolated group laboring under economic disadvantages" provided "an adequate explanation" [130, p. 19].

It is important to stress that the split between Frazier and Herskovits was not over whether African survivals existed in the culture of American Negroes. It was over *how much* of the African past had survived and over *how far-reaching* the impact of these retained elements had been. The issue was one of magnitude rather than of existence. Frazier had not excluded all African influences and Herskovits had not claimed that everything in Negro life was attributable to African influences. Just where the balance falls between these alternatives is still an unresolved issue.

The culmination of more than a half century of intellectual ferment among sociologists and anthropologists on the Negro question was reached with Gunnar Myrdal's epochal study, *An American Dilemma* [240]. That book has been so widely discussed that we will not attempt another review here. Its impact on historians of American Negro slavery and the responses it evoked were vividly described by Elkins [101, pp. 19-20]:

Meanwhile "science," in an all but fully popularized form, had come to dominate the argument and had in many ways taken charge of it. The Carnegie Foundation had decided by 1937 to sponsor a full-scale study of the "Negro problem" in the United States, an inquiry into the "American dilemma" between white democracy and second-class citizenship for Negroes. The Swedish scholar Gunnar Myrdal was engaged to conduct it, and it was imagined that the "neutral" and "non-imperialist" character of Myrdal's national background would eliminate any biases that might creep into the work of a more "committed" person. As it turned out, this was not much of a guaranty for or against anything, since what really set Myrdal's standards (and limits) was the contemporary academic and intellectual setting within which he would have to work while in this country and from which he would draw whatever advice and assistance were available to him. Among the men and women who advised and assisted him were Franz Boas, W. I. Thomas, Ruth Benedict, Ralph Bunche, W.E.B. Du Bois, E. Franklin Frazier, John Dollard, Melville Herskovits, Otto Klineberg, Louis Wirth, Charles S. Johnson, and Donald Young. The result was a detailed inquiry into the numerous phases of the Negro situation, touching at any number of points upon the experience and consequences of slavery, with all the lore and techniques of the social sciences – anthropology, sociology, and social psychology – at the service of this mammoth project.

Myrdal's own book, *An American Dilemma* (1944), was only one of five that came out of the enterprise, and all five strongly reflected the state which the debate on slavery had by then reached. The basic theme of Myrdal's study, and of those that followed it, is inequality and its impact on every phase of Negro life and Negro personality. In this sense it bears a resemblance to the abolitionist literature of antebellum times that is more than coincidental, despite its modern dress. The reader can hardly avoid feeling some measure of guilt for the burdens that American society has heaped upon the Negro; implicit throughout, moreover, is the assumption (similar to abolitionist assumptions on the nature of slavery) that if only these burdens were lifted, full equality on every level would be swift and sure. *An American Dilemma,* a general survey (the rest were more specialized), did retain a somewhat more dispassionate tone than the others, and a certain vein of European sophistication runs all through it. But the others, for all the protections of "science," were bound by the very dedication of the investigators, and by the very nature of what they were investigating, to tremble constantly on the verge of the polemic. There were in these studies numerous *obiter dicta* on the functional interchangeability of the human race (already proved many times over by then), and even the purely descriptive basis upon which the work rested was full of implications which the sensitive reader could not but take in their normative rather than their descriptive character.

5.3.1. Only two notable additions to the data base on slavery were made by the sociologists and anthropologists. One was the limited exploitation of the published narratives of ex-slaves carried out by Frazier. The other was the collection of over 100 interviews of surviving ex-slaves directed by Johnson under the aegis of the Social Science Institute of Fisk University (see [393, p. 343; 274, pp. i-v]). This effort led to the larger sample of approximately 2,000 interviews of ex-slaves collected by the Federal Writers' Project of the W.P.A. [393, pp. 1–6, 339–355]. Unfortunately very little use was made of these materials by either social scientists or historians until the 1960s [140; 141; 166; 273; 281; 393].

Beyond this, none of the sociologists or anthropologists discussed in 5.3 added to the body of evidence bearing on the American slave economy. While all were empirically oriented scholars, the antebellum period was, in each case, tangential to other interests. When they turned to the slave South, it was merely to extract from well-known sources (such as Olmsted) or secondary works (such as those of the Phillips school) the observations required for the construction of a theory of broader relevance.

The clash between Frazier and Herskovits involved no new information about antebellum times. It was a dispute over the interpretation of what was already familiar. The standards of evidence which Du Bois, Frazier, and Herskovits had each applied to the areas of their own expertise were abandoned when they dealt with the slave experience. Each could, and did, justly accuse the other of unsupported speculations.

"In the light of the data cited in earlier pages," said Herskovits in criticism of Frazier, "it is apparent that the 'favored position of the house servant' is taken for granted to a degree not justified by the facts. But beyond this, the assumption that in the slave cabins no 'moral instruction' took place will strike the critical reader as a highly questionable assumption" [178, p. 135]. Frazier had little difficulty in responding in kind: "These statements [of Herskovits] concerning the continuation in a diluted form of the African family in the United States are not based upon any data showing continuity between African traditions and the familial behavior of American Negroes." They were, Frazier continued, "only an ingenious attempt to show . . . supposed similarities in attitudes and behavior" [130, p. 12]. They were mere "speculation" [130, p. 19].

The contribution of the sociologists and anthropologists to the analysis of slavery was not in the evidence they offered but in the issues they raised — not in the conclusions but in the debate. For that debate shifted the spotlight from the master to the slave. The slave was no longer an unknown actor, lurking toward the rear of the historiographic stage. The debate had transformed him into a bright, new star.

5.4. Despite the developments within economic history, the substantial contributions of the Negro school, and the new view of "the Negro question" that was emerging from the work of sociologists and anthropologists, the work and views of Phillips and his school continued to dominate thought within the mainstream of the historical profession. This is not to say that historians were unaffected by the new developments. The revolution within anthropology and the changing concept of race, for example, slowly seeped into the thought of scholars. As Woodward has pointed out, it found reflection in Phillips's work. "One clear evidence of change," said Woodward recently of Phillips's final book, "is the degree to which the theme of racial inferiority had been subdued or eliminated" [263, p. v].

The new developments also contributed to a neoabolitionist resurgence within the historical profession. The reformation of a neoabolitionist camp was slow and uncertain. It began early in the 1930s with Bancroft's passionate study of the slave trade [11]. It gathered force with the work of Aptheker [4; 5; 6; 7] and Wish [371; 372] on Negro slave revolts toward the end of the 1930s. It became a self-conscious movement in the mid-1940s with the publication of Hofstadter's call for an attack on

"Phillips and the Plantation Legend" (see T.6, pp. 224–228). But it did not become triumphant until the publication of Stampp's *The Peculiar Institution* in the mid-1950s.

Bancroft, son of an abolitionist, reared in a town that had been "an important station on the underground railway" [55, p. 7], student of Burgess, Dunning, and von Holst, friend of Rhodes, biographer of Seward and Schurz, was 71 when he published his study of the slave trade. He was provoked to write it by his irritation with Phillips, who he felt had "calmly pre-empted the field of Southern history and told all persons of Northern birth that it would be hopeless for them to expect to learn or understand the facts until they had been interpreted by Southerners, etc.!" [55, p. 120].

Slave Trading in the Old South was a work of prodigious scholarship which rested on an extensive examination of advertisements for the sale of slaves in antebellum newspapers as well as on information obtained from commercial directories, interviews of "people whose memories stretched back to the ante-bellum era" [55, p. 121], correspondence of slave traders, travelers' reports, and abolitionists' critiques. Bancroft also made use of the coastwise manifests, then deposited at the Library of Congress, to obtain age breakdowns of the slaves involved in the interstate trade, and to determine the identities of the leading figures engaged in it. On the basis of these materials, Bancroft was able to specify the cities that were the principal centers of the trade, the types of firms involved in slave trading, and the mechanisms employed in buying and selling human beings.

Bancroft developed two major themes. The first made slave trading not just an aspect but the very core of the slave system. "Slave-rearing," he wrote, "early became the source of the largest and often the only regular profit of nearly all slaveholding farmers and of many planters in the upper South" [11, p. 68]. He estimated that toward the close of the antebellum era, the average annual transactions in slaves amounted to $100,000,000.

At that time, $100,000,000 was relatively a fabulous interest to the South. It represented about one-twenty-fifth of the entire value of the nearly four million slaves. And slave-trading was vastly more important than this suggests: it was absolutely necessary to the continuance of this most highly prized property and to the economic, social and political conditions dependent on it [11, p. 406].

The other theme stressed by Bancroft was that slave trading was extremely cruel and had a devastating impact on the lives of slaves. To show that "slavery maintained as a profitable and convenient institution was essentially ruthless in general and inhumane" [11, p. 197], he argued that the division of families, including the separation of mothers from their children, was common. "[T]o divide families," was "the everyday practice" [11, p. 199]. Bancroft vividly described the "demonstrations of grief" expressed by slave families "at the prospect of speedy and perpetual separation," "the deep sorrow of the husband and wife" which "became most hysterical" when the "importunate pleading of the husband" was ignored, and the vain attempt of a husband to have one more moment with his wife [11, pp. 290-291, 374]. He also described the ugliness of the jails and pens in which slaves awaiting sale were kept and the coffles in which they were transported. Perhaps most repulsive were the slave auctions [11, pp. 106-107]:

Hands were opened and shut and looked at inside and out. Arms and legs were felt of as a means of deciding whether they were muscular and regular. Backs and buttocks were scrutinized for the welts that heavy blows with a whip usually left. Necks were rubbed or pinched to detect any soreness or lumps. Jaws were grasped, fingers were run into negroes' mouths, which were widely opened and peered into. Lips were pressed back so that all the teeth and gums could be seen. This performance closely resembled that of an expert reading a horse's age. If there was any suspicion that one eye might not be good, a strange hand was clapped over the other and the slave was asked what object was held before him. The hearing was likewise tested. All such inquiries were made with equal freedom whether the slave was man, woman, boy or girl. . . .

Despite the impressive research which it embodies, *Slave Trading in the Old South* was paid little attention in the decade that followed its publication. The initial printing of 1,200 volumes "moved slowly" [11, p. ix]. The scholars who dominated antebellum history at the time ignored it. The book was not "rediscovered" until Stampp used it so effectively as a source for his chapter on slavemongering.

Slave insurrections had, of course, always been emphasized by Negro historians including Williams, Du Bois, and Woodson. Such insurrections, they argued, were a clear indication of the discontent of slaves with their lot, a form of "self-assertion" which proved that submissiveness was not an inborn characteristic of blacks, a demonstration of courage, and a part of the process through which a Negro culture evolved (see **5.2** and **5.3**). The most thorough examination of slave insurrections by a member of the Negro school was the study by Carroll [36], which appeared in 1938. This volume was based on a search of 70-odd newspapers published over the period between 1734 and 1865, as well as on the legal documents of the various slave states and a wide array of other sources. While Carroll concentrated mainly on the period after 1800, and especially on the conspiracies and insurrections of Gabriel, Vesey, and Turner, he also devoted two chapters to insurrectionary movements and seaboard mutinies running as far back as 1526.

His survey, said Carroll, showed that "there were Negroes who were held in physical bondage whose souls never bowed in obedience" [36, p. 10], and that the Negro "was ever ready to attempt any possible means at his disposal to emancipate himself" [36, p. 213]. On the other hand, Carroll did not view the many conspiracies and insurrections as part of a conscious political movement. While the leaders of some plots were influenced in various degrees by knowledge of revolts elsewhere, "most frequently they were unconscious of the general aspects of the movement" [36, p. 214].

The contribution of neoabolitionist writers, such as Aptheker and Wish, who took up the theme of Negro slave revolts was not, obviously, in their identification of a previously unknown phenomenon. Nor was it primarily in their addition to information on the scope of these insurrections, nor in their addition to knowledge regarding the details of particular events. Although Aptheker's extensive search of manuscript material and newspapers resulted in a significant addition to information on these matters, it did not markedly alter the main aspects of the description contained in Carroll's book.

The new element introduced by the neoabolitionist writers, particularly Aptheker, was the assertion that "acute fear" "of, or the actual outbreak of, militant concerted slave action" pervaded "ante-bellum Southern life and history" [7, pp. 368, 373]. In this view the antebellum South was an armed camp, which devoted a high proportion of its resources to the repression of ever-threatening rebellion. "Behind the owner, and his personal agents," wrote Aptheker, "stood an elaborate and complex system of military control. In the cities were guards and police, for the countryside there were the ubiquitous patrols, armed men on horseback. . . . Behind this were the state militias. . ." [7, p. 67]. The slave system was continuously under siege, not from without but from within, and extraordinary measures were required for the ruling class to retain its hegemony [7, p. 78]:

> ... [O]ne may say that the masters of the Southern states were not content to depend merely upon social inertia, or the power that their ownership of the means of production gave them in order to maintain their dominant position. On the contrary they called into play every trick, rule, regulation, and device that the human mind could invent to aid them; the attempted psychological, intellectual, and physical debasement of an entire people, the inculcating and glorifying of the most outrageous racial animosities buttressed by theological, historical, and anthropological theories, the dividing of the victims against themselves, the use of spies and the encouragement of traitors, the evolving of a rigid social code helpful for their purpose, the disdaining, tabooing, and finally repressing of all opposition thought and deed, the establishment of elaborate police and military systems, the enacting of innumerable laws of oppression and suppression; the developing, in short, of a social order within which the institution of Negro slavery became so deeply imbedded that it was true that to touch one was to move the other. . . .

5.4.1. Little was added to the basic body of data bearing on the operation of the slave economy by neoabolitionist writers of the 1930s and 1940s. The only serious attempt at analysis of numerical information is contained in the final chapter of Bancroft's book, where he attempted to estimate the volume of the interstate slave trade. Using a crude version of the forward survivor method [cf. **B.2.4**), he concluded that an average of about 18,000 slaves were sold interstate each year during the decade of the fifties. But this figure rested on the incorrect assumption that 70 percent of the slaves involved in the westward movement were sold in the market and that only 30 percent moved with their owners.

6. The neoabolitionist resurgence reached a climax in 1956 with the publication of Stampp's *The Peculiar Institution.* A powerfully written book, a product of great erudition and subtle insights, *The Peculiar Institution* rapidly replaced Phillips's *American Negro Slavery* as the most authoritative single volume on the nature of the slave economy. With Stampp's book, that which the neoabolitionist writers had striven to achieve throughout the 1930s and 1940s was finally realized: the Phillips school, the "southern view," was disenthroned. A new intellectual dominion was established. The scope of the triumph was assessed by Elkins [101, pp. 20-21] in this way:

217

There is now very little that Phillips did with the plantation regime that has not been done with greater thoroughness by his Northern successor. Not only has Phillips' moral position been overwhelmingly reversed, but even his scholarship — though nearly forty years would have to elapse before anyone finally accomplished it — has been left in the shade by scholarship more painstaking still. Not only has the challenge been successful; the victory is devastating. What is more, to carry the echoes back yet another quarter-century beyond Phillips, a further vindication has been achieved. The view of American Negro slavery presented by James Ford Rhodes in 1893 has acquired a new legitimacy which a generation and more of Southern-dominated writing had denied it.

6.1. Unlike neoabolitionist writers, such as Hofstadter and Schlesinger, who tenaciously defended the entire original economic indictment of slavery (see T.6, pp. 224–228; **4.2**), Stampp did not. He sharply rejected three of the principal points in that indictment and was ambiguous on the fourth (see T.6, p. 228). Stampp insisted on retaining only the proposition that slavery provided extremely harsh material conditions of life for slaves. In deviating from the rigid position of other neoabolitionist writers, Stampp gave explicit recognition to the fact that, for the most part, the traditional interpretation of the slave economy better served the defenders of slave society than its critics. "[T]he critics of slavery who argued that the institution was an economic burden to the master," said Stampp, "were using the weakest weapon in their arsenal" [303, p. 417].

Interestingly enough, Stampp's critique of the economic indictment is one of the least-mentioned aspects of his book. Descriptions of *The Peculiar Institution* more often stress its depiction of slavery "as a thoroughly cruel and brutal system of social control" [357, p. 79], "as primarily a harsh, repressive system for the exploitation of cheap labor" [223, p. 53], and "as the most bestial regime that has tarnished America" [27, p. 144]. While several of the chapters of *The Peculiar Institution* have been reprinted in the recent spate of readers on slavery, the chapter which focuses on the issues of profit, economic viability, efficiency, and economic growth has not, as far as we can determine, been one of them.

The neglect of Stampp on these issues is not due to mediocrity in his economic reasoning. On the purely theoretical level, he far surpasses Phillips. In some respects he even surpasses Gray, although, as Stampp acknowledged in his footnotes, he leaned heavily on the arguments of Gray, Govan, and Russel (see **5.1**). A case in point is Stampp's rejection of the proposition which Phillips uncritically accepted: that slavery prevented industrialization by absorbing capital. Stampp cogently revealed the error of this line of reasoning [303, p. 397]:

After the African slave trade was legally closed, the southern labor system absorbed little new capital that might have gone into commerce or industry. Then only the illegal trade carried on by northern and foreign merchants drained off additional amounts of the South's liquid assets. The domestic slave trade involved no further investment; it merely involved the transfer of a portion of the existing one between individuals and regions. Obviously, when one Southerner purchased slaves another liquidated part of his investment in slaves and presumably could have put his capital in industry if he cared to. . . . Southerners *did* have capital for investment in industry, and the existence of slavery was not the reason why so few of them chose to become industrialists.

But the economic issues could not be resolved on the level of theory alone. The facts of the matter had to be established. On the question of profitability, for example, it was not enough to expose the blunders of Phillips and Sydnor. To compute profit rates one needed reliable information on the typical value of the product of slaves by age and sex, the cost of investment in land and equipment, maintenance costs, depreciation rates, and mortality schedules. These issues, which were not pursued by Stampp, have, of course, been the ones which have occupied so much of the effort of the cliometricians over the past decade and a half (see **B.3.1**; **B.3.2**; **B.3.3**).

While Stampp, like Gray and Phillips, dealt with all five of the issues which constitute the traditional interpretation of the slave economy, his consideration of these issues was extremely uneven. His discussion of the efficiency of slave labor in the plantation context is completed in just four paragraphs [303, pp. 399–401]. On the other hand, his discussion of the material treatment of slaves constitutes the bulk of chapters 2, 3, 4, 5, 6, 7, and 8. In other words, some two thirds or more of *The Peculiar Institution* is concerned with the issue of material treatment.

This skewed distribution of effort cannot be explained by the intrinsic complexity of the issue of treatment and the simplicity of the issues of profitability, viability, efficiency, and growth. Nor is it true that material treatment is the issue on which the economic analysis of slavery turns. Indeed, the resolution of none of the other issues depends on the resolution of the question of material treatment. Slavery could have been profitable, economically viable, highly efficient, and the southern economy could have been rapidly growing under either a cruel or a mild regime.

Of course neither Stampp nor any other writer was obliged to deal with the full range of issues involved in the analysis of the slave system. The extent and implications of the maltreatment of slaves are important and difficult questions — important enough and difficult enough so that they might well be the sole subjects of more than one book. But *The Peculiar Institution* was not intended as an intensive exploration of a limited set of issues. Stampp's announced goal was a wide-ranging and fundamental reinterpretation of the slave system. His decision to concentrate on the issue of treatment apparently stemmed not only from his sense of moral outrage but also from his desire to end the intellectual hegemony of Phillips as well as from his strategy for achieving that objective.

Stampp recognized, more clearly than any writer before him, the basis of Phillips's success: the deft conversion of the traditional interpretation of slavery from an indictment into a justification. Stampp also recognized that the critical maneuver of the conversion had been Phillips's convincing argument that, in the treatment of their slaves, masters had been paternalistic rather than ruthless (see 3.2). Stampp therefore embarked on the refutation of all the principal elements of Phillips's version of the traditional interpretation as it was set forth in *American Negro Slavery*. Like Phillips, he concentrated on the issue of treatment. This is why the categories which Stampp adopted for "organizing his own work (food, shelter, police, medical care, etc.) had a very familiar look: they were the same that Phillips had used" [101, p. 22].

There was virtually no defense of the behavior of the slaveholding class put forward by Phillips that Stampp permitted to pass unanswered. Where Phillips pleaded that slaveowners had inherited the system, Stampp replied: "[T] hey built it little by little, step by step, choice by choice" [303, p. 6]. Where Phillips characterized slaveholders as men of goodwill whose treatment of slaves was generally "benevolent in intent and on the whole beneficial in effect," Stampp responded: "[C] ruelty was endemic in all slaveholding communities" and even those "concerned about the welfare of slaves found it difficult to draw a sharp line between acts of cruelty and such measures of physical force as were an inextricable part of slavery" [303, p. 185]. Where Phillips lauded the bountifulness of the food provided to slaves, Stampp countered: "On countless farms and plantations the laborers never tasted fresh meat, milk, eggs, or fruits, and rarely tasted vegetables" [303, pp. 284-285].

Why Stampp decided to hinge his strategy on the issue of treatment is not entirely clear. Some clues are contained in Stampp's 1952 article. The "fundamental problem" of the literature on Negro slavery, he wrote, was "the biased historian" [302, p. 613]. While he did not explicitly charge that Phillips had permitted his prejudices to misrepresent the evidence, he strongly implied that this was the case. In part, Stampp assumed, the misrepresentation arose from the convenient device of concentrating on large plantations. "The danger in generalizing about the whole regime from an unrepresentative sample is obvious enough" [302, p. 615]. In part, Stampp believed, the misrepresentation was due to the inaccurate reporting of the facts contained even in this sample, especially with respect to the issue of treatment. He asserted that "one of the chief faults of the classic portrayal of the slave regime," was its "tendency toward loose and glib generalizing" [302, p. 616].

If these are the assumptions which led Stampp to concentrate so heavily on the issue of treatment, they were unfortunate. While there were differences in behavior on small and large plantations, little evidence that we or any of the other cliometricians have thus far uncovered sustains the view that the treatment of slaves was markedly inferior on small than on large plantations, although we suspect that size may have affected the stability and quality of slave families (see [307]). As for the integrity of Phillips and the members of the institutionalist wing of his school in reporting the facts on material treatment, we have found nothing which justifies deprecation. This is not to say that they were without error in representing the central tendency of various characteristics, but that there is no evidence that these errors were biased in the direction of exaggerating the quality of slave treatment. Indeed, they made more errors which served to detract from the quality of slave treatment than to enhance it (cf. **B.4.5.2**; **B.4.5.3**; **B.4.6**; **B.4.8**; **3.1.1**; **4.1.2**).

The flaw in Stampp's strategy was his unwarranted belief that the issue of treatment was a stronger weapon with which to assail romanticizers of slavery than those propositions of the economic indictment which he had rightly discarded. By continuing to insist that the food, clothing, health care, and housing provided to slaves were much worse than to free laborers, by exaggerating the deleterious effects of slavery on the nature of the slave family, he misdirected the debate. For he distracted attention from such other abominations of the slave system as the barriers it raised to the education of blacks, its severe restrictions on opportunities for slave participation in the highest professions, and its insistence on the subordination of blacks to whites regardless of degree of black talent or achievement (except in narrowly defined occupations, and then only under quite restricted conditions).

Stampp's strategy also detracted attention from the most important new contributions of his book. One of these, as we have already noted, was the insightfulness of his critique of the greater part of the traditional interpretation of the economics of slavery. The second was his concerted effort to reassert the primacy of moral issues in evaluating the efficacy of slavery. The third was his effort to break away from racist depictions of black development under slavery and to uncover the positive aspects of black responses to the system.

Acutely aware of the extent to which Phillips had blunted the moral indictment of slavery, Stampp pressed, as he should have, to restore its primacy. Indignation against the system and the master class leaps out of nearly every page of *The Peculiar Institution.* Yet despite a language which has all the power that comes with deep and eloquently expressed moral rage, Stampp did not wholly succeed in attaining his objective. By continually linking the issue of morality with physical cruelty, with sexual abuses, or with mistreatment in respect to food, clothing, and shelter, Stampp inadvertently obfuscated rather than clarified the profound immorality of the *system.* His line of argument gave the impression that the issue of morality revolved primarily on such matters as the frequency of sexual abuse, the incidence of physical brutality, or the ratio of "good" to "bad" masters.

Stampp's error was not in his belief that cruel treatment and abuse, whether by few or by many slaveholders, compounded the immorality of slavery but in his failure to stress that proof of good treatment was insufficient to remove the moral brand. Even if slavery did produce, on the average, better material conditions than obtained for free Negro laborers, or white laborers for that matter, the *moral* indictment of slavery still prevails. For the moral indictment does not rest on the issue of treatment or on any of the other four propositions of the economic indictment evolved by the antislavery critics. The economic indictment was consciously forged as an expedient weapon in the ideological struggle to defeat slavery, a weapon which it was hoped would win the support of those who were unmoved by the purely moral arguments [T.5, pp. 159-161].

Today, as in the eighteenth and nineteenth centuries, the fundamental moral objection to slavery is still the one formulated by the radical Quakers: no person has the right to demand of another person such subordination as is required under slavery. These radicals were among the first to entertain a view that has since become a central moral premise of our age: however the variation in human ability or achievement, all people are entitled to equal opportunity (cf. [71]). What made Phillips's feint on the issue of morality so effective was his capacity to divert attention from the fact that slavery denied this premise. Phillips accomplished the diversion by his extraordinary success in reducing the question of morality to a debate on the quality of the material conditions of life provided to those who had been kept in bondage.

Perhaps Stampp's most important contribution was his unremitting assault on racist depictions of Negroes. The agenda of the stereotypes to be demolished was, once again, that provided by Phillips. Stampp pursued this agenda relentlessly.

He first attacked the basic racist premises that governed Phillips's characterizations of slaves. Against the belief that Negroes were biologically inferior to whites, Stampp pitted "an impressive accumulation of evidence" by "modern biologists, psychologists, sociologists, and anthropologists" that "Negroes and whites have approximately the same intellectual potentialities" [303, p. 10]. Against the belief that personality and temperament made the Negro "the natural slave of the white man," Stampp argued that variations in the "personalities of *individuals* within each race are as great as the variations in their physical traits. . . . Either slavery was a desirable status for some whites as well as for some Negroes, or it was not a desirable status for anyone" [303, pp. 10-11]. Against the belief that slaves had sprung from "barbarians" and therefore "needed" to be "civilized" by being "subjected to rigid discipline and severe controls," Stampp counterposed anthropological testimony that the "African ancestors of American Negroes had developed an economy based upon agriculture which in some places approached the complex organization of a plantation system," that African "[s]ocial and political institutions matched the complexity of the economy," and that in "the aesthetic sphere Africans expressed themselves through music, the dance, and the graphic and plastic arts" [303, pp. 11-13].

To emphasize the absence of either biological or cultural justifications for black enslavement, Stampp proclaimed "that the slaves were merely ordinary human beings, that innately Negroes *are,* after all, only white men with black skins, nothing more, nothing less" [303, pp. vii-viii]. This sentence has been widely criticized in recent years by both blacks and whites who have accused Stampp of denying the existence of a unique black culture — of depriving blacks of their cultural identity. Surely this is a misreading of Stampp's intent as well as of the exigencies of the ideological debate on race among historians of the South in the mid-1950s. The problem confronting Stampp was not that Phillips had denied American Negroes a distinct culture but that he had made the innate and immutable inferiority of blacks the source of a distinct culture which was defined by such characteristics as "cowardice," "docility," "proneness to superstition," "submissiveness," "inertness," "humble nonchalance," "licentiousness," and a proclivity for "lying," "shirking," and "stealing."

In attempting to resolve the issue of cultural identity, Stampp pursued two paths, neither of which was new. First, he took up the theme of "day-to-day resistance" which had been popularized by Herskovits and his students Bauer and Bauer (see **5.3**). Rather than challenging Phillips's contention that lying, stealing, shirking, and feigning illness were the characteristics of slave behavior, Stampp affirmed it. Much of Stampp's "resistance" chapter is spent recounting instances of such behavior, which in no way differ from those recounted by Phillips, except perhaps in their greater number. The question became not the appropriateness of Phillips's description of the behavior of slaves but the proper interpretation of the significance of this mutually agreed upon description.

Stampp's line of argument permitted the issue of racism to be confounded by a debate over value judgments. To Phillips the "good" Negro was the one "who was courteous and loyal to his master, and who did his work faithfully and cheerfully." But in a system-as evil as slavery, Stampp contended, normal ethical standards did not apply. In such a system the "good" slaves were those who "faked illness, loafed, sabotaged" [302, p. 618]. Indeed, Stampp made this precept part of the moral code of slaves. "For appropriating their master's goods they might be punished and denounced by him, but they were not likely to be disgraced among their associates in the slave quarters, who made a distinction between 'stealing' and 'taking'" [303, pp. 126–127]. And whom did slaves come most to venerate among their number? Some, Stampp said, admired the house slave who adopted "the white pattern of respectability." But the "generality of slaves believed that he who knew how to trick or deceive the master had an enviable talent, and they regarded the committing of petit larceny as both thrilling and praiseworthy" [303, pp. 334–335].

Of course Stampp was not the first scholar who attempted to transform planters' complaints about "errant" slaves into a resistance movement. But he pushed the theme farther than it had ever been taken before. Moreover, he added an element that was not present in the arguments of Herskovits or Bauer and Bauer. They had merely argued that laziness and irresponsibility were really forms of resistance to slavery. Stampp gave this resistance a moral twist. In effect, he attributed to slaves the morality of abolitionists. In so doing he not only gave to those engaged in resistance a political consciousness that Douglass did not find among his fellow bondsmen [81, p. 160], he simultaneously cast a stain on those who strove to improve themselves within the system.

Stampp's second path also led him to concede the truth of Phillips's description of the behavior of blacks, but to argue that it was *the system* rather than race which was to blame. Thus, if slaves exhibited a tendency to violence it was because of "the brutalizing effects of bondage" [303, p. 335]. If slaves had a "casual attitude" toward marriage, if husbands and wives failed to develop "deep and enduring affection" toward each other, it was because of "[t]he general instability of slave families" promoted by the system [303, p. 345], because of the forced "disintegration" of African "social organization" [303, p. 340], and because of the "easy access to female slaves" by "[u]nmarried slaveholders and the young males" [303, p. 355].

What of black achievements under slavery? A world in which good work is synonymous with betrayal and in which evasion, deception, and sabotage are the objectives to which to aspire leaves scant room for black achievement. There were, of course, those "who lacked the qualities which produce rebels." Such slaves "had to seek personal gratification and the esteem of their fellows in less spectacular ways. They might find these things simply by doing their work uncommonly well" [303, p. 336]. But *The Peculiar Institution* did not emphasize these accomplishments, as though they were of a lower order. Stampp's scattered references to the high skill of slave artisans, for example, hardly add up to two full pages in a book of over 400 pages.

Thus Stampp failed to effect a fundamental break with racist depictions of the antebellum Negro, despite his enormous desire to do so. All that Stampp was able to accomplish was to shift the blame for alleged Negro incompetence and moral turpitude from biological characteristics to sociological conditions — from God to the slaveholding class. Stampp was far less of a revisionist than he believed he was. Phillips — in his grave for a quarter of a century — still controlled the argument.

6.2. To what extent did Stampp extend the body of evidence bearing on the operation of the slave economy? In the preface to *The Peculiar Institution,* Stampp said only that he was embarked on "an attempt at a new synthesis" which drew on the methods, sources, and findings of

Table C.1

The Distribution of Footnote Citations in *The Peculiar Institution*

Primary Sources	Number of citations	Percent
Antebellum newspapers and journals	334	30
Plantation documents, unpublished	294	27
Travel and other "eyewitness" accounts	204	18
Court records, published (Catterall)	93	8
Ex-slave narratives (other than Fisk University and W.P.A.)	88	8
Plantation documents, published	49	4
U.S. census, published volumes	8	1
Court records, unpublished	6	1
Manuscript schedules of U.S. census	2	–
Ex-slave narratives (Fisk University and W.P.A.)	2	–
Other	27	2
Subtotal	1,107	100
Secondary Sources		
Phillips school	151	52
Economic historians	29	10
Neoabolitionist school (since 1918)	27	9
Negro school	24	8
Anthropologists and sociologists	10	3
Other	51	17
Subtotal	292	100
Total	1,399	

Notes:

1. The above count was based on the following rules:
   a. References to a given author within a single footnote were counted as a single citation, even if several books by that author were listed.
   b. References to a single journal within a given footnote were counted as single citation, even if pages widely separated in a single volume were

      involved or if pages in several different volumes were listed.

  c. References to a single manuscript record group within a given footnote were counted as a single citation even if several different documents within the record group were listed. (See notes to table C.2 for the definition of a record group.)

      Distributions based on alternative definitions of "a citation" were also constructed. While these alternative definitions changed the total number of citations, they had little effect on the basic pattern of the frequency distribution.

  2. The count of citations to unpublished plantation documents includes nine references made in the text but not cited in the footnotes.

  3. The two citations to *The Suppression of the African Slave Trade* are included under Negro school since the book does not reflect the sociological emphasis contained in the later work of Du Bois. The one reference to Frazier is included under anthropologists and sociologists.

Phillips as well as on a large number of books and articles written since 1918, and that "the best of them have pointed toward revisions of some of Phillips's conclusions" [303, p. viii]. On the other hand, Stampp's criticism of the representativeness of the sample of plantation documents employed by Phillips [302, pp. 614-615], together with the long list of plantation documents, census manuscript schedules, court records, and church records listed at the rear of *The Peculiar Institution,* suggested to some readers [101; 202] that Stampp's revisions rested, at least in part, on a substantial expansion of the evidential base.

    Some measure of the extent to which Stampp employed various sources of information may be obtained from an examination of the citations in his footnotes. Both the absolute and relative frequency of citations to eleven classes of primary materials and six classes of secondary materials are shown in table C.1. To avoid naïve or misleading interpretations of the information contained in this table, several caveats should be kept in mind. The frequency distributions pertain not to the sources that Stampp consulted but merely to the sources he *reported* as giving support to various statements made in *The Peculiar Institution.* The distributions indicate how often certain types of documents were cited, not the importance of the evidence reported. The most frequently cited sources need not contain the most critical evidence. The distributions do not by themselves indicate the manner in which evidence extracted from particular sources was employed.

    Where the frequency distributions indicated that certain sources or types of information were either heavily or lightly used, we sought confirmation through an examination of the discussion in the text, considering the subjects treated as well as the manner in which the evidence was related to these subjects. In various instances this examination led us to investigate the original sources, comparing the textual discussion with the nature of the information contained in the relevant sources. The results of several of these comparisons are set forth later in this section and in **6.3**.

There were several references to sources in the text that were not cited in the footnotes. These were added to the count of citations. The additions had little effect on the basic pattern of the distributions. The frequency distributions with which we actually worked were more elaborate than those shown here. They included cross tabulations by author, type of document, and by the ten chapters of *The Peculiar Institution.*

Table C.1 shows that the largest single category of primary sources employed by Stampp was antebellum journals and newspapers, especially agricultural journals and *DeBow's Review.* These accounted for 30 percent of all his citations of primary material. Since this source had also been heavily exploited by the Phillips school, there was little opportunity for the discovery of new information here, although, of course, Stampp could have, and did, interpret some of these articles differently.

Unpublished plantation documents are the second largest category of citations of primary materials. Of the 120 record groups listed by Stampp, only 35 were previously used either by Phillips or by one of the authors of the state studies (see **4.1**). This finding might appear to support the proposition that Stampp's conclusions were different from those reached by members of the Phillips school because he consulted a sample of plantations that was substantially different from their sample.

That possibility is diminished, however, by an analysis of Stampp's references to plantation documents. Of his 294 citations of unpublished plantation records, 62 (21 percent) pertained to just two record groups (Hammond and Pettigrew), both of which had been exploited previously by members of the Phillips school (see table C.2). Another 7 percent of the citations pertained to two additional record groups (Weeks and Thompson). A third group of 15 record sets accounted for another 34 percent of the citations. Thus 62 percent of Stampp's citations came from just 16 percent of the document collections listed at the rear of *The Peculiar Institution.* Of these heavily used collections, more than half the citations were to records which had been exploited previously by members of the Phillips school. Moreover, most of Stampp's new finds were never cited by him (35 of the record sets fall into this cate-

Table C.2

The Frequency Distribution of Citations to Unpublished Plantation Documents in *The Peculiar Institution*

Times cited	Number of record groups	Total number of citations
20 or more	2	62
10–19	2	22
5–9	15	100
2–4	30	81
1	29	29
0	42	0
Totals	120	294

Notes:

1. In constructing table C.2 the following definitions were employed:
   a. A *collection* is either one of the sets of manuscripts included by Stampp in his list of "Manuscripts Consulted" or three other manuscript collections referred to in the text but not listed in the rear of the book.
   b. A *record group* or record set consists of all records pertaining to a given family or plantation regardless of the archive at which it is located. Stampp listed two collections in each of the following cases: Ball, Hammond, Pettigrew, Ruffin, and Sparkman. Thus there are five less *record groups* than *collections*.
2. Only private papers of slaveholders are included in the documents analyzed in this table. Federal, state, county, court, and church records are excluded. Four collections of papers pertaining to slaveholders were treated as plantation documents, although they might more appropriately be classified in the category shown in table C.1 as "other primary sources." Such a reclassification would have little effect on the frequency distribution of either table C.1 or table C.2.
3. See the notes to table C.1 for the definition of a citation.
4. The count of citations includes nine references made in the text but not cited in the footnotes.

gory) or were cited only once each (17 record sets). In other words, the most valuable groups of plantation records had already been discovered and reported by the Phillips school. Like his predecessors, Stampp's analysis of plantation records was overwhelmingly drawn from a relatively small number of large plantations.

Nor should it be assumed that Stampp exploited all of the plantation records discovered by members of the Phillips school that were worth exploiting. A number of the record groups utilized by the Phillips school but omitted by Stampp contain much richer bodies of evidence than most of the plantations which Stampp substituted in their place. Among the records overlooked by Stampp were the Aventine, Canebrake, Elley, and Monette papers, which contain excellent daily work records and which permit analysis of the relative efficiency of male and female hands by age. They also bear on the intensity of the work schedule over the year. Other plantation records utilized by members of the Phillips school but not by Stampp, such as the Duncan, Furman, Kenner, Kleinpeter, MacKay, and Perry papers, contain excellent data on maternity patterns, family structure, morbidity, and mortality.

Stampp made little use of numerical information in the plantation manuscripts, preferring literary evidence. This was unfortunate since his penchant for apt phrases and striking language frequently misled him. For example, his four-page discussion of the extent of illness among slaves [303, pp. 296–300] draws on quotations from letters and personal diaries of ten manuscript collections.[1] As one might suspect, it was periods of unusually severe illness which were most likely to find their way into such documents. Stampp did not report systematic, year-long counts of morbidity experience which are contained in the account books of five of the record groups in his list (Bayside, Capell, Liddell, Marsten, and Newstead). Tabulating the time lost due to illness over a total of 834 man years, these records show an average morbidity rate of 11.9 days per man year. This systematic evidence gives a far less grim picture than the "frightful accounts of sickness" [303, p. 298] which Stampp extracted from vivid but misleading descriptions of epidemics or other brief periods of extensive illness.

In stressing Stampp's neglect of numerical evidence, we do not mean to imply that members of the Phillips school adequately mined all of the data in their samples of plantation records. They were nearly as deficient

---

[1] The endpoint of Stampp's discussion of morbidity rates is somewhat ambiguous. He passes from consideration of the *extent* of illness to consideration of the *types* of disease and other afflictions which beset slaves without a clear demarcation between the two matters. We interpret his discussion of morbidity rates to extend from line 7 of p. 296 through line 17 of p. 300.

as Stampp in making use of data bearing on such matters as the efficiency of slave labor and the demographic characteristics of slave families. Only Sydnor systematically exploited records on daily cotton picking rates [320, pp. 15-18], and he did not analyze adequately the effect of age and sex on these rates. No one in the Phillips school systematically utilized information in plantation documents on seasonal variations in births, kinship patterns, ages of mothers at last birth, the relationship between the fertility of women and the stability of marital bonds, or the effect of plantation size on the ages of mothers at the birth of their first children (cf. [165; 166; 307]). Both Stampp and the members of the Phillips school were generally too inexperienced in economics and demography to recognize the value of these data and too inexperienced in statistical methods to be able to exploit them.[2]

If Stampp did not succeed in overcoming his predecessors' concentration on large plantations, it was partly because of his superficial use of the manuscript schedules of the U.S. census and of probate records. These are the primary sources of information on small slaveholdings. Yet Stampp has only two citations to the manuscript schedules, and one of them [303, p. 53] is quite misleading (see **6.3**).

The neglect of the probate records in *The Peculiar Institution* is, in one respect, more surprising than the neglect of the manuscript schedules. For the probate records frequently do identify family groups and contain important evidence on such matters as the age of mothers at the births of various surviving children, age of husbands and wives, intervals between births of surviving children, and other demographic information vital to the analysis of slave families (see T.4, pp. 136-140; **B.2.5.4**; **B.4.8.3**; **B.4.11.2**). These records also make it possible to relate slave prices in both slave-exporting and -importing regions to age and sex and thus to obtain information highly relevant to the testing of the thesis that breeding for sale was an important source of plantation profit (see T.3, pp. 78-86; **B.1.8**; **B.2.6**; **B.3.5**; **B.4.11.2**).

Yet Stampp made no quantitative use of this type of evidence or, if he did, failed to report the results of his computations. In this respect his methodology was more deficient than that of Phillips and the institutionalist members of his school (see **3.1.1**; **4.1.1**). Stampp cites unpublished court records only six times. One is merely a reference to the location of

<hr/>

[2]Craven [61, chap. 4] and Johnson [195, p. 101] are exceptions; they noted the value of such data but made only slight use of them.

the records for the trial of Nat Turner [303, p. 134]. Two yield quotations bearing on the attitudes of masters toward slaves [303, pp. 323, 403]. And one provides two quotations of masters which are used to emphasize the strong affection of some slave mothers for their children [303, p. 348].

The remaining two citations to unpublished probate records pertain to a total of 10 wills [303, pp. 204, 231]. Stampp argues that wills show an overwhelming conflict between masters' interests in slaves as property and the integrity of slave families. He suggests that as a consequence of nine of the wills, slave families were broken up and that only in the tenth case was the entire plantation retained intact. Stampp's conclusions are not based on the actual disposition of the slaves but on such assumptions as the following: the division of eight slaves among three children, "in equal portions, share and share alike," necessarily "made the sale of all or part of these slaves inevitable" [303, p. 205]. Stampp gives no report of whether such a sale in fact took place, and if it did, whether it resulted in the breakup of the slave families. Nor does Stampp indicate whether his sample ratio of nine to one is to be taken as indicative of the population parameter. He never explicitly discusses how his sample of wills was drawn or its representativeness, although the conclusion that he reaches strongly implies that the sample was indeed representative [303, p. 231]:

Masters who ignored the demands of discipline by flagrantly violating the slave codes, who elevated their slaves to virtual freedom, who treated them with utter disregard for their status as property, and who strictly regulated their use when bequeathing them to heirs, are justly celebrated in the folklore of slavery. But they are celebrated because their conduct was so abnormal. Had other masters imitated them, the slave system would have disintegrated — and a nation might have been spared a civil war.

In pointing to the fact that Stampp did not systematically exploit highly relevant numerical data contained in the census and probate records, we wish to call attention to a limitation, not in his scholarship, but in the evidence on which his conclusions were based. Even if Stampp had possessed the requisite training in quantitative methods, he could not have duplicated recent work on the data contained in these documents (see, for example, T.3, pp. 73-85; T.4, pp. 111-113, 137, 153-156; T.6, pp. 191-196, 200-202; **B.P.2**; **B.2.2**; **B.3.4**; **B.4.2**; **B.4.5, B.6.2.3; B.6.2.4;**

B.6.3.1; B.6.4; B.6.5). At the time Stampp carried out his research, in the late 1940s and early 1950s, the large grants required for the retrieval and processing of data were not available, computers were slow and very expensive, and they lacked the capacity to hold the amount of information that had to be analyzed or to perform the type of operations that have now been carried out.

Unlike most members of the Phillips school, Stampp persistently sought to view slavery from the standpoint of the slaves. This effort is reflected in Stampp's frequent use of the narratives of ex-slaves, particularly those written during the antebellum era. Altogether Stampp has 90 references to these narratives, only two of which come from the interviews collected under the Federal Writers' Project. These materials are used mainly in three chapters. Some 47 percent of the citations are in chapter 8, which deals with slave culture. An additional 20 percent are in chapter 3, which focuses on slave resistance. And 12 percent are cited in chapter 4, which describes the methods used to control slaves.

Stampp employs the narratives primarily as evidence that slavery warped the personalities and culture of Negroes, to show that slavery transformed many Negroes into awestruck, fear-ridden beings [303, pp. 145–46], who were "extremely uncomfortable" in the presence of whites [303, p. 331], who admired "petit larceny" [303, p. 335], who were tyrannical toward each other [303, p. 335], who "'put on airs' in imitation of the whites" [303, p. 338], and who were "culturally rootless people" [303, p. 364] whose unstable families resulted in "widespread sexual promiscuity" [303, p. 346] because marriage "had no existence among slaves" [303, p. 347].

The point is not that the ex-slave narratives cannot be used as a source for such characterizations, but that these are by no means all that appear in the narratives (cf. [21]). It is illuminating to compare Stampp's treatment of the narratives with Frazier's 1930 paper on the slave family, which was also based on the ex-slave narratives. Frazier found more evidence than did Stampp of the emergence of a distinct, positive culture and of "the solidarity of the slave family" [128, p. 234]. Interestingly enough, Stampp has no reference to this article.

That *The Peculiar Institution* does not emphasize the work of Negro writers such as Frazier (who is cited only once) points to another issue. Stampp does not appear to have fully appreciated the significance of the central thrust of the members of the Negro school – the emphasis on the achievements of Negroes. Woodson is cited only twice. The first reference is to Woodson's listing of free Negroes who were slaveholders [303, pp. 194-195] and the second to Woodson's explanation for the success of Baptist and Methodist missionaries among slaves [303, pp. 372-373].

Nowhere does Stampp take up Woodson's emphasis on the thirst of slaves for education and the remarkably large number who achieved it, given the obstacles placed in their way [376, pp. 85, 228; cf. 96, chap. 9]. Nowhere does Stampp recognize that there could have been "a rapid mental development" of Negroes under slavery or that slaves could have been not only effective laborers but that many did acquire an "administrative ability adequate to the management of business establishments and large plantations" [376, pp. 5-6]. He says little about the remarkable achievements of those slaves who were able to buy their way out of bondage through accumulated earnings. Nothing is said of the equally notable commercial successes of many free Negroes, North and South, in the face of obstacles almost as severe as those which confronted slaves (cf. [123; 126; 188; 360; 381; 382; 383]). Nor can one learn from Stampp's book that many southern crafts were dominated by slaves, that slaves may have even accounted for the majority of southern artisans [360, p. 142; B.2.1.3]. Despite Stampp's emphasis on the nature of Negro culture, members of the Negro school who focused on this question are cited only 24 times. That this is less than a fifth as many citations as are made to the Phillips school is another indication of the difficulty Stampp had in making an intellectual break with those who were the main targets of his fire.[3]

Stampp's inadequate definition of black accomplishments under slavery may have been related to his approach to the issue of racism. While Stampp unequivocally rejected the contention that Negroes were biologically inferior to whites, he did not inquire very deeply into the forms which racism assumed during the antebellum era, or consider how it might have affected the views of both the "eyewitnesses" and the historians that he invoked as authorities. Stampp was most alert to the racism of slaveholders, of southern historians, and of northern historians, such as Burgess and Fiske, who defended the slaveholding South (see [303, pp. 6-12]). But nowhere in *The Peculiar Institution* did he question the effect of racism on the views of Olmsted, whom he cited 81 times, nor of Kemble, who is cited 18 times (see T.4, pp. 143-144; T. 5, pp. 177-181; T.6, pp. 216-218). Stampp reported as fact, untinged by racism, Olmsted's descrip-

[3] Even so, Stampp was well ahead of most of his contemporaries in making use of the findings of Negro scholars.

tions of slaves as "chronic" malingerers [303, pp. 96, 100, 103], as untrustworthy with anything other than "crude, clumsy tools" [303, p. 103], as "excessively careless and wasteful" [303, p. 103], as embracing a moral code that justified theft [303, p. 127], as untrustworthy in the exercise of their "own discretion" [303, p. 148], as unwilling to "labor at all except to avoid punishment" [303, p. 171], as possessed of childlike personalities [303, p. 328], as "not severely disturbed by forced separation" of husbands and wives [303, pp. 345-346].

Stampp discussed racism as if it were a southern phenomenon rather than a national one. *The Peculiar Institution* reports the restrictions against the free Negroes in the South, but not in the North. Such discrimination is attributed, not to the racism which dominated the thoughts of nearly all whites in all regions, but to slaveholders who feared that the existence of some free blacks would undermine the entire system of bondage, and who sought "to convince slaves that winning freedom was scarcely worth the effort" [303, p. 216; cf. pp. 88, 149-150, 222, and 232]. Thus Northerners are inadvertently relieved of complicity in the establishment of the network of anti-Negro discrimination.

6.3. Although Stampp did not pursue or systematically employ numerical data, quantitative issues play an important role in his book. Certain of his conclusions depend critically on his assessment of the absolute or relative magnitudes of particular variables. Of the authors of the three landmark contributions to the economics of slavery (Phillips, Gray, and Stampp), Stampp was the most casual — least systematic — in the treatment of quantitative evidence. As a result his errors were the most serious.

Stampp was persistently faced with the problem of how to represent the main features of large distributions of characteristics. How could he best describe, in a simple way, the pertinent dimensions of the diet of slaves, the experience with morbidity, and the incidence of mortality? More complicated was the issue of the relationship between variables. What was the most effective way to compare the productivity of large and small farms, to evaluate the effect of plantation size on the infant death rate, or to determine whether the destabilizing effects of slavery on family life were more severe on large plantations where the relationship between masters and slaves was remote or small ones where contact was more immediate? There was still another set of problems. Given the incomplete nature of much of the available data and the absence of adequate breakdowns of the data, could any valid inferences be made? Could one, for example, infer the incidence of overseers on large plantations merely from the data contained in the published census? When many variables were likely to impinge on infant mortality, was it possible to separate out the influence of treatment from the epidemiological environment and genetic characteristics?

The need for measures which are capable of summarizing accurately and simply the information contained in a large distribution is well-known. Statisticians usually regard measures of central tendency, such as the mean, median, or mode, as the single most informative statistic. For some issues a measure of the degree of variation, such as the standard deviation, the mean deviation, or the interquartile range, is more relevant. Other important statistics are those designed to measure the skewness of a distribution and its degree of peakedness. With these four measures it is usually possible to characterize most of the relevant features of a distribution of thousands of observations. Statisticians have also developed procedures for dealing with more complex issues, such as the relationship between variables, the distribution of errors in attempting to infer the values of population parameters from samples, and the quantification of qualitative evidence.

For many of the issues taken up in *The Peculiar Institution,* the crucial statistic was the mean. For other questions, however, such as the relationship between plantation size and mortality, more complex statistical procedures — including regression analysis, analysis of variance, and chi-square tests — were called for.

Stampp never employed these more elaborate statistical procedures. He rarely even computed means. In general he shunned formal statistics, relying merely on his impressions of various bodies of evidence. It was this willingness to trust his senses — his intuition about the characteristics of large bodies of data — which was the crux of Stampp's difficulty in the resolution of quantitative issues. Time and again his intuition misled him. He frequently fell into the trap of believing that extreme observations were in fact the central tendencies of entire distributions. He assumed, without investigation, that the deliberate decisions of planters, or of slaves, were more important in explaining observed differences in mortality and morbidity experience than epidemiological or genetic factors. He never explicitly confronted issues which arose out of the incompleteness of data or out of the high level at which data in the published census are aggregated.

An example of Stampp's tendency to confuse extreme observations with central tendencies arises early in the book. On page 53, Stampp wrote:

Table C.3

Indexes of Cotton Output per Capita and per Equivalent Full Field Hand on Cotton Farms, by Size of Farm, in 1860

(1) *Number of* *slaves per farm*	*(2)* *Bales produced* *per capita*	*(3)* *Bales produced* *per equivalent* *full field hand*
1–19	100	100
20–49	164	168
50 +	214	204

Source: Parker-Gallman sample (see **B.P.2**).

In cotton production those with modest slaveholdings faced no overwhelming competitive disadvantage. Some of the smaller cotton growers were as preoccupied with this staple as were their neighbors on the large plantations. Some even depended upon outside supplies of food. Many of them reported astonishing cotton-production records to the census takers, the number of bales per hand easily matching the records of the planters.

The thrust of this paragraph appears to be that cotton productivity was, on the average, roughly as great on "modest" slaveholdings as on plantations (Stampp defined a "planter" as a farmer with "at least twenty slaves" [303, p. 30]). But to establish the validity of such a conclusion various questions have to be confronted. How many is "many"? Is cotton output per hand an adequate measure of productivity? What is the definition of "hand"? Was the labor input adjusted for age and sex? How was the labor of whites treated?

Stampp answers none of these questions. The only information provided about his procedures is contained in the following brief footnote [303, p. 53]:

This information about small slaveholders was derived from a study of their production records in representative counties throughout the South as reported in the manuscript census returns for 1860.

Table C.4

Farms with 1–19 Slaves Arrayed according to Their Productivity in Cotton Production and Compared with the Average Cotton Productivity on Medium and Large Plantations, 1860 (in bales)

	Decile averages for farms with 1–19 slaves	
Decile	*Output of cotton per capita*	*Output of cotton per equivalent field hand*
highest	4.1	9.3
second	1.9	4.9
third	1.4	3.6
fourth	1.1	2.8
fifth	0.8	2.1
sixth	0.6	1.5
seventh	0.4	1.0
eighth	0.1	0.4
ninth	0.0	0.0
tenth	0.0	0.0
	Averages for medium and large slaveholdings	
Farms with 20–49 slaves	1.7	4.5
Farms with 50 or more slaves	2.3	5.5

Source: Parker-Gallman sample (see **B.P.2**).

As pointed out in chapter 6 (pp. 192–194) and in appendix B (**B.6.2**; **B.6.3**), large slaveholdings did have a marked competitive advantage over small ones. The result is the same whether one uses a partial measure of labor productivity as suggested by Stampp or the more complete measure that we employed. Why, then, did Stampp err so badly?

The problem is not lodged in a failure to take account of products other than cotton nor in a lack of sophistication in the measurement of the labor input. These conclusions arise from a consideration of table C.3, which shows that even if one restricts output just to cotton, large plantations, as a group, are strikingly more productive than small ones — the advantage being on the order of 2 to 1. Indeed, omission of other crops and livestock actually serves to exaggerate the advantage of large over small holdings (cf. **B.6.2.4**). Comparison of columns 2 and 3 of table C.3 shows that the results are also insensitive to the adjustments for the labor input. As it turns out, the higher ratio of women and children to adult males in the labor forces of large plantations is offset by a lower labor force participation rate of both male and female whites and a larger proportion of workers involved in nonfield activities.

The key to Stampp's error is suggested by table C.4, which reveals that only a very small proportion of "modest" slaveholdings matched the average productivity of the larger plantations. Whether arrayed according to cotton production per capita or per equivalent full field hand, less than 20 percent of the small holdings were as productive as the average medium-size plantation. When the comparison shifts to large plantations (those with 50 or more slaves) less than 12 percent of the small holdings equaled or exceeded the average of that class.

Stampp apparently did not calculate a proper frequency distribution. If he had, he would have known that only the top 10 or 20 percent of "modest" slaveholders attained levels of cotton productivity that matched the records of the typical medium or large planters. These were the "many" small slaveholdings whose cotton productivity "astonished" him. The other 80 percent of the small slaveholders did not reach 60 percent of the level of productivity that prevailed on the typical large plantation. "Modest" slaveholders who achieved levels "of bales per hand" that "easily" matched "the records of planters" were exceptional not only in the sense of rare but also in the sense that they probably included many of those especially talented entrepreneurs who, had the system continued, would have risen into the ranks of medium and large planters.

Of course a frequency distribution by itself would not have revealed that "modest" slaveholders did face an "overwhelming" disadvantage in cotton production. More complex procedures would have been necessary to resolve that issue (see **B.6.1–B.6.3**). But a frequency distribution would have revealed that farms of "modest" size had in fact been overwhelmed (submerged) as cotton producers. For while those with 19 or fewer slaves represented 88 percent of the farms of the cotton belt, they produced only 37 percent of the cotton. On the other hand, planters with 20 or more slaves produced 63 percent of the cotton, although they represented just 12 percent of the farms. Not only did large-scale farms dominate the raising of this crop, but there is no evidence that the process of concentrating the production of cotton on large plantations had come to an end by 1860 (see **B.6.3.2**).

It is difficult to assess fully the consequence of Stampp's confusion of the exceptional and the typical on his perception of the economic efficiency of plantations, since his discussion of the question of efficiency is so limited. However, the same confusion arose in Stampp's assessment of the material conditions of life for slaves. Here the consequences of his failure to follow established statistical procedures are more apparent.

We have already referred to the exaggeration of slave morbidity which arose because *The Peculiar Institution* reports letters and diaries describing exceptional periods of illness instead of providing a computation of the mean number of days lost per man year derived from systematic data (see **6.2**).

Stampp's conclusion that the diet of slaves was inadequate is supported by citations to one article in an agricultural journal which gave questionable nutritional advice to planters, reports in two slave narratives, reports by three planters (that may be incomplete) of the food fed to slaves on their estates, and critical statements made by six other observers along the lines that the slave diet was "coarse, crude, and wanting in variety" and that there were "many farmers" who "feed their negroes sparingly, believing that it is economy" [303, pp. 283–286].

Of course, many reports in the same sources give a quite different picture. For example, the majority of ex-slaves who commented on their diet in the W.P.A. narratives indicated that it was good or very good [104]. Stampp did not seek to resolve these conflicting claims, as he could have, by using the U.S. Department of Agriculture method for estimating food consumption on data in the manuscript schedules. For reasons stated in appendix B (see **B.4.2.2.1**), this technique can only be applied to large plantations. Since Stampp believed that the diet of slaves was poorer on large than on small plantations [303, p. 288], a test based on large plantations would have been appropriate. If nothing more, the issue of the average diet of slaves for at least this class of plantations would have been resolved on a more satisfactory basis than the arbitrary selection of a few quotations.

On no issue did Stampp make greater use of quantitative evidence than on the question of slave mortality. He drew data from three sources. First, he cited Sydnor's estimate of the expectation of life for Mississippi slaves aged 20. Second, he presented a series of statistics which he obtained from the published census for 1850. Third, he reported findings obtained from the records of six plantations. Each of these efforts was flawed either by failures to adjust for various biases in the data, by the unrepresentativeness of his samples, or by errors in computational procedures.

The most serious computational errors were not Stampp's but Sydnor's. Sydnor attempted to compute life expectations in two different ways, both of which were wrong [319]. The standard definition of life expectation at age i is, of course,

$$(C.1) \quad E_i = \sum_{j=i+1}^{m} P_j X_j$$

where

E_i = the life expectation at age i

P_j = the probability of just surviving from age i to age j

$X_j = j - i$ years.

Sydnor made two attempts at carrying through the procedure indicated by equation C.1. In his first attempt Sydnor based himself not on equation C.1 but on

$$(C.2) \quad E_i = \frac{\sum_{j=i+1}^{m} L_j}{L_i}$$

where L_j is the number of persons alive at age j. Equation C.2 is an approximation to C.1 which, under certain circumstances, gives good results while reducing the complexity of the computation. Three conditions are required for the approximation to work well. One is the availability of information on the age distribution of the population by single years of age. The second is that the population in question is stationary (not increasing). The third is that the population is closed (that there is no in- or out-migration).

None of these conditions were met in Sydnor's case. The censuses of 1850 and 1860 reported the ages of persons over 20 only by ten-year intervals. And, of course, the slave population of Mississippi was growing quite rapidly, because of both a high rate of natural increase and a high rate of net in-migration. Equation C.2 could have been adjusted to take account of these difficulties but Sydnor did not do so. As a consequence his calculations on the 1850 data yielded life expectations at age 20 of 14.23 years for free persons and 12.53 years for slaves. The same computation on the 1860 data yielded corresponding figures of 14.54 and 12.65 years.

Sydnor's second attempt was based on the verbal explanation contained in his sources of the formula for life expectation. Unfortunately, Sydnor was no better at understanding verbal mathematics than he was at symbolic mathematics. He also misinterpreted the verbal discussion. This time the error was in his manner of estimating P_j. Instead of finding the percentage of persons just surviving from age i to age j, he computed

$$(\text{C.3}) \quad \frac{d_j}{\sum\limits_{j=20}^{100} d_j}$$

where d_j was the number of persons aged j who died during the census year 1850. Sydnor's second computation yielded free and slave life expectations at age 20 of 27.72 years and 22.30 years respectively.

Both of Sydnor's computations resulted in gross underestimates of life expectations. Evans, who carried out the calculations correctly, found that life expectations at age 20 were 40.9 years for whites and 39.0 years for slaves in 1850 [105, p. 212].

Sydnor's two alternative methods for computing life expectations appear to have puzzled Stampp. For Sydnor provided no explanation as to why the two alternative methods should yield such large differences. Stampp did not report the results of either of the two attempts nor did he question why they differed. He resolved the problem by averaging Sydnor's 1860 result under the first calculation with the result under the second calculation, reporting that in Mississippi "[T]he life expectancy of slaves at this age was 17.5 years, of whites 19.2 years" [303, p. 319].

Sydnor's extremely low estimates of life expectation may have spurred Stampp's partial resurrection of the old abolitionist charge that slaveholders maximized profit by working slaves to death in seven years. "[N]either public opinion," wrote Stampp, nor high prices prevented some of the bondsmen from suffering physical breakdowns and early deaths because of overwork. The abolitionists never proved their claim that many sugar and cotton growers deliberately worked their slaves to death every seven years with the intention of replacing them from profits. Yet some of the great planters came close to accomplishing that result without designing it. In the "race for wealth" in which, according to one Louisiana planter, all were enlisted, few proprietors managed their estates according to the code of the patricians. They were sometimes remarkably shortsighted in the use of their investments [303, pp. 81–82].

The only quantitative evidence that Stampp cited, other than Sydnor's, which might be construed as support for this thesis, is of questionable relevance. Stampp was impressed by the fact that in 1860 only 3.5 percent of slaves were over 60 while 4.4 percent of whites exceeded that age [303, p. 318]. These percentages are, of course, quite useless as proxies for the life expectations of the elderly, since the percentage of the aged among slaves could have differed from the percentage among whites, even if expectations were identical, both because the slave birthrate exceeded the white birthrate [307] and because of white immigration. Evans's life table for 1850 shows that at age 60 white life expectation differed from that of slaves by just six tenths of a year. The respective figures were 16.0 years and 15.4 years. At age 70, slave life expectation exceeded that of whites by a quarter of a year [105, p. 212].

Stampp also emphasized the census of 1860 report of a higher crude death rate for slaves (1.8 percent) than for whites (1.2 percent) [303, p. 318]. But the inference that these differences were necessarily due to poor treatment of slaves is, again, unwarranted. Stampp did not realize that the slave death rate had to be adjusted for the higher fertility rates among slaves than among free women. Given the extremely high infant death rate, greater slave fertility would have made the crude death rate of slaves higher than that of whites even if both groups had had identical *age-specific* death rates. Moreover, Stampp made no effort to adjust for the difference in the epidemiological environments of the North and South. Since virtually all slaves lived in the South, while only a third of the white population lived there, the slave death rate would exceed the national white death rate even if both groups had identical *region-specific* death rates. Work is now underway to determine the death rate of whites in the South for 1850 and 1860. As reported in appendix B, it will be several years before this work is completed. Preliminary results suggest that within the South, white and slave death rates were not significantly different (see **B.4.5.3** and T.4, pp. 123–126).

Stampp's tendency to confuse the exceptional with the typical reappears in his discussion of infant mortality. In support of his contention that the comparison between the infant death rate of slaves and whites was "fantastic" [303, p. 319], Stampp offered the following [303, p. 320]:

Slaveholders who kept their own vital statistics produced grim documentation of these conditions. William J. Minor had one of the least disheartening records on his Louisiana sugar plantation, "Waterloo," where out of 209 live births between 1834 and 1857, only 44 (21 per cent) died before the age of five. In Bertie County, North Carolina, Stephen A. Norfleet listed 24 births during the 1850's, of whom sixteen (67 per cent) died in infancy. In Charleston District, South Carolina, Keating S. Ball recorded 111 births during an eleven-year period, of whom 38 died before the age of one and 15 more between the ages of one and four. On St. Simon Island, Georgia, Fanny Kemble interviewed 9 slave women who together had had 12 miscarriages and 55 live births; 29 of their children were dead. These infants were the victims of the ignorance that made tetanus such a killer, of neglect by slave mothers whose days were spent in the fields, and of "mismanagement" by their masters.

One problem with this paragraph is the inconsistency in the measure of infant deaths. Demographers define "infant" deaths as those which occur before age one. In this paragraph Stampp befuddles "infant" and "child" death rates in three of the five plantations to which he refers. On the Waterloo plantation his death statistic is for children under five. In Kemble's case, the ages of the children at time of death are unknown since Kemble provided no information on this matter and the demographic records of her husband's plantation are not available. In the case of Norfleet, we have been unable to reconstruct Stampp's count. Part of the difficulty arises from the unsuitability of that plantation for the calculation of infant death rates. The Norfleet records frequently list deaths by year only, not by month and day. When both birth and death occur in the same calendar year, no ambiguity arises. In half of the eligible cases, however, death occurred in the calendar year following that of birth. There is no way of knowing which of these ambiguous cases was actually an infant death. But even if all of them are included in the category of infant deaths, the count still falls short of the figure of 16 listed by Stampp. This suggests that Stampp again included child deaths in his count.

The main shortcoming of Stampp's paragraph, however, is that his discussion revolves around the exceptional rather than the average. Stampp reported on the death rates in only 3 of the record groups (Minor, Norfleet, and Ball) in his sample of plantation documents. However, 10 additional record groups among those he examined also contained data on infant mortality. Had he used all of the data available to him, he would have discovered that Norfleet and Ball were far above the mean infant death rate for his total sample. The mean infant death rate, Norfleet included, is 19.5 percent. If the Norfleet plantation is dropped because of the dubious nature of its entries, the mean becomes 18.5 percent. Currently available estimates indicate that the Southwide infant death rate among whites in 1850 was 17.7 percent (see **B.4.5.3**). The small difference between this figure and the average in the Stampp sample might well be explained by the fact that a number of the entries in the sample pertain to years much earlier than 1850 as well as to years of epidemics.

Nor does the available evidence sustain Stampp's claim that morbidity and mortality rates were most severe on sugar and rice plantations [303, pp. 296-299]. In regressions containing dummy variables for such plantations, the dummies are not statistically significant. The dummy for rice is small and positive while the dummy for sugar is small and negative. The effect of treatment and of the size and type of plantation on the demographic experience of slaves must remain a moot issue, at least until current efforts to probe more deeply into available data on mortality are completed (see T.4, pp. 123-126; **B.4.5**).

6.4. Despite the fact that *The Peculiar Institution* attacked four of the five propositions of Phillips's version of the traditional interpretation of the slave economy, the initial effect of Stampp's book was to reinforce rather than to undermine the tradition. What appears to have impressed readers most was not Stampp's rejection of the traditional view on profit, viability, and growth but his forceful reiteration of the abolitionist contention of extremely cruel, harsh treatment. As a consequence, the immediate impact of *The Peculiar Institution* was the restoration of the traditional interpretation in its original, pre-Phillips form.

On the other hand, Stampp contributed powerfully to shifting historical concern from the planter to the slave. Whatever the limitations of his discussion of slave culture, he did help to push this issue to the center of attention. Whatever the limitations of his discussion of the moral issue, he did succeed in reasserting its primacy. No historian who turned to the question of slavery after the publication of Stampp's book could again afford to treat slaves merely as ill-defined, shadowy objects. Stampp, to paraphrase Woodson, made the revelation of the slave mind the order of the day among historians of the antebellum South. Of course Elkins [101], among other writers, Negro and white, as well as broader social forces, also contributed to the new direction. But Stampp's influence on the discussions that have ensued during the seventeen years following the publication of *The Peculiar Institution* has been pervasive.

7. Since the mid-1950s there has, of course, been an enormous expansion of research into black history in general and into the slave era in particular. As a consequence it is impossible for us to discuss adequately, within the confines of this book, the many directions of recent thought.

We have in the main text, and in appendix B, attempted to set forth the most important new contributions to those questions which bear directly on economic matters. But we have, at best, only adumbrated some of the considerable advances that have been made in the study of comparative systems of slavery, the reconstruction of the history of slavery in particular areas of the Caribbean and South America, the inquiry into the effect of slavery on black personalities, the analysis of black cultural development during the antebellum era (including the rediscovery of Negro achievements under slavery), the re-examination of the nature of the slave family and the challenge of the old belief regarding matriarchal domination of the black family, the reconsideration of the sources and manifestations of racism (North and South) including the reconsideration of the motivation for political opposition to slavery in the antebellum North, the unfolding of the process of emancipation in the northern states and in the rest of the Western Hemisphere, the delineation of the various postemancipation restrictions on black labor throughout the hemisphere, and the re-evaluation of the treatment of slave labor within the system of sanctions applied against all labor from the seventeenth through the nineteenth centuries.

During much of the past seventeen years this rich and many-sided re-examination of the slave experience took place independent of, or only marginally influenced by, the work of the cliometricians. As pointed out in appendix B, until the mid-1960s the cliometricians tended to focus on a fairly limited set of issues, and were involved with rather esoteric (but quite important) problems of economic theory and measurement. It was only after they began to collect large samples of new data from manuscript records, and as they sought to use these data to determine the

246

sources of the southern food supply, to estimate production functions, to measure the inequality of the wealth distribution, and to compare the relative efficiency of slave and free agriculture that cliometric research became strongly connected with the mainstream of research into black history. For in the course of examining these new bodies of data, the cliometricians discovered much new information bearing on the composition of slave diets, the distribution of slave skills, demographic characteristics of the slave population, slave health experience, the nature of slave families, and the quality of slave labor.

List of References

The list that follows is not a complete bibliography of sources relevant to an understanding of American Negro slavery. It is limited to items cited in appendixes B and C. See the bibliographies in [223] and [357] for relevant works not listed here.

1. Adamson, Alan H. *Sugar Without Slaves: The Political Economy of British Guiana, 1838-1904.* New Haven: Yale University Press, 1972.
2. *American Historical Review* 55 (July, 1950).
3. Anstey, Roger T. "The Volume and Profitability of the British Slave Trade, 1761-1807," in Stanley L. Engerman and Eugene D. Genovese (eds.). *Race and Slavery in the Western Hemisphere: Quantitative Studies.* Princeton: Princeton University Press, 1974.
4. Aptheker, Herbert. "American Negro Slave Revolts." *Science and Society* I (Summer, 1937): 512-538.
5. —— *Negro Slave Revolts in the United States, 1526-1860.* New York: International Publishers, 1939.
6. —— "Maroons Within the Present Limits of the United States." *Journal of Negro History* XXIV (April, 1939): 167-184.
7. —— *American Negro Slave Revolts.* ("Studies in History, Economics and Public Law, edited by the Faculty of Political Science of Columbia University," No. 501.) New York: Columbia University Press, 1943.
8. Ashley, W.J. "On the Study of Economic History." *Quarterly Journal of Economics* VII (January, 1893): 115-136.
9. Awad, Mohamed. *Report on Slavery.* United Nations, Economic and Social Council, Special Rapporteur on Slavery. New York: United Nations, 1966.
10. Ballagh, James Curtis. *A History of Slavery in Virginia.* ("Johns Hopkins University Studies in Historical and Political Science," Extra Vol. XXIV.) Baltimore: Johns Hopkins Press, 1902.

11. Bancroft, Frederic. *Slave Trading in the Old South.* Introduction by Allan Nevins. New York: Frederick Ungar, 1959.

12. Bassett, John Spencer. *Slavery in the State of North Carolina.* ("Johns Hopkins University Studies in Historical and Political Science," Series XVII, No. 7–8.) Baltimore: Johns Hopkins Press, 1899.

13. Bateman, Fred. "Improvement in American Dairy Farming, 1850–1910: A Quantitative Analysis." *Journal of Economic History* XXVIII (June, 1968): 255–273.

14. Battalio, Raymond C. and Kagel, John. "The Structure of Antebellum Southern Agriculture: South Carolina, A Case Study." *Agricultural History* XLIV (January, 1970): 25–37.

15. Bauer, Raymond A. and Bauer, Alice H. "Day to Day Resistance to Slavery." *Journal of Negro History* XXVII (October, 1942): 388–419.

16. Beale, Howard K. "What Historians Have Said About the Causes of the Civil War," in *Theory and Practice in Historical Study.* Social Science Research Council Bulletin No. 54. New York: Social Science Research Council, 1946, pp. 55–102.

17. Bean, Richard Nelson and Thomas, Robert Paul. "The Fishers of Men: The Profits of the Slave Trade." Unpublished paper, 1973.

18. Bennett, Merrill K. and Peirce, Rosamond H. "Change in the American National Diet, 1879–1959." *Food Research Institute Studies* II (May, 1961): 95–119.

19. Bergman, Abraham B. and Beckwith, J. Bruce. "Sudden Death Syndrome of Infancy," in Morris Green and Robert J. Haggerty (eds.). *Ambulatory Pediatrics.* Philadelphia: W.B. Saunders Co., 1968, pp. 777–780.

20. Bidwell, Percy Wells and Falconer, John I. *History of Agriculture in the Northern United States, 1620–1860.* Washington, D.C.: Carnegie Institution, 1925.

21. Blassingame, John W. *The Slave Community: Plantation Life in the Antebellum South.* New York: Oxford University Press, 1972.

22. Blum, Jerome. *Lord and Peasant in Russia from the Ninth to the Nineteenth Century.* Princeton: Princeton University Press, 1961.

23. Boas, Franz. "Anthropology," in Edwin R. A. Seligman (ed.). *The Encyclopedia of the Social Sciences.* Vol. II. New York: Macmillan, 1930, pp. 73–110.

24. Bonner, James C. "Plantation and Farm: The Agricultural South," in Arthur S. Link and Rembert W. Patrick (eds.). *Writing Southern History: Essays in Historiography in Honor of Fletcher M. Green.* Baton Rouge: Louisiana State University Press, 1965, pp. 147–174.

25. Bornet, Vaughn D. Review of *The Health of Slaves on Southern Plantations* by William Dosite Postell. *American Historical Review* 57 (July, 1952): 1063–1064.

26. Brackett, Jeffrey R. *The Negro in Maryland: A Study of the Institution of Slavery.* ("Johns Hopkins University Studies in Historical and Political Science," Extra Vol. VI.) Baltimore: Johns Hopkins Press, 1889.

27. Brewer, William M. Review of *The Peculiar Institution: Slavery in the Ante-Bellum South* by Kenneth M. Stampp. *Journal of Negro History* XLII (April, 1957): 142–144.

28. Brown, William Garrott. *The Lower South in American History.* New York: Macmillan, 1902.

29. Budd, Edward C. "Factor Shares, 1850–1910," in Conference on Research in Income and Wealth, *Trends in the American Economy in the Nineteenth Century.* Studies in Income and Wealth, Vol. 24. Princeton: Princeton University Press, 1960, pp. 365–406.

30. Burgess, John W. *The Middle Period, 1817–1858.* Vol. 4 of *The American*

History Series. New York: Charles Scribner's Sons, 1897.

31. Butlin, N.G. *Ante-bellum Slavery – Critique of a Debate.* Canberra: Department of Economic History, Australian National University, 1971.

32. Cade, John B. "Out of the Mouth of Ex-Slaves." *Journal of Negro History* XX (July, 1935): 294–337.

33. Cairnes, J.E. *The Slave Power: Its Character, Career, and Probable Designs: Being an Attempt to Explain the Real Issues Involved in the American Contest.* Introduction by Harold D. Woodman. New York: Harper & Row, 1969.

34. Calderhead, William. "How Extensive Was the Border State Slave Trade?: A New Look." *Civil War History* XVIII (March, 1972): 42–55.

35. Carey, Henry C. *The Slave Trade, Domestic & Foreign.* Philadelphia: A. Hart, 1853.

36. Carroll, Joseph Cephas. *Slave Insurrections in the United States, 1800–1865.* Boston: Chapman & Grimes, 1938.

37. Catterall, Helen Tunicliff (ed.). *Judicial Cases Concerning American Slavery and the Negro.* 5 vols. Washington, D.C.: Carnegie Institution, 1926–1937.

38. Cauthen, C.E., with the collaboration of Lewis P. Jones. "The Coming of the Civil War," in Arthur S. Link and Rembert W. Patrick (eds.). *Writing Southern History: Essays in Historiography in Honor of Fletcher M. Green.* Baton Rouge: Louisiana State University Press, 1965, pp. 224–248.

39. Channing, Edward. *A History of the United States.* 6 vols. New York: Macmillan, 1905–1925.

40. Chapin, Robert Coit. *The Standard of Living among Workingmen's Families in New York City.* New York: Charities Publication Committee, 1909.

41. Clapham, J.H. "Economic History: Survey of Development to the Twentieth Century," in Edwin R.A. Seligman (ed.). *The Encyclopedia of the Social Sciences.* Vol. V. New York: Macmillan, 1931, pp. 315–320.

42. —— "Economic History as a Discipline," in Edwin R.A. Seligman (ed.). *The Encyclopedia of the Social Sciences.* Vol. V. New York: Macmillan, 1931, pp. 327–330.

43. Clark, Blanche Henry. *The Tennessee Yeoman, 1840–1860.* Nashville: Vanderbilt University Press, 1942.

44. Clark, Victor S. *History of Manufactures in the United States.* 3 vols. Washington, D.C.: Carnegie Institution, 1916–1929.

45. Coale, Ansley J. and Demeny, Paul. *Regional Model Life Tables and Stable Populations.* Princeton: Princeton University Press, 1966.

46. Cole, Arthur H. "Economic History in the United States: Formative Years of a Discipline." *Journal of Economic History* XXVIII (December, 1968): 556–589.

47. —— "The Committee on Research in Economic History: An Historical Sketch." *Journal of Economic History* XXX (December, 1970): 723–741.

48. Coleman, J. Winston, Jr. *Slavery Times in Kentucky.* Chapel Hill: University of North Carolina Press, 1940.

49. Coles, Harry L., Jr. "Some Notes on Slaveownership and Landownership in Louisiana, 1850–1860." *Journal of Southern History* IX (August, 1943): 381–394.

50. Collins, Winfield H. *The Domestic Slave Trade of the Southern States.* New York: Broadway Publishing Company, 1904.

51. Commons, John R., et al. *A Documentary History of American Industrial Society.* 11 vols. Cleveland: The A. H. Clark Co., 1910–1911.

52. ——*History of Labour in the United States.* 4 vols. New York: MacMillan, 1918–1935.

53. Conrad, Alfred H. and Meyer, John R. "The Economics of Slavery in the

Ante Bellum South." *Journal of Political Economy* 66 (April, 1958): 95-130. Reprinted in their book, *The Economics of Slavery and Other Studies in Econometric History.* Chicago: Aldine, 1964, pp. 43-92.

54. Conrad, Alfred H., et al. "Slavery as an Obstacle to Economic Growth in the United States: A Panel Discussion." *Journal of Economic History* XXVII (December, 1967): 518-560.

55. Cooke, Jacob E. *Frederic Bancroft, Historian.* Norman: University of Oklahoma Press, 1957.

56. Cooley, Henry S. *A Study of Slavery in New Jersey.* ("Johns Hopkins University Studies in Historical and Political Science," 14th Series, IX-X.) Baltimore: Johns Hopkins Press, 1896.

57. Cooper, Martin R., Barton, Glen T., Brodell, Albert P. *Progress of Farm Mechaniza tion.* U.S. Department of Agriculture, Miscellaneous Publication No. 630. Washington, D.C.: 1947.

58. Craton, Michael. "Jamaican Slave Mortality: Fresh Light from Worthy Park, Longville, and the Tharp Estates." *Journal of Caribbean History* 3 (November, 1971): 1-27.

59. —— "Jamaican Slavery," in Stanley L. Engerman and Eugene D. Genovese (eds.). *Race and Slavery in the Western Hemisphere: Quantitative Studies.* Princeton: Princeton University Press, 1974.

60. Craven, Avery. *The Repressible Conflict, 1830-1861.* University: Louisiana State University Press, 1939.

61. —— *The Coming of the Civil War.* New York: Charles Scribner's Sons, 1942.

62. —— *The Growth of Southern Nationalism, 1848-1861.* Vol. VI of *A History of the South.* Edited by Wendell Holmes Stephenson and E. Merton Coulter. Baton Rouge: Louisiana State University Press, 1953.

63. Cruden, Robert. "James Ford Rhodes and the Negro: A Study in the Problem of Objectivity." *Ohio History* 71 (July, 1962): 129-137.

64. Curlee, Abigail. "A Study of Texas Slave Plantations, 1822 to 1865." Unpublished Ph.D. dissertation, University of Texas, 1932.

65. Curtin, Philip D. *The Atlantic Slave Trade: A Census.* Madison: University of Wisconsin Press, 1969.

66. —— "Measuring the Atlantic Slave Trade," in Stanley L. Engerman and Eugene D. Genovese (eds.). *Race and Slavery in the Western Hemisphere: Quantitative Studies.* Princeton: Princeton University Press, 1974.

67. David, Paul A. "The Growth of Real Product in the United States Before 1840: New Evidence, Controlled Conjectures." *Journal of Economic History* XXVII (June, 1967): 151-197.

68. Davis, Charles S. *The Cotton Kingdom in Alabama.* Montgomery: Alabama State Department of Archives and History, 1939.

69. Davis, David Brion. "James Cropper and the British Anti-Slavery Movement, 1821-1823." *Journal of Negro History* XLV (October, 1960): 241-258.

70. —— "James Cropper and the British Anti-Slavery Movement, 1823-1833." *Journal of Negro History* XLVI (July, 1961): 154-173.

71. —— *The Problem of Slavery in Western Culture.* Ithaca: Cornell University Press, 1966.

72. Davis, Edwin Adams (ed.). *Plantation Life in the Florida Parishes of Louisiana 1836-1844, as Reflected in the Diary of Bennet H. Barrow.* New York: Columbia University Press, 1943.

73. Deane, Phyllis and Cole, W.A. *British Economic Growth, 1688-1959: Trends and Structure.* Second edition. Cambridge: University Press, 1967.

74. Deerr, Noel. *The History of Sugar.* 2 vols. London: Chapman and Hall, 1949-1950.

75. Denison, Edward F. *Why Growth Rates Differ: Postwar Experience in Nine Western Countries.* Washington, D.C.: Brookings Institution, 1967.
76. Dickey, G. Edward and Wilson, Warren W. "Economies of Scale in Cotton Agriculture, 1850–1860." Unpublished paper, 1972.
77. Dodd, William E. *The Cotton Kingdom: A Chronicle of the Old South.* Vol. 27 of *The Chronicles of America.* Edited by Allen Johnson. New Haven: Yale University Press, 1919.
78. Domar, Evsey D. "On the Measurement of Technological Change." *Economic Journal* 71 (December, 1961): 709–729.
79. —— "On Total Productivity and All That." *Journal of Political Economy* 70 (December, 1962): 597–608.
80. Donnan, Elizabeth. *Documents Illustrative of the History of the Slave Trade to America.* 4 vols. Washington, D.C.: Carnegie Institution, 1930–1935.
81. Douglass, Frederick. *My Bondage and My Freedom.* Introduction by Philip S. Foner. New York: Dover Publications, 1969.
82. Dowd, Douglas F. "A Comparative Analysis of Economic Development in the American West and South." *Journal of Economic History* XVI (December, 1956): 558–574.
83. Dowson, J.L. and De Saussare, H.W. *Census of Charleston for 1848.* Charleston: J.B. Nixon, 1849.
84. Doyle, Bertram Wilbur. *The Etiquette of Race Relations in the South: A Study in Social Control.* Chicago: University of Chicago Press, 1937.
85. Drake, St. Clair and Cayton, Horace R. *Black Metropolis: A Study of Negro Life in a Northern City.* New York: Harcourt, Brace, 1945.
86. Du Bois, W.E. Burghardt. *The Suppression of the African Slave-Trade to the United States of America, 1638–1870.* ("Harvard Historical Studies," Vol. 1.) New York: Longmans, Green and Co., 1896.
87. —— *The Philadelphia Negro: A Social Study.* ("Series in Political Economy and Public Law," No. 14.). Philadelphia: University of Pennsylvania, 1899.
88. Du Bois, W.E. Burghardt (ed.). *The Negro American Family.* ("The Atlanta University Publications," No. 13.) Atlanta: Atlanta University Press, 1908.
89. Du Bois, W.E. Burghardt. "Reconstruction and Its Benefits." *American Historical Review* 15 (July, 1910): 781–799.
90. —— *The Souls of Black Folk: Essays and Sketches.* Chicago: A.C. McClurg & Co., 1911.
91. —— *The Negro.* New York: Henry Holt and Co., 1915.
92. —— Review of *American Negro Slavery* by Ulrich Bonnell Phillips. *American Political Science Review* XII (November, 1918): 722–726.
93. Easterlin, Richard A. "Interregional Differences in Per Capita Income, Population, and Total Income, 1840–1950," in Conference on Research in Income and Wealth. *Trends in the American Economy in the Nineteenth Century.* Studies in Income and Wealth, Vol. 24. Princeton: Princeton University Press, 1960, pp. 73–140.
94. —— "Regional Income Trends, 1840–1950," in Seymour Harris (ed.). *American Economic History.* New York: McGraw Hill, 1961, pp. 525–547.
95. —— "Farm Production and Income in Old and New Areas at Mid-Century," in David C. Klingaman and Richard K. Vedder (eds.). *The Old Northwest: Essays in Economic History.* Unpublished manuscript, 1973.
96. Eaton, Clement. *The Mind of the Old South.* Revised edition. Baton Rouge: Louisiana State University Press, 1967.
97. —— *The Waning of the Old South Civilization 1860–1880.* Athens: University of Georgia Press, 1968.

98. Eaton, John. *Political Economy: A Marxist Textbook.* New York: International Publishers, 1949.

99. Eblen, Jack Ericson. "On the Natural Increase of Slave Populations: The Example of the Cuban Black Population, 1775–1900," in Stanley L. Engerman and Eugene D. Genovese (eds.). *Race and Slavery in the Western Hemisphere: Quantitative Studies.* Princeton: Princeton University Press, 1974.

100. Edwards, G. Franklin. "E. Franklin Frazier," in David L. Sills (ed.). *International Encyclopedia of the Social Sciences.* Vol. 5. New York: Macmillan, 1968, pp. 553–554.

101. Elkins, Stanley M. *Slavery: A Problem in American Institutional and Intellectual Life.* Chicago: University of Chicago Press, 1959.

102. Engerman, Stanley L. "The Antebellum South: What Probably Was and What Should Have Been." *Agricultural History* XLIV (January, 1970): 127–142.

103. —— "The Slave Trade and British Capital Formation in the Eighteenth Century: A Comment on the Williams Thesis." *Business History Review* XLVI (Winter, 1972): 430–443.

104. Eriksen, Gary H. "Problems and Prospects in Quantifying the WPA Slave Narratives." Unpublished paper, University of Chicago, 1973.

105. Evans, Robert, Jr. "The Economics of American Negro Slavery," in Universities-National Bureau Committee for Economic Research. *Aspects of Labor Economics.* Princeton: Princeton University Press, 1962, pp. 185–243.

106. Farnam, Henry W. *Chapters in the History of Social Legislation in the United States to 1860.* Washington, D.C.: Carnegie Institution, 1938.

107. Ferguson, James M. (ed.). *Public Debt and Future Generations.* Chapel Hill: University of North Carolina Press, 1964.

108. Fielding, Ronald H. "American Slave Emancipation: The Costs in the South, the District of Columbia, and the North." Unpublished paper, 1973.

109. Fishlow, Albert. "Antebellum Interregional Trade Reconsidered," in Ralph L. Andreano (ed.). *New Views on American Economic Development: A Selective Anthology of Recent Work.* Cambridge: Schenkman Publishing Company, 1965, pp. 187–200.

110. —— "Postscript on Antebellum Interregional Trade," in Ralph L. Andreano (ed.). *New Views on American Economic Development: A Selective Anthology of Recent Work.* Cambridge: Schenkman Publishing Company, 1965, pp. 209–212.

111. Fishlow, Albert and Fogel, Robert W. "Quantitative Economic History: An Interim Evaluation: Past Trends and Present Tendencies." *Journal of Economic History* XXXI (March, 1971): 15–42.

112. Flanders, Ralph Betts. *Plantation Slavery in Georgia.* Chapel Hill: University of North Carolina Press, 1933.

113. Fogel, Robert William. *Railroads and American Economic Growth: Essays in Econometric History.* Baltimore: Johns Hopkins Press, 1964.

114. —— "A Provisional View of the 'New Economic History,'" in Ralph L. Andreano (ed.). *New Views on American Economic Development: A Selective Anthology of Recent Work.* Cambridge: Schenkman Publishing Company, 1965, pp. 201–208.

115. —— "American Interregional Trade in the 19th Century," in Ralph L. Andreano (ed.). *New Views on American Economic Development: A Selective Anthology of Recent Work.* Cambridge: Schenkman Publishing Company, 1965, pp. 213–224.

116. —— "The Reunification of Economic History and Economic Theory." *American Economic Review* LV (May, 1965): 92–98.

117. Fogel, Robert William and Engerman, Stanley L. "The Economics of Slavery,"

in Robert William Fogel and Stanley L. Engerman (eds.). *The Reinterpretation of American Economic History*. New York: Harper & Row, 1971, pp. 311–341.

118. —— "The Relative Efficiency of Slavery: A Comparison of Northern and Southern Agriculture in 1860." *Explorations in Economic History* 8 (Spring, 1971): 353–367.

119. —— "A New Index of Slave Prices in New Orleans." Forthcoming.

120. Food and Nutrition Board, National Academy of Sciences. *Recommended Dietary Allowances*. Publication 1146. 6th revised edition. Washington, D.C.: National Academy of Science, National Research Council, 1964.

121. Foust, James D. "The Yeoman Farmer and Westward Expansion of U.S. Cotton Production." Unpublished Ph.D. dissertation, University of North Carolina, 1967.

122. Foust, James D. and Swan, Dale E. "Productivity and Profitability of Antebellum Slave Labor: A Micro Approach." *Agricultural History* XLIV (January, 1970): 39–62.

123. Franklin, John Hope. *The Free Negro in North Carolina, 1790–1860*. Chapel Hill: University of North Carolina Press, 1943.

124. —— "Slaves Virtually Free in Ante-Bellum North Carolina." *Journal of Negro History* XXVIII (July, 1943): 284–310.

125. —— "The Enslavement of Free Negroes in North Carolina." *Journal of Negro History* XXIX (October, 1944): 401–428.

126. —— *From Slavery to Freedom: A History of American Negroes*. New York: Alfred A. Knopf, 1947.

127. —— "The New Negro History." *Journal of Negro History* XLII (April, 1957): 89–97.

128. Frazier, E. Franklin. "The Negro Slave Family." *Journal of Negro History* XV (April, 1930): 198–259.

129. —— *The Negro Family in the United States*. Chicago: University of Chicago Press, 1939.

130. —— *The Negro in the United States*. New York: Macmillan, 1949.

131. Frederickson, George M. and Lasch, Christopher. "Resistance to Slavery." *Civil War History* XIII (December, 1967): 315–329.

132. Galambos, Louis. *American Business History*. ("Service Center for Teachers of History," Publication Number 70.) Washington, D.C.: American Historical Association, 1967.

133. Gallman, Robert E. "Gross National Product in the United States, 1834–1909," in Conference on Research in Income and Wealth. *Output, Employment, and Productivity in the United States After 1800*. Studies in Income and Wealth, Vol. 30. New York: Columbia University Press, 1966, pp. 3–76.

134. —— "Trends in the Size Distribution of Wealth in the Nineteenth Century: Some Speculations," in Conference on Research in Income and Wealth. *Six Papers on the Size Distribution of Wealth and Income*. Studies in Income and Wealth, Vol. 33. New York: Columbia University Press, 1969, pp. 1–25.

135. —— "Self-Sufficiency in the Cotton Economy of the Antebellum South." *Agricultural History* XLIV (January, 1970): 5–23.

136. Gallman, Robert E. and Howle, Edward S. "Trends in the Structure of the American Economy since 1840," in Robert William Fogel and Stanley L. Engerman (eds.). *The Reinterpretation of American Economic History*. New York: Harper & Row, 1971, pp. 25–37.

137. Gallman, Robert E. and Weiss, Thomas J. "The Service Industries in the Nineteenth Century," in Conference on Research in Income and Wealth. *Production and Productivity in the Service Industries*. Studies in Income and Wealth,

Vol. 34. New York: Columbia University Press, 1969, pp. 287–352.

138. Genovese, Eugene D. "The Medical and Insurance Costs of Slaveholding in the Cotton Belt." *Journal of Negro History* XLV (July, 1960): 141-155.

139. —— *The Political Economy of Slavery: Studies in the Economy & Society of the Slave South.* New York: Pantheon, 1965.

140. —— *In Red and Black: Marxian Explorations in Southern and Afro-American History.* New York: Pantheon, 1971.

141. —— *Roll, Jordan, Roll: Afro-American Slaves in the Making of the Modern World.* New York: Pantheon, 1974.

142. Gibson, Arthur H. *Human Economics.* London: Longmans, Green and Co. 1909.

143. Gilbert, Milton and Kravis, Irving B. *An International Comparison of National Products and the Purchasing Power of Currencies: A Study of the United States, the United Kingdom, France, Germany & Italy.* Paris: Organization for European Economic Cooperation, 1954.

144. Gilbert, Milton and Associates. *Comparative National Products and Price Levels: A Study of Western Europe and the United States.* Paris: Organization for European Economic Cooperation, 1958.

145. Glass, Bentley and Li, C.C. "The Dynamics of Racial Intermixture – an Analysis Based on the American Negro." *American Journal of Human Genetics* V (March, 1953): 1-20.

146. Goldin, Claudia Dale. "The Economics of Urban Slavery: 1820 to 1860." Unpublished Ph.D. dissertation, University of Chicago, 1972.

147. —— "The Economics of Emancipation." *Journal of Economic History* XXXIII (March, 1973): 66-85.

148. —— "A Model to Explain the Relative Decline of Urban Slavery: Empirical Results," in Stanley L. Engerman and Eugene D. Genovese (eds.). *Race and Slavery in the Western Hemisphere: Quantitative Studies.* Princeton: Princeton University Press, 1974.

149. Goodrich, Carter. "Recent Contributions to Economic History: The United States, 1789-1860." *Journal of Economic History* XIX (March, 1959): 25-43.

150. Govan, Thomas P. "Was Plantation Slavery Profitable?" *Journal of Southern History* VIII (November, 1942): 513-535.

151. —— "Comments" [to Robert Evans, Jr., "The Economics of American Negro Slavery"], in Universities-National Bureau Committee for Economic Research. *Aspects of Labor Economics.* Princeton: Princeton University Press, 1962, pp. 243-246.

152. Gras, N.S.B. "The Rise and Development of Economic History." *Economic History Review* I (January, 1927): 12-34.

153. —— "Economic History in the United States," in Edwin R.A. Seligman (ed.). *The Encyclopedia of the Social Sciences.* Vol. V. New York: Macmillan, 1931, pp. 325-327.

154. Gray, Lewis Cecil. *History of Agriculture in the Southern United States to 1860.* 2 vols. Washington, D.C.: Carnegie Institution, 1933.

155. Gray, Wood. "Ulrich Bonnell Phillips," in William T. Hutchinson (ed.). *The Marcus W. Jernegan Essays in American Historiography.* Chicago: University of Chicago Press, 1937, pp. 354-373.

156. Greene, Lorenzo Johnston. *The Negro in Colonial New England, 1620-1776.* ("Studies in History, Economics and Public Law, edited by the Faculty of Political Science of Columbia University," No. 494.) New York: Columbia University Press, 1942.

157. —— "The New England Negro as Seen in Advertisements for Runaway Slaves." *Journal of Negro History* XXIX (April, 1944): 125-146.
158. Greene, Lorenzo J. and Woodson, Carter G. *The Negro Wage Earner*. Washington, D.C.: The Association for the Study of Negro Life and History, 1930.
159. Greenidge, C.W.W. *Slavery*. London: George Allen & Unwin, 1958.
160. Griliches, Zvi. "The Sources of Measured Productivity Growth: United States Agriculture, 1940-60." *Journal of Political Economy* 71 (August, 1963): 331-346.
161. —— "Research Expenditures, Education, and the Aggregate Agricultural Production Function." *American Economic Review* LIV (December, 1964): 961-974.
162. Gross, Nachum T. "An Estimate of Industrial Product in Austria in 1841." *Journal of Economic History* XXVIII (March, 1968): 80-101.
163. —— "Economic Growth and the Consumption of Coal in Austria and Hungary, 1831-1913." *Journal of Economic History* XXXI (December, 1971): 898-916.
164. Gunderson, Gerald. "Southern Ante-bellum Income Reconsidered." *Explorations in Economic History* 10 (Winter, 1973): 151-176.
165. Gutman, Herbert G. "Le phénomène invisible: la composition de la famille et du foyer noirs après la Guerre de Sécession." *Annales, E. S. C.* 26 (Juillet-Octobre, 1972): 1197-1218.
166. —— *Afro-Americans: Their Families During and After Enslavement, 1760-1930: A New View*. New York: Pantheon, forthcoming.
167. Hacker, Louis M. *The Triumph of American Capitalism: The Development of Forces in American History to the End of the Nineteenth Century*. New York: Simon and Schuster, 1940.
168. Hart, Albert Bushnell. *Slavery and Abolition, 1831-1841*. Vol. XVI of *The American Nation: A History*. Edited by Albert Bushnell Hart. New York: Harper & Brothers, 1906.
169. Hart, Hornell and Hertz, Hilda. "Expectation of Life as an Index of Social Progress." *American Sociological Review* 9 (December, 1944): 609-621.
170. Hasse, Adelaide R. *Index of Economic Materials in Documents of the States of the United States: California, 1849-1904; Delaware, 1789-1904; Illinois, 1809-1904; Kentucky, 1792-1904; Maine, 1820-1904; New Hampshire, 1789-1904; New Jersey, 1789-1904; New York, 1789-1904; Ohio, 1787-1904; Pennsylvania, 1790-1904; Rhode Island, 1789-1904; Vermont, 1789-1904*. Washington, D.C.: Carnegie Institution, 1907-1919.
171. Heaton, Herbert. "Recent Developments in Economic History." *American Historical Review* 47 (July, 1942): 727-746.
172. Helper, Hinton Rowan. *The Impending Crisis of the South: How to Meet It*. Edited by George M. Frederickson. Cambridge: Belknap Press, 1968.
173. Henry, H.M. *The Police Control of the Slave in South Carolina*. Emory, Va.: 1914.
174. Hershberg, Theodore. "Free Blacks in Antebellum Philadelphia: A Study of Ex-Slaves, Freeborn, and Socioeconomic Decline." *Journal of Social History* 5 (Winter, 1971-1972): 183-209.
175. —— "Free-Born and Slave-Born Blacks in Antebellum Philadelphia," in Stanley L. Engerman and Eugene D. Genovese (eds.). *Race and Slavery in the Western Hemisphere: Quantitative Studies*. Princeton: Princeton University Press, 1974.
176. Herskovits, Melville J. "A Preliminary Consideration of the Culture Areas of

Africa." *American Anthropologist.* New Series 26 (January–March, 1924): 50-63.

177. —— *The American Negro: A Study in Racial Crossing.* New York: Alfred A. Knopf, 1928.

178. —— *The Myth of the Negro Past.* New York: Harper & Brothers, 1941.

179. Higman, Barry W. "Slave Population and Economy in Jamaica at the Time of Emancipation." Unpublished Ph.D. dissertation, University of the West Indies, 1970.

180. Hilliard, Sam Bowers. *Hog Meat and Hoecake: Food Supply in the Old South, 1840-1860.* Carbondale: Southern Illinois University Press, 1972.

181. Hofstadter, Richard. "U.B. Phillips and the Plantation Legend." *Journal of Negro History* XXIX (April, 1944): 109-124.

182. Holland, Dorothy F. and Perrott, George St. J. "Health of the Negro." *Milbank Memorial Fund Quarterly* XVI (January, 1938): 5-38.

183. Holmes, George K., et al. *Meat Situation in the United States.* U.S. Department of Agriculture: Report No. 109, 5 parts. Washington, D.C., 1916.

184. von Holst, H. *The Constitutional and Political History of the United States.* Translated by John J. Lalor. 8 vols. Chicago: Callaghan and Company, 1876-1892.

185. Homer, Sidney. *A History of Interest Rates.* New Brunswick: Rutgers University Press, 1963.

186. Hughes, Helen MacGill. "Robert E. Park," in David L. Sills (ed.). *International Encyclopedia of the Social Sciences.* Vol. 11. New York: Macmillan, 1968, pp. 416-419.

187. Hutchinson, William K. and Williamson, Samuel H. "The Self-Sufficiency of the Antebellum South: Estimates of the Food Supply." *Journal of Economic History* XXXI (September, 1971): 591-612.

188. Jackson, Luther Porter. *Free Negro Labor and Property Holding in Virginia, 1830-1860.* New York: Appleton-Century, 1942.

189. Jacobson, Paul H. "An Estimate of the Expectation of Life in the United States in 1850." *Milbank Memorial Fund Quarterly* XXXV (April, 1957): 197-201.

190. Jaffe, A.J. and Lourie, W.I., Jr. "An Abridged Life Table for the White Population of the United States in 1830." *Human Biology* XIV (September, 1942): 352-371.

191. Johnson, Charles S. *Shadow of the Plantation.* Chicago: University of Chicago Press, 1934.

192. —— *Growing Up in the Black Belt: Negro Youth in the Rural South.* Washington, D.C.: American Council on Education, 1941.

193. Johnson, D. Gale. "Allocation of Agricultural Income." *Journal of Farm Economics* XXX (November, 1948): 724-749.

194. Johnson, Emory R., et al. *History of Domestic and Foreign Commerce of the United States.* 2 vols. Washington, D.C.: Carnegie Institution, 1915.

195. Johnson, Guion Griffis. *A Social History of the Sea Islands: With Special Reference to St. Helena Island, South Carolina.* Chapel Hill: University of North Carolina Press, 1930.

196. —— *Ante-Bellum North Carolina: A Social History.* Chapel Hill: University of North Carolina Press, 1937.

197. Jones, Bobby F. "A Cultural Middle Passage: Slave Marriage and Family in the Ante-Bellum South." Unpublished Ph.D. dissertation, University of North Carolina, 1965.

198. Kaser, David. "Nashville's Women of Pleasure in 1860." *Tennessee Historical Quarterly* XXIII (December, 1964): 379-382.

199. Kemble, Frances Anne. *Journal of a Residence on a Georgian Plantation in*

1838-1839. Edited, with an introduction, by John A. Scott. New York: Alfred A. Knopf, 1961.

200. Kendrick, John W. *Productivity Trends in the United States.* Princeton: Princeton University Press, 1961.

201. Klein, Herbert S. "The Trade in African Slaves to Rio de Janeiro, 1795–1811: Estimates of Mortality and Patterns of Voyages." *Journal of African History* X (1969): 533–549.

202. Klingberg, Frank W. Review of *The Peculiar Institution: Slavery in the Ante-Bellum South* by Kenneth M. Stampp. *American Historical Review* 63 (October, 1957): 139–140.

203. Kuznets, Simon. *Economic Change: Selected Essays in Business Cycles, National Income, and Economic Growth.* New York: W.W. Norton, 1953.

204. —— *Economic Growth of Nations: Total Output and Production Structure.* Cambridge: Belknap Press, 1971.

205. Lang, Edith Mae. "The Effects of Net Interregional Migration on Agricultural Income Growth: The United States, 1850–1860." Unpublished Ph.D. dissertation, University of Rochester, 1971.

206. Lave, Lester B. *Technological Change: Its Conception and Measurement.* Englewood Cliffs: Prentice-Hall, 1966.

207. Lebergott, Stanley. *Manpower in Economic Growth: The American Record Since 1800.* New York: McGraw-Hill, 1964.

208. —— "Labor Force and Employment, 1800–1960," in Conference on Research in Income and Wealth. *Output, Employment, and Productivity in the United States After 1800.* Studies in Income and Wealth, Vol. 30. New York: Columbia University Press, 1966, pp. 117–204.

209. Lee, Everett S. "Migration Estimates," in Everett S. Lee, et al. *Population Redistribution and Economic Growth, United States, 1870–1950.* Vol. I: *Methodological Considerations and Reference Tables.* Philadelphia: American Philosophical Society, 1957, pp. 9–361.

210. Lesser, Alexander. "Franz Boas," in David L. Sills (ed.). *International Encyclopedia of the Social Sciences.* Vol. 2. New York: Macmillan, 1968, pp. 99–110.

211. Linden, Fabian. "Economic Democracy in the Slave South: An Appraisal of Some Recent Views." *Journal of Negro History* XXXI (April, 1946): 140–189.

212. Lindstrom, Diane L. "Southern Dependence upon Interregional Grain Supplies: A Review of the Trade Flows, 1840–1860." *Agricultural History* XLIV (January, 1970): 101–113.

213. Loomis, Ralph A. and Barton, Glen T. *Productivity of Agriculture: United States, 1870–1958.* U.S. Department of Agriculture, Technical Bulletin No. 1238. Washington, D.C.: 1961.

214. Maddison, Angus. *Economic Progress and Policy in Developing Countries.* London: George Allen & Unwin, 1970.

215. —— *Class Structure and Economic Growth: India and Pakistan Since the Moghuls.* London: George Allen & Unwin, 1971.

216. Marketti, Jim. "Black Equity in the Slave Industry." *Review of Black Political Economy* II (Winter, 1972): 43–66.

217. Martin, Edgar W. *The Standard of Living in 1860: American Consumption Levels on the Eve of the Civil War.* Chicago: University of Chicago Press, 1942.

218. Marx, Karl. *Capital: A Critique of Political Economy.* Vol. I: *The Process of Capitalist Production.* Translated by Samuel Moore and Edward Aveling. Chicago: Charles H. Kerr, 1906.

219. Massell, Benton F. "A Disaggregated View of Technical Change." *Journal of Political Economy* 69 (December, 1961): 547-557.
220. McCusker, John James, Jr. "The Rum Trade and the Balance of Payments of the Thirteen Continental Colonies, 1650-1775." Unpublished Ph.D. dissertation, University of Pittsburgh, 1970.
221. McDougle, Ivan E. *Slavery in Kentucky, 1792-1865.* Lancaster: Press of the New Era Printing Company, 1918.
222. McMaster, John Bach. *A History of the People of the United States, from the Revolution to the Civil War.* 8 vols. New York: D. Appleton and Company, 1883-1913.
223. McPherson, James M., et al. *Blacks in America: Bibliographic Essays.* Garden City: Doubleday & Company, 1971.
224. Menn, Joseph Karl. *The Large Slaveholders of Louisiana, 1860.* New Orleans: Pelican Publishing Company, 1964.
225. —— "The Large Slaveholders of the Deep South, 1860." Unpublished Ph.D. dissertation, University of Texas, 1964.
226. Meyer, Balthasar Henry, et al. *History of Transportation in the United States Before 1860.* Washington, D.C.: Carnegie Institution, 1917.
227. Mintz, Sidney W. "Melville J. Herskovits and Caribbean Studies: A Retrospective Tribute." *Caribbean Studies* IV (July, 1964): 42-51.
228. Mitchell, B.R. "Statistical Appendix: 1700-1914," in Carlo M. Cipolla (ed.). *The Emergence of Industrial Societies, 1700-1914.* Volume 4 of *The Fontana Economic History of Europe.* Edited by Carlo M. Cipolla. London: Collins, 1971.
229. Mitchell, B.R., with the collaboration of Phyllis Deane. *Abstract of British Historical Statistics.* Cambridge: University Press, 1962.
230. Moody, V. Alton. "Slavery on Louisiana Sugar Plantations." *Louisiana Historical Quarterly* 7 (April, 1924): 191-301.
231. Moohr, Michael. "The Economic Impact of Slave Emancipation in British Guiana, 1832-1852." *Economic History Review,* Second Series, XXV (November, 1972): 588-607.
232. Mooney, Chase C. *Slavery in Tennessee.* ("Indiana University Publications, Social Science Series," No. 17.) Bloomington: Indiana University Press, 1957.
233. Moore, John Hebron. "A Review of Lewis C. Gray's *History of Agriculture in the Southern United States to 1860.*" *Agricultural History* XLVI (January, 1972): 19-28.
234. Morris, Laura Newell (comp.). *Human Populations, Genetic Variation, and Evolution.* San Francisco: Chandler Publishing Co., 1971.
235. Morris, Richard B. *Government and Labor in Early America.* New York: Columbia University Press, 1946.
236. —— "The Measure of Bondage in the Slave States." *Mississippi Valley Historical Review* XLI (September, 1954): 219-240.
237. Morris, William (ed.). *The American Heritage Dictionary of the English Language.* New York: American Heritage Publishing Co., 1969.
238. Mulhall, Michael G. *The Dictionary of Statistics.* Fourth edition. London: George Routledge and Sons, 1899.
239. Mullin, Gerald W. *Flight and Rebellion: Slave Resistance in Eighteenth Century Virginia.* New York: Oxford University Press, 1972.
240. Myrdal, Gunnar. *An American Dilemma: The Negro Problem and Modern Democracy.* New York: Harper & Brothers, 1944.
241. *Negro History Bulletin* 13 (May, 1950).
242. Newton, Lewis W. and Gambrell, Herbert P. *A Social and Political History of Texas.* Dallas: Southwest Press, 1932.

243. North, Douglass C. *The Economic Growth of the United States, 1790-1860.* Englewood Cliffs: Prentice-Hall, 1961.
244. Olmsted, Frederick Law. *A Journey in the Seaboard Slave States.* New York: Dix & Edwards, 1856.
245. —— *A Journey Through Texas.* New York: Dix, Edwards & Co., 1857.
246. —— *A Journey in the Back Country.* New York: Mason Brothers, 1860.
247. —— *The Cotton Kingdom.* Edited, with an introduction, by Arthur M. Schlesinger. New York: Alfred A. Knopf, 1953.
248. Owsley, Frank Lawrence. "The Irrepressible Conflict," in Twelve Southerners. *I'll Take My Stand: The South and the Agrarian Tradition.* New York: Harper & Brothers, 1930, pp. 61-91.
249. —— "The Fundamental Cause of the Civil War: Egocentric Sectionalism." *Journal of Southern History* VII (February, 1941): 3-18.
250. —— *Plain Folk of the Old South.* Baton Rouge: Louisiana State University Press, 1949.
251. Owsley, Frank L. and Owsley, Harriet C. "The Economic Basis of Society in the Late Ante-Bellum South." *Journal of Southern History* VI (February, 1940): 24-45.
252. Park, Robert E. "The Conflict and Fusion of Cultures with Special Reference to the Negro." *Journal of Negro History* IV (April, 1919): 111-133.
253. Parker, William N. "Slavery and Southern Economic Development: An Hypothesis and Some Evidence." *Agricultural History* XLIV (January, 1970): 115-126.
254. Passell, Peter and Wright, Gavin. "The Effects of Pre-Civil War Territorial Expansion on the Price of Slaves." *Journal of Political Economy* 80 (November/December, 1972): 1188-1202.
255. Patterson, Caleb Perry. *The Negro in Tennessee, 1790-1865.* ("University of Texas Bulletin," No. 2205.) Austin: The University, 1922.
256. Patterson, Orlando. "Rethinking Black History." *Harvard Education Review* 41 (August, 1971): 297-315.
257. Phillips, Ulrich Bonnell. "The Economic Cost of Slaveholding in the Cotton Belt." *Political Science Quarterly* XX (June, 1905): 257-275.
258. —— "The Origin and Growth of the Southern Black Belts." *American Historical Review* 11 (July, 1906): 798-816.
259. —— *A History of Transportation in the Eastern Cotton Belt to 1860.* New York: Columbia University Press, 1908.
260. Phillips, Ulrich Bonnell (ed.). *Plantation and Frontier Documents 1649-1863.* Vols. I and II of John R. Commons, et al. *A Documentary History of American Industrial Society.* Cleveland: The A.H. Clark Co., 1910.
261. Phillips, Ulrich Bonnell. *American Negro Slavery: A Survey of the Supply, Employment and Control of Negro Labor As Determined by the Plantation Regime.* New York: D. Appleton and Company, 1918.
262. —— "The Central Theme of Southern History." *American Historical Review* 34 (October, 1928): 30-43.
263. —— *Life and Labor in the Old South.* Boston: Little, Brown, 1963.
264. Pollard, Sidney. *The Genesis of Modern Management: A Study of the Industrial Revolution in Great Britain.* London: Edward Arnold, 1965.
265. Pope, Clayne. "The Impact of the Ante-Bellum Tariff on Income Distribution." *Explorations in Economic History* 9 (Summer, 1972): 375-421.
266. Postell, William Dosite. *The Health of Slaves on Southern Plantations.* ("Louisiana State University Studies, Social Science Series," No. 2.) Baton Rouge: Louisiana State University Press, 1951.
267. Postma, Johannes. "The Origin of African Slaves: The Dutch Activities on the

Guinea Coast, 1675–1795," in Stanley L. Engerman and Eugene D. Genovese (eds.). *Race and Slavery in the Western Hemisphere: Quantitative Studies.* Princeton: Princeton University Press, 1974.

268. Pressly, Thomas J. *Americans Interpret Their Civil War.* Princeton: Princeton University Press, 1954.

269. Primack, Martin Leonard. "Farm Formed Capital in American Agriculture: 1850 to 1910." Unpublished Ph.D. dissertation, University of North Carolina, 1962.

270. Ramsdell, Chas. W. "The Natural Limits of Slavery Expansion." *Mississippi Valley Historical Review* XVI (September, 1929): 151–171.

271. Randall, J.G. *The Civil War and Reconstruction.* Boston: D.C. Heath, 1937.

272. —— "The Blundering Generation." *Mississippi Valley Historical Review* XXVII (June, 1940): 3–28.

273. Rawick, George P. (ed.). *The American Slave: A Composite Autobiography.* Vol. I: *From Sundown to Sunup: The Making of the Black Community.* Westport: Greenwood Publishing Co., 1972.

274. —— *The American Slave: A Composite Autobiography.* Vol. XVIII: *Unwritten History of Slavery.* Westport: Greenwood Publishing Co., 1972.

275. Reed, T. Edward. "Caucasian Genes in American Negroes." *Science* 165 (August, 1969): 762–768. Reprinted in [234], pp. 427–446.

276. Reynolds, Marcus T. "The Housing of the Poor in American Cities." *Publications of the American Economic Association.* Vol. III. Baltimore: American Economic Association, 1893, pp. 131–262.

277. Rhodes, James Ford. *History of the United States from the Compromise of 1850.* Vol. I: *1850–1854.* New York: Harper & Brothers, 1893.

278. Roberts, George W. *The Population of Jamaica.* Cambridge: University Press, 1957.

279. Robinson, Joan. *The Economics of Imperfect Competition.* London: Macmillan, 1954.

280. —— *An Essay on Marxian Economics.* London: Macmillan, 1957.

281. Rose, Willie Lee. *Rehearsal for Reconstruction: The Port Royal Experiment.* Indianapolis: Bobbs-Merrill, 1964.

282. Rosenblat, Angel. *La Población Indígena y El Mestizaje en America.* 2 vols. Buenos Aires: Editorial Nova. 1954.

283. Roughley, Thomas. *The Jamaica Planter's Guide.* London: Longman, Hurst, Rees, Orme, and Brown, 1823.

284. Russel, Robert R. "The General Effects of Slavery Upon Southern Economic Progress." *Journal of Southern History* IV (February, 1938): 34–54.

285 Russell, Robert. *North America: Its Agriculture and Climate.* Edinburgh: Adam and Charles Black, 1857.

286. Ruttan, Vernon W. and Stout, Thomas T. "Regional Differences in Factor Shares in American Agriculture: 1925–1957." *Journal of Farm Economics* XLII (February, 1960): 52–68.

287. Saraydar, Edward. "A Note on the Profitability of Ante Bellum Slavery." *Southern Economic Journal* XXX (April, 1964): 325–332.

288. Saving, T. R. "Estimation of Optimum Size of Plant by the Survivor Technique." *Quarterly Journal of Economics* LXXV (November, 1961): 569–607.

289. Scarborough, William Kauffman. *The Overseer: Plantation Management in the Old South.* Baton Rouge: Louisiana State University Press, 1966.

290. Schlesinger, Arthur M., Jr. "The Causes of the Civil War: A Note on Historical Sentimentalism." *Partisan Review* XVI (October, 1949): 969–981.

291. Schouler, James. *History of the United States of America Under the Constitution.* 7 vols. New York: Dodd, Mead and Company, 1880–1913.

292. Seagrave, Charles Edwin. "The Southern Negro Agricultural Worker: 1850–1870." Unpublished Ph.D. dissertation, Stanford University, 1971.

293. Sellers, James Benson. *Slavery in Alabama.* University: University of Alabama Press, 1950.

294. Sheridan, R.B. "The Wealth of Jamaica in the Eighteenth Century." *Economic History Review,* Second Series, XVIII (August, 1965): 292–311.

295. —— "The Wealth of Jamaica in the Eighteenth Century: A Rejoinder." *Economic History Review,* Second Series, XXI (April, 1968): 46–61.

296. Simon, Julian L. "The Worth Today of United States Slaves' Imputed Wages." *Journal of Economic Issues* V (September, 1971): 110–113.

297. Sitterson, J. Carlyle. *Sugar Country: The Cane Sugar Industry in the South, 1753–1950.* Lexington: University of Kentucky Press, 1953.

298. Smith, William W. *Pork Production.* Revised edition. New York: Macmillan, 1937.

299. Soltow, Lee. *Patterns of Wealthholding in Wisconsin Since 1850.* Madison: University of Wisconsin Press, 1971.

300. —— "Economic Inequality in the United States in the Period from 1790 to 1860." *Journal of Economic History* XXXI (December, 1971): 822–839.

301. —— "The Wealth, Income, and Social Class of Men in Large Northern Cities of the United States in 1860," in Conference on Research in Income and Wealth. *Personal Distributions of Income and Wealth.* Studies in Income and Wealth, Vol. 39. New York: Columbia University Press, 1974.

302. Stampp, Kenneth M. "The Historian and Southern Negro Slavery." *American Historical Review* 57 (April, 1952): 613–624.

303. —— *The Peculiar Institution: Slavery in the Ante-Bellum South.* New York: Alfred A. Knopf, 1956.

304. Starobin, Robert S. *Industrial Slavery in the Old South.* New York: Oxford University Press, 1970.

305. Stavisky, Leonard Price. "The Negro Artisan in the South Atlantic States, 1800–1860." Unpublished Ph.D. dissertation, Columbia University, 1958.

306. Steckel, Richard. "Negro Slavery in the Western Hemisphere." Unpublished paper, University of Chicago, 1971.

307. —— "The Economics of U.S. Slave and Southern Free-White Fertility." Unpublished paper, University of Chicago, 1973.

308. Steiner, Bernard C. *History of Slavery in Connecticut.* ("Johns Hopkins University Studies in Historical and Political Science," 11th Series, IX–X.) Baltimore: Johns Hopkins Press, 1893.

309. Stephenson, Wendell Holmes. *Isaac Franklin: Slave Trader and Planter of the Old South.* University: Louisiana State University Press, 1938.

310. —— *The South Lives in History: Southern Historians and Their Legacy.* Baton Rouge: Louisiana State University Press, 1955.

311. —— *Southern History in the Making: Pioneer Historians of the South.* Baton Rouge: Louisiana State University Press, 1964.

312. Stetson, Kenneth Winslow. "A Quantitative Approach to Britain's American Slave Trade, 1700–1773." Unpublished Master's thesis, University of Wisconsin, 1967.

313. Stigler, George J. "The Economies of Scale." *Journal of Law and Economics* I (October, 1958): 54–71.

314. Stocking, George W., Jr. *Race, Culture, and Evolution: Essays in the History of Anthropology.* New York: Free Press, 1968.

315. Strauss, Frederick and Bean, Louis H. *Gross Farm Income and Indices of Farm Production and Prices in the United States 1869–1937.* U.S. Department of Agriculture, Technical Bulletin No. 703. Washington, D.C.: 1940.

316. Sutch, Richard. "The Profitability of Ante Bellum Slavery – Revisited." *Southern Economic Journal* XXXI (April, 1965): 365-377.

317. —— "The Breeding of Slaves for Sale and Westward Expansion of Slavery, 1850-1860," in Stanley L. Engerman and Eugene D. Genovese (eds.). *Race and Slavery in the Western Hemisphere: Quantitative Studies.* Princeton: Princeton University Press, 1974.

318. Swan, Dale E. "The Structure and Profitability of the Antebellum Rice Industry: 1859." Unpublished Ph.D. dissertation, University of North Carolina, 1972.

319. Sydnor, Charles S. "Life Span of Mississippi Slaves." *American Historical Review* 35 (April, 1930): 566-574.

320. —— *Slavery in Mississippi.* New York: Appleton-Century, 1933.

321. Taylor, Alrutheus Ambush. *The Negro in South Carolina During the Reconstruction.* Washington, D.C.: The Association for the Study of Negro Life and History, 1924.

322. —— *The Negro in the Reconstruction of Virginia.* Washington, D.C.: The Association for the Study of Negro Life and History, 1926.

323. Taylor, Clara Mae and Pye, Orrea Florence. *Foundations of Nutrition.* 6th edition. New York: Macmillan, 1966.

324. Taylor, Joe Gray. *Negro Slavery in Louisiana.* Baton Rouge: Louisiana Historical Association, 1963.

325. Taylor, Orville W. *Negro Slavery in Arkansas.* Durham: Duke University Press, 1958.

326. Taylor, Rosser Howard. *Slaveholding in North Carolina: An Economic View.* ("The James Sprunt Historical Publications Published Under the Direction of the Department of History and Government, University of North Carolina," Vol. 18, Nos. 1-2.) Chapel Hill: University of North Carolina Press, 1926.

327. Thorpe, Earle E. *Black Historians: A Critique.* New York: William Morrow, 1971.

328. Tindall, George B. "Southern Negroes Since Reconstruction: Dissolving the Static Image," in Arthur S. Link and Rembert W. Patrick (eds.). *Writing Southern History: Essays in Historiography in Honor of Fletcher M. Green.* Baton Rouge: Louisiana State University Press, 1965, pp. 337-361.

329. Towne, Marvin W. and Rasmussen, Wayne D. "Farm Gross Product and Gross Investment in the Nineteenth Century," in Conference on Research in Income and Wealth. *Trends in the American Economy in the Nineteenth Century.* Studies in Income and Wealth, Vol. 24. Princeton: Princeton University Press, 1960, pp. 255-312.

330. Trent, William P. *William Gilmore Simms.* "American Men of Letters." Edited by Charles Dudley Warner. Boston: Houghton Mifflin, 1892.

331. Trexler, Harrison Anthony. *Slavery in Missouri, 1804-1865.* ("Johns Hopkins University Studies in Historical and Political Science," Series XXXII, No. 2.) Baltimore: Johns Hopkins Press, 1914.

332. Turner, Edward Raymond. *The Negro in Pennsylvania: Slavery – Servitude – Freedom, 1639-1861.* (Prize Essays of the American Historical Association, 1910.) Washington, D.C.: American Historical Association, 1911.

333. Twyman, Robert W. "The Clay Eater: A New Look at an Old Southern Enigma." *Journal of Southern History* XXXVII (August, 1971): 439-448.

334. United Nations, Department of Economic and Social Affairs. *The Determinants and Consequences of Population Trends.* Population Studies, No. 17. New York: United Nations, 1953.

335. —— Department of Economic and Social Affairs. *Methods of Estimating*

Basic Demographic Measures from Incomplete Data. Population
Studies, No. 42. New York: United Nations, 1967.

336. U.S. Bureau of the Census, Seventh (1850). *Statistical View of the United
States.* Washington, D.C.: 1854.

337. U.S. Bureau of the Census, Eighth (1860). *Agriculture of the United States
in 1860.* Washington, D.C.: 1864.

338. —— *Population of the United States in 1860.* Washington, D.C.: 1864.

339. —— *Manufactures of the United States in 1860.* Washington, D.C.: 1865.

340. —— *Statistics of the United States in 1860.* Washington, D.C.: 1866.

341. U.S. Bureau of the Census, Twelfth (1900). *Agriculture, Part I.* Vol. V.
Washington, D.C.: 1902.

342. U.S. Bureau of the Census, Sixteenth (1940). *Population: Comparative Occupation Statistics for the United States, 1870 to 1940.* Washington, D.C.: 1943.

343. U.S. Bureau of the Census. *Historical Statistics of the United States,
Colonial Times to 1957.* Washington, D.C.: 1960.

344. U.S. Commissioner of Labor. *Seventh Special Report of the Commissioner of
Labor.* House Executive Document, No. 257 (53rd Cong. 2nd Sess.) (Ser. 3228).
Washington, D.C.: 1894.

345. U.S. Department of Agriculture, Bureau of Agricultural Economics. *Consumption of Food in the United States, 1909-1948.* Miscellaneous Publication No.
691. Washington, D.C.: 1949.

346. —— *Consumption of Food in the United States, 1909-1952.* Agricultural
Handbook No. 62. Washington, D.C.: 1953.

347. U.S. Department of Agriculture, Agricultural Marketing Service. *Livestock and
Meat Statistics, 1957.* Statistical Bulletin No. 230. Washington, D.C.: 1958.

348. U.S. Department of Health, Education, and Welfare. *Disability Days, United
States – 1968.* Series 10, Number 67. Rockville: 1972.

349. U.S. Department of Labor. "Conditions of the Negro in Various Cities."
Bulletin No. 10. Washington, D.C.: 1897, pp. 257–369.

350. —— *How American Buying Habits Change.* Washington, D.C.: 1959.

351. Wall, Bennett H. "African Slavery," in Arthur S. Link and Rembert W. Patrick
(eds.). *Writing Southern History: Essays in Historiography in Honor of
Fletcher M. Green.* Baton Rouge: Louisiana State University Press, 1965,
pp. 175–197.

352. Ward, Edward G., Jr. *Milk Transportation: Freight Rates to the Largest Fifteen
Cities in the United States.* U.S. Department of Agriculture, Division of Statistics, Bulletin No. 25. Washington, D.C.: 1903.

353. Washington, Booker T. *The Story of the Negro: The Rise of the Race from
Slavery.* 2 vols. New York: Doubleday, Page & Company, 1909.

354. Watkins, James L. *Production and Price of Cotton for One Hundred Years.*
U.S. Department of Agriculture, Miscellaneous Series, Bulletin No. 9. Washington, D.C.: 1895.

355. Watt, Bernice K., et al. *Composition of Foods – Raw, Processed, Prepared.*
U.S. Department of Agriculture, Agricultural Handbook No. 8. Washington,
D.C.: 1950.

356. Weaver, Herbert. *Mississippi Farmers, 1850-1860.* Nashville: Vanderbilt University Press, 1945.

357. Weinstein, Allen and Gatell, Frank Otto (eds.). *American Negro Slavery: A
Modern Reader.* Second edition. New York: Oxford University Press, 1973.

358. Weiss, Leonard W. "The Survival Technique and the Extent of Suboptimal
Capacity." *Journal of Political Economy* 72 (June, 1964): 246–261.

359. Weld, Theodore D. *American Slavery As It Is: Testimony of a Thousand Witnesses.* New York: American Anti-Slavery Society, 1839.

360. Wesley, Charles H. *Negro Labor in the United States, 1850-1925: A Study in American Economic History.* New York: Vanguard Press, 1927.

361. —— "Manifests of Slave Shipments Along the Waterways, 1808-1864." *Journal of Negro History* XXVII (April, 1942): 155-174.

362. —— "Carter G. Woodson – As a Scholar." *Journal of Negro History* XXXVI (January, 1951): 12-24.

363. —— "Creating and Maintaining an Historical Tradition." *Journal of Negro History* XLIX (January, 1964): 13-33.

364. West, Robert Craig. "Social, Political, and Economic Factors Concerning the Feasibility of Compensated Emancipation During the 1860's." Unpublished paper, Northwestern University, 1972.

365. Williams, Eric. "The Golden Age of the Slave System in Britain." *Journal of Negro History* XXV (January, 1940): 60-106.

366. Williams, Faith M. and Zimmerman, Carle C. *Studies of Family Living in the United States and Other Countries: An Analysis of Material and Method.* U.S. Department of Agriculture, Miscellaneous Publication No. 223. Washington, D.C.: 1935.

367. Williams, George W. *History of the Negro Race in America from 1619 to 1880.* 2 vols. New York: G.P. Putnam's Sons, 1883.

368. ——*A History of the Negro Troops in the War of the Rebellion, 1861-1865.* New York: Harper & Brothers, 1888.

369. Williams, Mary Wilhelmine. "The Treatment of Negro Slaves in the Brazilian Empire: A Comparison with the United States of America." *Journal of Negro History* XV (July, 1930): 315-336.

370. Wilson, Woodrow. *Division and Reunion, 1829-1889.* "Epochs of American History." Edited by Albert Bushnell Hart. 4th edition, revised. New York: Longmans, Green and Company, 1893.

371. Wish, Harvey. "American Slave Insurrections Before 1861." *Journal of Negro History* XXII (July, 1937): 299-320.

372. —— "Slave Disloyalty Under the Confederacy." *Journal of Negro History* XXIII (October, 1938): 435-450.

373. —— *The American Historian: A Social-Intellectual History of the Writing of the American Past.* New York: Oxford University Press, 1960.

374. Woodman, Harold D. "The Profitability of Slavery: A Historical Perennial." *Journal of Southern History* XXIX (August, 1963): 303-325.

375. Woodruff, William. *Impact of Western Man: A Study of Europe's Role in the World Economy, 1750-1960.* New York: St. Martin's Press, 1967.

376. Woodson, Carter G. *The Education of the Negro Prior to 1861: A History of the Education of the Colored People of the United States from the Beginning of Slavery to the Civil War.* Second edition, Washington, D.C.: The Associated Publishers, 1919.

377. —— Review of *American Negro Slavery. Journal of Negro History* IV (January, 1919): 102-103.

378. —— Review of *American Negro Slavery. Mississippi Valley Historical Review* V (March, 1919): 480-482.

379. —— *The History of the Negro Church.* Washington, D.C.: The Associated Publishers, 1921.

380. Woodson, Carter G. (ed.). *Free Negro Owners of Slaves in the United States in 1830 together with Absentee Ownership of Slaves in the United States in 1830.* Washington, D.C.: The Association for the Study of Negro Life and History, 1924.

381. Woodson, Carter G. *Free Negro Heads of Families in the United States in 1830 together with a Brief Treatment of the Free Negro*. Washington, D.C.: The Association for the Study of Negro Life and History, 1925.

382. Woodson, Carter G. (ed.). *The Mind of the Negro as Reflected in Letters Written during the Crisis, 1800-1860*. Washington, D.C.: The Association for the Study of Negro Life and History, 1926.

383. Woodson, Carter G. *The Negro in Our History*. Sixth edition. Washington, D.C.: The Associated Publishers, 1931.

384. —— "An Accounting for Twenty-Five Years." *Journal of Negro History* XXV (October, 1940): 422–431.

385. Woodward, C. Vann. *Origins of the New South, 1877-1913*. Volume IX of *A History of the South*. Edited by Wendell Holmes Stephenson and E. Merton Coulter. Baton Rouge: Louisiana State University Press, 1951.

386. Wright, Carroll D. "An Economic History of the United States." *Papers and Proceedings of the Seventeenth Annual Meeting of the American Economic Association*. Vol. VI, Part II, pp. 160–198.

387. Wright, Gavin. "The Economics of Cotton in the Antebellum South." Unpublished Ph.D. dissertation, Yale University, 1969.

388. —— " 'Economic Democracy' and the Concentration of Agricultural Wealth in the Cotton South, 1850–1860." *Agricultural History* XLIV (January, 1970): 63–94.

389. —— "Note on the Manuscript Census Samples Used in These Studies." *Agricultural History* XLIV (January, 1970): 95–100.

390. — — "An Econometric Study of Cotton Production and Trade, 1830–1860." *Review of Economics and Statistics* LIII (May, 1971): 111–120.

391. —— "New and Old Views on the Economics of Slavery." *Journal of Economic History* XXXIII (June, 1973): 452–466.

392. Yasuba, Yasukichi. "The Profitability and Viability of Plantation Slavery in the United States." *The Economic Studies Quarterly* XII (September, 1961): 60–67. Reprinted in Robert William Fogel and Stanley L. Engerman (eds.). *The Reinterpretation of American Economic History*. New York: Harper & Row, 1971, pp. 362–368; and Hugh G.J. Aitken (ed.). *Did Slavery Pay?* Boston: Houghton Mifflin, 1971, pp. 186–196.

393. Yetman, Norman R. (ed.). *Life Under the "Peculiar Institution": Selections from the Slave Narrative Collection*. New York: Holt, Rinehart and Winston, 1970.

394. Zanger, Jules. "Crime and Punishment in Early Massachusetts." *William and Mary Quarterly*, Series 3, XXII (July, 1965): 471–477.

395. Zelinsky, Wilbur. "The Historical Geography of the Negro Population of Latin America." *Journal of Negro History* XXXIV (April, 1949): 153–221.

396. Zevin, Robert Brooke. "The Growth of Cotton Textile Production After 1815," in Robert William Fogel and Stanley L. Engerman (eds.). *The Reinterpretation of American Economic History*. New York: Harper & Row, 1971, pp. 122–147.

397. Zilversmit, Arthur. *The First Emancipation: The Abolition of Slavery in the North*. Chicago: University of Chicago Press, 1967.

398. Zimmerman, Carle C. *Consumption and Standards of Living*. New York: Van Nostrand, 1936.